POLITICS AND JOBS

POLITICS AND JOBS

THE BOUNDARIES OF EMPLOYMENT
POLICY IN THE UNITED STATES

Margaret Weir

PRINCETON UNIVERSITY PRESS   PRINCETON, NEW JERSEY

Copyright © 1992 by Princeton University Press
Published by Princeton University Press, 41 William Street,
Princeton, New Jersey 08540
In the United Kingdom: Princeton University Press, Oxford
All Rights Reserved

Library of Congress Cataloging-in-Publication Data
Weir, Margaret
Politics and jobs : the boundaries of employment policy
in the United States / Margaret Weir
p.   cm.
Includes index.
ISBN 0-691-07853-X (alk. paper)
1. United States—Full employment policies.
2. Manpower policy—United States.   3. Public service
employment—United States.   I. Title.
HD5724.W38   1991
339.5′0973—dc20   91-18287   CIP

This book has been composed in Adobe Utopia

Princeton University Press books are printed
on acid-free paper, and meet the guidelines
for permanence and durability of the Committee
on Production Guidelines for Book Longevity
of the Council on Library Resources

Printed in the United States of America

10 9 8 7 6 5 4 3 2 1

For My Parents

_____

Contents

Figures

Tables

Preface

THIS BOOK examines the politics of active employment policies in the United States. It asks why the range of policies that seek to promote employment or modify the operation of the labor market has been so truncated in America and why the policies that were enacted unraveled soon after their inauguration. I argue that this enduring pattern in economic policy can be understood by examining how citizens and politicians come to define public problems, how they understand the range of choices open to them, and how they interpret their interests within a given range of possible policies. As I examine major turns in policy from the New Deal to the 1980s, I ask why debates about employment became framed in particular ways and why the range of politically acceptable government action expanded or shrank at particular moments.

This approach contrasts with much of the current literature on policy, which explains policy as the product of the preferences of politicians or voters. Rather than take definitions of problems as given and preferences as established, I examine how notions of what is possible become established, and explore how these notions in turn affect policy. In E. E. Schattschneider's words, "What people do about the government depends on what they think the government is able to do."[1] This book asks how the realm of the possible is created and how it shapes public decisions about what is desirable.

The approach I take is fundamentally historical; I show how policy decisions reached in the 1940s restricted the scope for later initiatives by channeling thinking and political activity along distinctive paths. Employment policy was organized and implemented in ways that progressively narrowed the realm of the possible and the desirable. Because it emphasized racial differences, employment policy drew opposition for being a special interest measure for African-Americans. Because it highlighted the limited capacities of the American national state, it attracted charges of waste, fraud, and corruption. Antipathy to the federal government and racial antagonism became the dominant features in the politics of employment policy by the 1970s.

To understand how this occurred, I address two sets of questions left unexplored in much of the political economy literature. The first concerns the role of ideas. How do policy ideas become influential, and in what ways do ideas shape views about how to define public problems and select appropriate policies? The second set of questions explores the way different social groups come to understand their interests with regard to employment. How does the process of building coalitions of support for policy in the United States affect possibilities for joining diverse interests around employment policies?

I examine these questions by studying the development of active employment policies from the New Deal to the Reagan administration. This period begins with the federal government's assumption of a responsibility to intervene in the economy in order to reduce unemployment, and it ends with the political failure of employment policy in the late 1970s. I examine two of the most important active employment policies—Keynesianism and labor market policy—at critical points in their development, and explore failed efforts to create planning mechanisms and tripartite cooperation in the late 1970s.

Chapter One analyzes the broad pattern of American employment policy, pointing to the remedial, ad hoc nature of these measures and to the cycle of innovation and frustration that has characterized policy in this area. It briefly discusses several ways to account for this pattern and lays out the analytic framework that will guide this study. Chapter Two asks how a relatively noninterventionist version of Keynesian stabilization policy emerged as the central employment policy in the United States. It examines early experiments with a social Keynesianism that joined social and economic objectives, considering why the United States eventually adopted an alternative version of Keynesianism that severed the social and economic domains and deemphasized the public role in the economy.

Chapters Three and Four discuss the evolution of labor market policies in the United States. Chapter Three examines how these policies became subsumed into the War on Poverty and assesses the political and institutional ramifications of incorporating labor market policies into a racially identified program. Chapter Four examines the revival of labor market policies in the form of public service employment during the 1970s. It asks why public employment became the dominant response to rising unemployment, and shows how the organization of this policy tapped into a recurrent theme in American politics, the crusade against corruption.

The failure of attempts to establish planning mechanisms and forums for tripartite cooperation during the latter half of the 1970s is explored in Chapter Five. The chapter asks why congressional and executive initiatives in these directions failed to take root. Chapter Six considers what the experience of employment policy reveals about the construction of policy boundaries and the possibilities for innovation in the United States.

Acknowledgments

IN THE COURSE of writing this book I have benefited from the intellectual support and assistance offered by a variety of institutions, colleagues, and friends. One of the rewards of completing the book is to be able to thank them.

This book had its origins in my Ph.D. thesis at the University of Chicago. I owe a special debt to the members of my dissertation committee, Ira Katznelson, Theda Skocpol, William Julius Wilson, and Gary Orfield; they provided a rare blend of intellectual guidance and personal support as I worked on the dissertation, and they have continued to offer encouragement and advice.

As a graduate student at the University of Chicago, I was immersed in a stimulating intellectual and political environment that influenced the problems addressed and the approach taken in this book. Collaborative work with Ira Katznelson and Theda Skocpol taught me how to do historical institutional work. Much of my thinking about policy innovation was first influenced by Theda Skocpol. I have benefited greatly from her generosity as a colleague and as a friend. I owe special thanks to Ira Katznelson, who read several drafts of each chapter. His guidance, encouragement, and good cheer over many years have been central to my intellectual development and were especially helpful as I completed this book. Classes with Lloyd Rudolph introduced me to issues in public administration and seminars with Adam Przeworski first sparked my interest in employment policy.

A number of fellow graduate students provided a strong intellectual community in Chicago. I would particularly like to thank Kathy Gille, whose critical eye and warm friendship sustained me while I was writing the dissertation and later as I revised the manuscript. I benefited from numerous conversations with Kim Stanton, Jack Knight, John Echeverri-Gent, and Ed Amenta. I would also like to thank Alan Pifer and Forrest Chisman of the Project on the Federal Social Role for sponsoring conferences at Chicago, at which some of this work was first presented. Dan Kurtz, Kim Mathews, Judy Hertz, Chuck Harrison, Hallie Segal, and Martha Rose all kept me in touch with the real worlds of city politics, community organizing, and cars. My students at the Instituto del Progreso Latino also helped me keep academic endeavors in perspective.

As I undertook my research I was aided by a number of librarians, archivists, and colleagues. I am particularly grateful to Judson Mac-

Laury and Hank Guzda, librarians in the Historical Office of the Department of Labor, who efficiently and cheerfully helped me locate a variety of materials. I also owe thanks to Gary Mucciaroni, who first took me to the Department of Labor and has since been a valued colleague. The librarians at the John F. Kennedy Library and the Lyndon Baines Johnson Library and Jerry Hess at the National Archives all provided helpful assistance.

As I revised the manuscript, a number of scholars took time from their own work to read chapters and offer advice. I received valuable comments on the manuscript from Ellen Immergut, Hugh Heclo, Charles Perrow, H. W. Perry, Jr., Doug Price, Joe Schwartz, Martin Shefter, Jim Shoch, Sven Steinmo, Jeff Tulis, Gavin Wright, and Sid Verba. Their criticisms and insights have improved the book.

Discussions with colleagues at Harvard were helpful in thinking though the arguments and evidence presented in the book. I would particularly like to thank Jim Alt, Peter A. Hall, Mark A. Peterson, and Shannon Stimson. I have also benefited from the perspectives and advice of Chris Allen, Ken Finegold, Vicky Hattam, Ann Shola Orloff, and Ann Withorn. Nick Ziegler offered intellectual and moral support during the final stages of the project. Sara Beckman and Neil Bennett gave me useful advice on preparing the charts and Matt Dickinson, Vindu Goel, Peter Yu, and Paul Hess provided research assistance.

Financial and institutional assistance came from a variety of sources. I am grateful to the American Council of Learned Societies for a grant to support the dissertation revision. I also received financial and institutional support from the Institute for Advanced Study in Princeton, New Jersey, which provided an idyllic setting for undertaking revisions. I would particularly like to thank Albert Hirschman for his hospitality and intellectual guidance while I was at the Institute.

I owe thanks to the Faculty Aide Program at Harvard University, which provided funds for research assistance and to the Lyndon Baines Johnson Foundation, which supported travel to the Johnson Library. The final touches were put on the manuscript at the Russell Sage Foundation, where Pauline Rothstein and Camille Yezzi provided valuable assistance. Thanks are also due to Gail Ullman of Princeton University Press for her encouragement and to Lyn Grossman for editorial assistance.

Finally, I would like to acknowledge the continuing support and encouragement of my parents, to whom this book is dedicated.

Abbreviations

AAA	Agricultural Adjustment Administration
AFDC	Aid to Families with Dependent Children
ASPER	Assistant Secretary for Policy, Evaluation, and Research
AVA	American Vocational Association
BAC	Business Advisory Council
BES	Bureau of Employment Security
BLS	Bureau of Labor Statistics
CAP	Community Action Program
CEA	Council of Economic Advisers
CED	Committee for Economic Development
CEP	Concentrated Employment Program
CETA	Comprehensive Employment and Training Act
COWPS	Council on Wage and Price Stability
CWA	Civil Works Administration
EEA	Emergency Employment Act
ICESA	Interstate Conference of Employment Security Agencies
JOBS	Job Opportunities in the Business Sector
MDTA	Manpower Development and Training Act
NAB	National Alliance of Businessmen
NIRA	National Industrial Recovery Act
NMAC	National Manpower Advisory Committee
NRA	National Recovery Administration
NRPB	National Resources Planning Board
OEO	Office of Economic Opportunity
OMB	Office of Management and Budget
PCJD	President's Committee on Juvenile Delinquency
PEP	Public Employment Program
PWA	Public Works Administration
TAA	Trade Adjustment Assistance
USES	United States Employment Service
WIN	Work Incentive Program
WPA	Works Progress Administration

POLITICS AND JOBS

One

Innovation and Boundaries in American Policymaking

DURING the 1980s, American policymakers sought to break with the past. Democratic and Republican politicians alike claimed that a bloated federal government had weakened the national economy, had distorted the conduct of politics, and ultimately had damaged the moral character of the American citizenry. Their solution was to curb government activity. Nowhere was this aim more successfully realized than in the domain of employment policy. Congress dismantled existing employment and training programs, economic policymakers officially repudiated Keynesian prescriptions for managing the national economy, and executive agencies abandoned sectoral initiatives to control inflation.

These changes marked more than an incremental shift in policy: taken together they represented a rejection of the notion that the government could—and should—directly intervene in the economy to ensure adequate employment for its citizens. Thus, the social and economic policy shifts of the 1980s signaled the political failure of a set of ideas that had helped to organize the relationship among the federal government, the economy, and American citizens for more than four decades. With the supremacy of the market rhetorically confirmed, deliberate efforts to create an American employment policy diminished sharply in the 1980s. Instead, as massive deficits drove unemployment down by the mid-1980s, debate about the government's role in the domain of employment all but vanished from the national agenda.[1]

The shifts in perspective and policy were not simply the product of a new president's political wizardry: existing employment policies found few articulate and energetic advocates. Only a handful in Congress were prepared to defend deficit spending as a regular and necessary tool of economic management; even enthusiastic supporters of employment and training policies were hard pressed to stand behind existing programs. Given the dearth of alternatives, market strategies easily prevailed.

The turn away from government action in the 1980s reflected deeper, long-standing problems with active employment policies in the United States. Although concern about employment issues became a staple in the political rhetoric of postwar America, that concern was unevenly reflected in policy. Despite forty years of experimentation, the United States drew on a truncated repertoire of policies to cope with employment issues; moreover, the measures that were adopted managed to achieve only a tenuous foothold. American employment policy was always an unsettled area, characterized by false starts, poorly implemented programs, and a vacillating national commitment.

This pattern of policy is puzzling when we examine the importance of work in American political culture. For a nation that claims the work ethic as a central feature of its political identity, the United States has been remarkably lax in introducing and sustaining policies that actively promote employment.[2] The fitful course of experimentation with and abandonment of employment policies has limited the government's role in facilitating entry into the labor market and easing transitions for those already working. Moreover, heavy reliance on macroeconomic policy has meant that the government has often deliberately restricted the supply of jobs to control inflation. As a result, American policy has by default taken a more passive approach, with policies that simply dole out funds to those in need (for a limited time and, for most programs, in ungenerous amounts) or regulatory policies that monitor hiring practices and working conditions. It has not emphasized policies that promote self-reliance by creating jobs, easing transitions into the labor market for those already working, and facilitating movement into employment for those entering the labor force.

The underemphasis on active employment measures has created a policy configuration curiously out of step with dominant American values. Americans have consistently expressed distaste for programs that provide income assistance for the able-bodied; by contrast, public support for government intervention in the area of employment has been strong.[3] But such support has been "a broadly sweeping and vague preference in search of a viable policy": policymakers have not translated such support into policy.[4] As a result, American policies have paradoxically operated to promote dependency rather than to encourage economic independence.

This book explores this paradox in American social and economic policy, asking why the scope of employment policy has been so limited in the United States. I examine the development of Keynesian macroeconomic policy and labor market policy, two policy areas central to American efforts to address employment problems after the New Deal, and I analyze failed efforts to extend policy in the

1970s to include economic planning and tripartite cooperation. I argue that the pattern of innovation and failure in each of these domains can be understood by examining how policy problems became framed in particular ways that limited their further development. To make sense of this process, I explore the creation of institutionally based policy networks, the organization of political competition, and the formation of political alliances for each of these policy areas. My approach is historical: I treat the development of policy as a sequential process in which new initiatives created boundaries that restricted the shape of future innovation.

In the United States, I show, such sequences of development had important ramifications for the contours of employment policy. First, American employment policy settled on a narrow definition of the problem to be solved: policy focused on "unemployment," as defined by a single aggregate figure. Second, policymakers concerned with employment policy rarely conceived their task as one of institution building. Finally, employment issues became partitioned into an "economic" component and a "social" component, each cast into a distinct orbit of politics and administration. Over time, this institutional and political segmentation systematically bounded employment policy and narrowed the possibilities for adapting policy to new political and economic conditions.

In the 1930s, when the federal government first entered the field of employment policy, there was some possibility that economic and social policies relevant to employment would be institutionally and politically linked as mutually reinforcing endeavors, allowing for a broad and flexible approach to employment problems. The initial failure to join these arenas spurred the development of fragmented intellectual, institutional, and interest configurations that left the United States poorly equipped to devise employment policies under the changing political and economic circumstances of the next decades. Instead, employment policies became entangled with two concerns pivotal in American politics: the economic and political position of African-Americans and the role of the federal government. Conflicts in each of these areas stymied the development of institutions to implement employment policy and unraveled the coalitions needed to sustain government action. By the end of the 1970s, racial divisions and government incompetence had set the terms for debates about employment policies, which were increasingly portrayed as wasteful, special interest programs standing in the way of the broad public interest in a prosperous economy peopled by resourceful individuals.

Employment Policy and the American National Community

In the decades after the New Deal, fundamental issues about how the American government should enter the realm of employment remained unsettled. Although much of the policy debate was conducted in technical language, conflicts about employment policy raised fundamental issues, which had implications for the relationship between state and society and ultimately for the meaning of national community in America.

States, Citizens, and Employment Policy

Employment policy provides a context for studying patterns of national policymaking, but it also offers a window onto the fundamental character of a political regime. Because work is at the core of social activity, decisions about employment policies touch on the most basic features of social organization. Public debates about employment can thus be read as struggles to define the proper relationship between states and markets, to extend or contract the meaning of citizenship, and to determine the public role in the ostensibly private sphere of family life.

The pattern of government involvement in employment signals the way a society constructs the boundaries between public and private; embedded in debates about employment issues are assumptions about the status of markets and states. Markets may be defended as a set of private relationships over which the state has no legitimate claim. Alternatively, they may be defined as social constructs, which the state creates and sustains, and over which the state may exercise authority.[5] Such public authority over markets may be justified on the grounds of national interest. Concerns about national security, both economic and military, provide the rationale for promoting some economic sectors over others to ensure a desired mix of activities.

Because workers are citizens, employment policies also provoke questions about the rights of citizenship and the rights of private employers. How far does the government's role in ensuring the welfare of its citizens extend into the private marketplace? How a government answers this question will have important ramifications for the relative power of different social groups. By altering the terms on which employers and workers confront each other in the labor market, decisions to intervene in the realm of employment may decisively shift the balance of power in society and alter the contours of politics.

Employment policies also reveal much about social conceptions of family.[6] Definitions of work, beliefs about who should work, and perceptions of appropriate levels of compensation reflect and in turn influence the economic strategies of families. Modifications in the organization of family life, including changes in the economic roles of women and children, have important implications for how governments intervene in employment matters and for the kinds of demands that emerge from society. Likewise, shifts in family patterns alter the effects of government intervention. Policies premised on particular forms of family may have quite different consequences when the organization of family life changes.

The employment policies adopted in the United States since World War II have embodied ambiguities in each of these spheres. The federal government emerged from the war with an enhanced but vague commitment to watch over the economy; the principles that would guide government action were left murky, and the instruments of intervention remained unspecified. Similarly, the responsibility of the state to the citizen in the realm of employment was never spelled out. Although the federal government professed concern about unemployment, efforts to establish a legal right to a job were repeatedly defeated, and no public response to employment problems was guaranteed. Finally, like the rest of American social policy, employment policy was silently premised on the two-parent, male-headed household. At the same time, however, employment policy appeared blind to the effects of the economy on families and to the way that changes in families might alter the role of employment policy.[7]

The vague purview, unspoken assumptions, and blind spots in American employment policy reflect the limits of New Deal reform and the consequent bounds of political debate in postwar America.[8] The lack of a firm political and institutional foundation hindered incremental policy development; moments of political opportunity permitted innovation, but new policies remained ad hoc initiatives, unconnected to any broader justification of the state's obligation to citizens in the realm of employment. Policy innovations were, accordingly, perpetually vulnerable to political redefinition and contestation.

American ambiguity and vacillation in the sphere of employment contrasts markedly with the better-elaborated policies and forthright commitments characteristic of many European industrial democracies in the postwar era. In some nations, government action rested on a political commitment to provide full employment; in others, established forms of intervention allowed further development of policies relevant to employment. Sweden combined a firm commitment to full employment with an elaborate set of active labor market policies. West Germany developed a weaker version of labor market policy but politically downplayed the centrality of full employment. In Britain, full employment was central to postwar politics, but policies remained limited and, for the most part, short-lived. France eschewed public commitment to full employment but developed extensive planning policies that allowed the government control over important aspects of employment.[9]

Despite this considerable variation in the lines of policy stressed and in the political prominence accorded employment efforts in European nations, nowhere was government intervention in the realm of employment as politically contested and as institutionally anchorless as in the United States. American employment policy reveals a pattern of frustration evident in each of the major initiatives of the postwar era.

The American Pattern of Employment Policy

Since the 1930s, diverse initiatives and often unexpected innovations in American employment policy have suggested that policy in this area has not been bound by some set of predetermined limits. Nonetheless, over time, a pattern of frustration and political failure has characterized active employment policies in the United States. Initiatives typically were launched in a burst of innovation, followed by abandonment or significant dilution. Underlying this pattern was the inability of these policies to sustain the political support that marked their initial reception. Active employment policies have also been remedial; they targeted "losers" in the economic system as opposed to being universally available, and they were typically enacted after economic problems emerged, rather than being preventive or proactive policies.

These features of individual employment policies influenced the broader pattern of policy over time: although American policymakers often treated them as separate realms, these policy areas were in fact closely connected. Decisions about macroeconomic management made in the 1940s narrowed the possibilities for decisionmaking about labor market policy in the 1960s; decisions about both shaped the debates about planning and tripartite (government-

business-labor) cooperation in the 1970s. To make sense of employment policy in the United States, we need to understand the repeated cycle of innovation and abandonment that characterized
individual policies as well as the connections among policies that led
to the broader pattern of frustration that developed over time.

The cycle of innovation followed by dilution and loss of political
support clearly represents the fate of Keynesianism in the United
States. In *The General Theory*, Keynes challenged classical economic
theory, arguing that unemployment was not voluntary, but stemmed
from insufficient demand in the economy. Thus, governments did
not have to wait for markets to right themselves but could take action to reduce unemployment by increasing overall demand. These
ideas meshed well with similar perspectives being developed in the
United States, and in 1938 the United States became one of the first
Western nations deliberately to undertake deficit spending in order
to promote employment.[10] Alvin Hansen, the leading American
Keynesian, saw Keynesianism as a way of resolving the "apparent
conflict between the humanitarian and social aims of the New Deal
and the dictates of 'sound economics.' "[11]

After World War II, however, the "social Keynesianism" of the
1930s, which tied economic objectives to social welfare initiatives by
using spending to create deficits, was rejected with the defeat of the
Full Employment bill and passage of the much watered-down Employment Act.[12] Although tools of Keynesian analysis became part of
the national economic policymaking apparatus, it was an "automatic" version of Keynesian policy, relying on variations in government income and spending that occur automatically with the
business cycle, that emerged after the war. Not until 1964 was a deliberate effort to stimulate the economy enacted, and then it took the
form of tax cuts, not government spending.[13]

Even after the landmark tax cut, active use of Keynesian principles
to combat unemployment enjoyed only a precarious status in American economic policymaking. Each decision to raise or lower taxes in
accordance with Keynesian principles continued to provoke controversy and vocal opposition in Congress; calls for balanced budgets
threatened even the use of automatic stabilizers. Fiscal adjustments
rarely anticipated economic activity; instead they were far more
likely to take place after declines or surges in the private economy.[14]
In this context, Keynesian economics fared poorly in the economic
turmoil of the late 1970s. During the Reagan administration, it was
formally abandoned in favor of supply-side economics and the rhetoric, if not the reality, of balanced budgets.[15]

Labor market policies, too, exhibited a pattern of intense activity followed by dilution and near-abandonment. Each wave of labor market policy was preceded by sufficient support to launch the new policy, and in the case of the public employment policies of the 1930s and the 1970s, that backing was initially broad based and enthusiastic. In each instance, however, these new programs ended in a cloud of disillusion only a few years after they had been inaugurated.

The Works Progress Administration (WPA) of the 1930s generated sufficient animosity to be credited with taking public employment off the national agenda for a generation.[16] The second and third waves of labor market policy fared little better. Initially, enthusiasm accompanied the various job-training programs launched in the 1960s, most of which were eventually folded into the War on Poverty and the public employment and training programs of the 1970s, largely implemented under the auspices of the Comprehensive Employment and Training Act of 1973 (CETA).[17] But the flurry of new programs was followed only a few years later by disillusionment and a sharp scaling down of resources devoted to them. The Reagan administration essentially abandoned active labor market policies; CETA was one of the first programs totally eliminated when Reagan took office.[18] Although individual programs—such as the Job Corps—have occasionally attracted enough allies to survive for many years, enduring support for a broad and systematic labor market policy never emerged from these episodes of policy experimentation.

Labor market policies in the United States have generally been remedial in both the population served and the timing of initiatives. After the New Deal, job placement and job-training activities concentrated on those at the lower end of the labor market. Although some advocates of public employment during the Depression saw the programs as a means of stimulating the economy, for the most part they were designed and administered as social policies to provide temporary help to those thrown out of work by the Depression.[19] During World War II, however, the job placement activities of the U.S. Employment Service were widely viewed as essential to the health of the war economy.

But during the War on Poverty in the 1960s, labor market policies were definitively cast into the realm of social policy. In fact, by targeting poor urban African-Americans and setting up new "poverty institutions," labor market policies of the 1960s became strongly associated with welfare policy, the most despised segment of social policy in America. These remedial features are not intrinsic to labor market policy; other nations have historically used training and job placement activities at various levels of the labor market.[20] Because they functioned as remedial programs, American labor market policies were not used in any systematic way to anticipate labor bottlenecks or surpluses.[21] Instead, policymakers turned to them after problems, such as unemployment, appeared.

During the 1970s, rising inflation and sharpened international economic competition provoked new interest in expanding the tools available to the federal government for promoting employment objectives. In Congress, interest centered on economic planning, while support for establishing new forums for tripartite cooperation emerged within the executive branch. Each of these efforts sought to extend the scope of economic policymaking beyond the framework established at the end of World War II.

The Humphrey-Hawkins Act, first proposed in the mid-1970s, sought to create a national planning process to reach the goal of full employment.[22] The act envisioned a cooperative effort in which the federal government, state and local officials, and private actors would agree on how to achieve employment objectives. Spiraling unemployment gave the bill considerable momentum in Congress, but support evaporated in a matter of months as the 1976 election approached. Only after it had stripped the bill of content did Congress enact Humphrey-Hawkins in 1978. First proposed as a strong planning initiative to achieve full employment, the act passed as a toothless measure, without clear ultimate objectives.

In place of planning, policymakers produced a patchwork of remedial programs and initiatives, focusing on the losers in economic competition. The 1979 bailout of the Chrysler corporation provides a classic example.[23] The apparent success of the Chrysler rescue notwithstanding, this type of intervention did not constitute the planned use of government authority to influence private economic decisionmaking. Such interventions were not part of an overall vision of the economy, and they were typically enacted at the last possible moment, when industry was on the brink of failure.

Efforts to create forums for tripartite cooperation were no more successful than planning ones. These initiatives, which emerged primarily from the Labor Department, were founded on the belief that inflation could be controlled by developing new frameworks that would encourage labor and management to reach a consensus about wages and prices.[24] The government would act as a facilitator. Initial steps to move in this direction during the Ford and Carter administrations were unsuccessful. Instead of creating new patterns of interaction, the Carter administration sought to control prices and wages with government-issued guidelines, which did little more than antagonize both business and labor. Lacking support from either politicians or the private sector, the apparatus administering guidelines was quickly dismantled after Reagan took office.

This pattern of failure compounded over time marks employment policy as archetypical of one path in American policy evolution. The cycle of innovation followed by dilution or abandonment is a recurrent strand in American social and economic policy.[25] Counterposed to this pattern of contested and unsettled policy is an alternative one in which policies attract sufficient support to dig in and survive, often in the face of sharp challenge. Some policies, such as Social Security, develop strong public backing and bureaucratic protection that allows them to expand and shields them from attack. In other cases, even unpopular policies with weak constituencies, such as Aid to Families with Dependent Children (AFDC), can endure and actually expand with a measure of bureaucratic and legal protection. Understanding why active employment policies were not able to become entrenched in the same manner as did Social Security and even AFDC offers a way to make sense of the distinctive restrictions on the range of choice in American social and economic policy during the postwar period.

Explaining the American Pattern of Employment Policy

What this book aims to do, then, is to account for the emergence of a broad pattern of policy over time by probing relationships between policy areas that are often viewed as separate and by scrutinizing the historical sequences that sent policy off in particular channels. This task defines a broad focus of inquiry that is not often found in individual case studies of policy. But it raises concerns that are addressed by broad theories about American politics and by general models of policymaking.

These two literatures take quite different approaches to explaining the dominant features of American social and economic policy. Broad theories of American politics, which examine cultural norms or the power of social interests, highlight the restrictions on innovation posed by enduring features of the American regime. General theories of policymaking, by contrast, say little about the boundaries of policy; instead, they envision policymaking as a process with multiple determinants, without characteristic restrictions. By examining what each of these approaches tells us about policymaking and what each leaves unsaid, we can begin to build a research strategy that accounts for policy boundaries as well as the possibilities for innovation.

Values and Power as Policy Explanations

VALUES

Values deeply embedded in American political culture are often called upon to explain the distinctive features of social and economic policy in the United States.[26] Two cultural traits in particular are credited with shaping American policy. The first is what Louis Hartz called "the liberal tradition in America"—an antistatist individualist strain running deep in the American political character; the second is a pervasive work ethic that prizes advancement through individual effort.[27]

Such broad cultural accounts are quite limited as explanations for policy because they are poorly equipped to explain variations in the shape and timing of particular policies. Although observers of American politics from Tocqueville on have been struck by the antistatism, individualism, and work ethic that seem imprinted in the American national character, the social and economic policies that bear on these values have changed substantially over time. The federal role in social welfare provision has grown dramatically over the past half-century with the enactment of major social welfare and economic policy initiatives. Likewise, the work ethic has found expression in diverse policies. At times it has served to justify support for full employment, in which jobs would be provided for all who want to work; at other times, the work ethic has primarily found expression in support for "workfare" programs in which work is mandated as a condition for receiving welfare benefits.[28]

To understand such variation in policy, we need to understand the links between values and government action. One way that political analysts have sought to draw these connections is by operationalizing values as public opinion. But using public opinion as a proxy for values creates new problems.[29] For one thing, policy does not always reflect public opinion. Moreover, for a variety of reasons, opinion and policy are often only loosely linked. Several policies may be compatible with a particular opinion; additionally, survey researchers have found a persistent disjuncture between abstract general values, such as liberty and freedom, and the policy preferences that people express.[30] Finally, public opinion is "often diffuse and labile."[31] In Robert Reich's words, policymaking does not simply respond "to pre-existing public wants"; instead, it gives "voice to these half-articulated fears and hopes, . . . embodying them in convincing stories about their sources and the choices they represent."[32]

The limitations of cultural explanations suggest that we must examine the intervening processes by which values enter into policy debates and shape outcomes. Central to this task, I shall argue, is the need to make sense of the way cultural symbols are used in conflicts over policy-relevant ideas. Does the cultural repertoire make some ways of understanding social problems more compelling than others? To answer such questions we need to understand how political and social institutions reproduce some cultural definitions over others and facilitate particular forms of political activity and marginalize others.[33] This calls for a developmental perspective that shows how possibilities for policy innovation have opened and closed over time and how, once put into place, policy changes have themselves affected interpretations of cultural values. When tied to institutions and to political strategies in specific historical settings, cultural traditions can become a useful element of explanation because they define the repertoire of symbols, attitudes, and styles with which institutions identify and out of which social and political actors fashion their activity.[34]

POWER

A second broad theory of politics highlights the power of social interests and identifies the disproportionate influence of business as the dominant influence on American politics and policy. In this perspective, the distinctive limits of American employment policy and politics can be understood by reference to the strength of business. This contention parallels a prominent argument made by the Polish economist Michael Kalecki in 1943.[35] Kalecki argued that full employment would inevitably confront political problems because business would oppose policies to reach full employment, fearing that low rates of joblessness would increase the bargaining power of workers as the reserve army of labor was depleted. Drawing inspiration from Marxism, a variety of like-minded arguments have maintained that the balance of power between business and labor is the key to understanding the limits of economic and social policy. This perspective has provided the foundation for a wealth of studies seeking to account for cross-national variations in the size of the welfare state and in unemployment and inflation rates.[36]

This focus on only two main actors, business and labor, creates problems for explaining policy. Even in the United States, where business has often played a prominent role in blocking or limiting employment policies, it has rarely done so alone. The ability to attract allies is an important component of success, but the balance of power approach says little about it. Moreover, these theories make several unwarranted assumptions about interests. By tying interests to the mode of production in such a broad way, they assume a commonality of interests within business and labor and, conversely, antagonism between business and labor. In fact, businesses differ greatly, both cross-nationally and within individual countries, in the support they have lent to welfare state and employment measures; labor positions on these issues have likewise varied.[37] The assumption that business and labor are necessarily in conflict over welfare state and employment measures is equally problematic. On such issues as Keynesianism, labor market policy, or industrial policy, where business or sectors of business stand to gain by government intervention, the assumption of zero-sum conflict between labor and business is misleading.

Economic coalition arguments remedy some of these problems by dividing business and labor—along with other relevant economic interests, such as agriculture—into different sectors based on their economic interests.[38] Because they recognize that business and labor are not monolithic, or the only important actors in policymaking, and because they allow for the possibility of common interests between sectors of business and labor, economic coalition arguments avoid making the sweeping assumptions about policy interests evident in arguments that focus on business and labor alone. Consequently their analyses are more readily able to make sense of the circumstances under which labor and business will cooperate on policy issues. They are also able to address the often critical role that other groups play in policy decisions.

Despite the more nuanced analyses they produce, arguments that emphasize economic coalitions remain limited. One problem emerges from the way these explanations treat ideas. By assuming that ideas enter politics on the shoulders of influential social groups, economic coalition arguments cannot take into account the more independent role that new ideas can play in causing existing groups to rethink their interests and form alliances that would not be possible under an older system of ideas. In contrast to this vision of ideas as the property of particular social groups, I suggest that, at times, ideas can become influential through processes that are not under the direct control of politicians or of any single social group.[39] To make sense of coalitions, the processes by which ideas come to guide policy therefore need to be understood.

Questions about ideas suggest that closer attention be paid to professional groups. These groups often play an important role in constructing the framework within which economic groups identify their interests. Experts are often instrumental in defining problems and establishing the scope of alternative policies; they may even prove decisive in determining which definition of policy interests economic groups ultimately embrace. In the field of employment policy, the influence of economists is particularly important to understand because they early on established themselves as intellectual gatekeepers for discussions of policy. Their approaches to employment issues have shaped the language in which the problems are discussed and the terms in which policy options are debated and evaluated. Economic coalition arguments provide little insight into the potentially independent contributions of such groups in policymaking if they simply assume that they serve as proxies for various economic interests.[40]

Another problem with economic coalition arguments is that they often fail to consider how political and policymaking institutions can affect a group's capacity to influence policy and shape the probability that diverse interests will form policy coalitions.[41] When they do not analyze paths of influence, these arguments imply that adoption of a policy is evidence that the groups supporting it caused it to pass. Unless they can also show how the group inflenced decisionmaking and weigh its influence against other factors, explanations of this sort end up presenting a simple, instrumental view of politics.[42] This lack of theorizing about institutions also means that economic coalition arguments offer only a limited perspective on how coalitions form. Political institutions will affect the way a group weighs the need for cooperation with other interests by shaping the costs and benefits of alliances forged along different lines.

These gaps in economic coalition arguments suggest that the role economic interests have in shaping policy is heavily mediated and that it is essential to understand the links between economic interests and political choices in order to make sense of policy. Highlighting the importance of these links does not mean that explanation should ignore the role that economic interest plays, nor does it deny that policy outcomes may disproportionately benefit some groups and harm others. It does, however, suggest that power over policy cannot be assumed on the basis of statements by business executives or other economically powerful interests. Instead, policy explanations need to examine how political conflicts over policy lead some definitions of interest to win out over others. This requires an understanding of how different groups come to have particular conceptions of their policy interests and how the arena in which policy is debated affects the formation of alliances.

Models of Policymaking

General models of policymaking offer a quite different perspective from which to view employment policies. Rather than identifying key enduring features of American politics or culture, they seek to explain outcomes on the basis of characteristic modes of decisionmaking. These models often identify different factors as the central components of decisionmaking and they have different visions of how they merge to produce policy. What they share, however, is a view of policy innovation that is not systematically constrained by deep-seated features of American politics or culture. The particular features of employment policy and changes in design are more easily accounted for in these types of explanation.

A recent influential approach to policymaking in the United States has been offered by John Kingdon.[43] Focusing on the process of agenda setting, Kingdon explores an often neglected aspect of policymaking, particularly important for examining questions about the boundaries and possibilities of policy. Kingdon rejects rational models of decisionmaking as too orderly to capture the complexity and uncertainty that pervade policymaking. Incremental models, he argues, come closer to describing the way policy is actually made, but they do not encompass all of policymaking. Indeed, incremental models fail to explain some of the most striking policy innovations in the United States, which seem to occur in a "big bang" rather than through gradual change.[44]

What Kingdon proposes instead is a variant of the "garbage can" model of decisionmaking, in which several separate processes merge to produce policy.[45] He identifies three "streams" that must come together for a policy to find a place on the nation's agenda: problem recognition, generation of policy proposals, and political events. Each of these streams is largely independent of the other two, and their joining is fundamentally unpredictable. The emergence of new problems or significant political changes are the most frequent preconditions for merging the streams, but their joining often depends on the actions of skillful policy entrepreneurs.

Kingdon's model of agenda setting incorporates important elements that broad theories of American politics leave out. Because it pays attention to the influence of ideas on policy, it can say more about why social groups interpret their interests in particular ways. Moreover, because Kingdon highlights the variability and flux possible in each of the "streams" he examines, he can account for change more readily than can culture- or interest-based theories.

But because Kingdon's model is ahistorical, it is in many ways too fluid. The problems that result are clearest in his contention that problems, politics, and policy are fundamentally independent. On the contrary, a historical perspective shows that these streams are linked in important ways over time. Policies from an earlier period can affect each of these streams at a later time. The conception of what the problems are and how they should be defined very often depends on previous policies, which establish some groups as authoritative voices in a particular field and make other perspectives less credible. Earlier policies also provide politicians and policymakers with analogies that they use to judge future policy options.[46] Likewise, the range of appropriate solutions to a problem can be affected by earlier policies, which direct research along particular lines by making funding and other resources available. Policies introduced at one time can also powerfully shape the politics at a later moment. Similar influences across time can be traced to the problem recognition and politics streams.

This account of the way that problems, policies, and politics are linked over time is not meant to suggest that the past uniquely determines what is possible at a later moment. Rather, it shows how action taken at one time can make some perceptions and decisions more plausible at a later time. A historical perspective is needed to understand the ways in which ideas and action may be channeled by earlier policies and politics.

Innovation and the Boundaries of Policy

The approach I take in this study aims to make sense of innovation as well as boundaries in American policymaking. This objective directs attention to the diverse links among ideas, political institutions, political actors, networks of experts, and social interests that are often overlooked in culture- or interest-based accounts of policymaking. But it also entails an understanding of how, over time, some avenues of policy become increasingly blocked, if not entirely cut off. Central among the questions I ask are, How do social phenomena become "policy problems," and how do particular understandings of problems emerge to guide policymaking? How do such understandings affect the way groups identify their policy interests, in the process facilitating some alliances and discouraging others?

Answering such questions requires an approach that is fundamentally historical, looking for connections among policies over time. Such a perspective is essential for understanding how opportunities for innovation arise and for assessing the range of policy possibilities open at any particular moment. Inherent in this approach is the notion that individual innovations are part of a "policy sequence" in which institutional development renders some interpretations of problems more persuasive and some prospective policies more politically viable than others.[47] Underlying the concept of a policy sequence is the notion of "path dependence": decisions at one point in time can restrict future possibilities by sending policy off onto particular tracks, along which ideas and interests develop and institutions and strategies adapt.[48]

To understand how a sequence develops requires examination of not only the direct antecedents of innovation but also policies formally classified in other arenas, which may nonetheless shape the problem itself, thinking about the problem, or the politics of the issue.[49] This calls for casting a broad eye over politics to understand how developments in different domains of politics and policy collide with one another to create outcomes that cannot be readily anticipated or easily controlled by individual actors. Such "collisions" can become turning points in a sequence by creating opportunities for political actors seeking to promote new ideas and different visions of politics.[50]

We can get a better sense of how this process works in the United States by taking a close look at how American political institutions affect the entry of ideas into policy debate, the terms of political competition, and the process of alliance formation. In each area, we will consider how the organization of institutions relevant to employment policy has created opportunities for some kinds of innovation and how their development has also set boundaries on the types of innovation possible.

Political Institutions and the Production of Ideas

Two features of American political institutions have influenced the range of ideas that have been considered in national policymaking about employment. The first is the relative openness of the federal government to new ideas; the second is the limited capacity of the government to serve as a site for the production of ideas about employment.

The mode of bureaucratic recruitment and the procedures that govern advancement within the federal government both facilitate consideration of innovative ideas in national policymaking. The American practice of recruiting "inners and outers," whose primary identification and prospects for career advancement lie in their professional expertise, provides a hospitable setting for introducing new ways of looking at problems. In contrast to systems where recruitment into government is governed by strict guidelines emphasizing conformity to established civil service norms, the American federal bureaucracy is routinely refreshed with ideas from outside government.[51]

A second aspect of American institutions that facilitates the entry of new ideas is the way politicians are linked to bureaucracies. The often freewheeling relationship between politics and administration in the United States allows American presidents routinely to solicit ideas from different levels of the bureaucracy; rarely do they restrict themselves to interaction with those at the apex, as is customary in systems with stricter norms of hierarchy.[52] This diversity in potential sources of advice increases the pool of ideas likely to receive serious consideration in American policymaking.

Finally, the permeability of the federal government by social groups expands the range of ideas that receive a hearing in American policymaking. One characterization of the relationship between interest groups and the bureaucracy is the "capture" theory, which argues that bureaucracies and politicians become the captives of the social interests whose activities they are supposed to regulate.[53] But even if we reject this extreme version of the relationship between socioeconomic interests and government, Congress and many areas of the American federal bureaucracy are very much open to the participation and potential influence of economic interests, which may serve to bring new ideas into government.

These features of American political institutions mean that a wide range of ideas have a chance of influencing American policy. Ideas that are formulated and advocated by preexisting interests as well as those devised by professional groups without direct ties to interests may find their way onto the policy agenda. But such openness is bounded by the particular history of an issue. As resources, expertise, and institutions become invested in particular courses of action, ideas that envision substantial reorganizations of these elements may be blocked by institutional obstacles and/or institutional hostility.

One of the most important determinants of whether a new idea is deemed appropriate for coping with a particular issue is its relationship to previously dominant ways of understanding problems. Such relationships are not purely intellectual but are embedded in a variety of institutional practices. Which lessons are drawn from past policy interventions depends on who has established authority to speak to these issues and how institutions divide responsibility for them. The way a problem is initially understood and classified will give some professional groups a dominant voice in interpreting the problem and devising solutions and will grant particular agencies jurisdiction over the issue.[54] Further developments in a policy area are thus powerfully influenced by how the problem was conceived in the first place, since institutional and professional holds on issues are not readily relinquished or easily reorganized.

In employment policy, professional economists became critical in setting limits on the kinds of ideas that would be most influential in policymaking. To make sense of how policy was limited, we must understand how particular networks of expertise arose, how cohesive they were, and how they established channels of communication to the government.[55]

The range of ideas is constrained not only by the establishment of professional authority but also by the range of institutional sites for producing ideas. In the United States, a critical factor has been the limited role played by the federal bureaucracy in producing ideas about employment policy since World War II.[56] The major institution created to oversee employment issues, the Council of Economic Advisers, is a small agency with limited resources. And as government operating agencies concerned with employment issues became increasingly preoccupied with short-range routine work and the tasks of program evaluation and cost-benefit analyses during the 1970s, the bureaucratic "space" for investigating new policy approaches within the government shrank.

In this vacuum, private think tanks and university researchers—often operating with government contracts but little direct supervision—took much of the initiative in formulating innovative ideas about employment policy.[57] The split between idea-producing agencies and the operating branches of government exacerbated the characteristic difficulties that American institutions have in joining ideas, politics, and administration.[58] At the same time, it handicapped policies that proposed using government institutions in more extensive and innovative ways. Arguments in favor of government action were less likely to be voiced if governmental actors did not play an important role in generating policy alternatives. Moreover, ideas that did call for innovative uses of existing agencies or the creation of new institutions were handicapped by the absence of bureaucratic actors, whose support would be essential for establishing the political and practical feasibility of such policy.

Thus, the organization of American national political institutions has generally encouraged consideration of a range of ideas in national policymaking. However, over time, the central role that relatively independent networks of professional economists played in setting the terms of employment policy and the confined role of the state as a producer of ideas narrowed the scope of policy and, in particular, worked to disadvantage ideas that sought to use government institutions to achieve policy goals.

Political Competition and Policy Choice

Because political actors link policy and politics by choosing to support some ideas over others, their motivations and concerns are central to an understanding of policy innovation. In nations with strong party systems, political parties play the key role in linking ideas and politics: their competition spurs policy innovation. In the United States, parties are too diffuse as organizations to take up this role in a predictable or consistent manner.[59] Instead, individual presidents often have considerable leeway in defining issues and setting policy agendas. Consequently, we must examine the activities of both parties and presidents to see how political competition affects the fate of policy in the United States.[60]

To understand how parties and presidents make choices about policy ideas requires knowledge of the organizational context within which they operate. Explanations of strategy need to specify how actors choose courses of action; public choice theorists have solved this problem simply (and parsimoniously) by adopting the assumption of individual rational action.[61] Such theoretical elegance comes at a cost, however. Many rational choice theorists now argue the importance of organizational setting and institutional structure in creating the terms of rationality.[62] I draw on this perspective by looking to the organizational context within which political actors operate as the key to understanding how they choose to embrace some policy ideas and reject others. Unlike rational choice theorists, however, I argue that a variety of motives, including personal beliefs and ethical judgments apart from electoral success, may underlie the way political actors approach policy choices.[63]

Two features of American politics offer clues to the conditions under which parties and presidents have evaluated choices about employment policy. The first is the fragmented structure of national political institutions, which creates a wealth of opportunities for mobilizing opposition. The ease of organizing opposition encourages politicians to adopt a shortened time horizon and makes short-term coalitions the bread and butter of American policymaking. Such arrangements do not encourage attention to the long-range repercussions of policy. The second feature of American politics that affects politicians' evaluations of policy is the federal system, which can create formidable political and procedural barriers to implementing policy. The need to negotiate the different levels of the federal system affects the way political actors decide how policy goals should be achieved or, indeed, whether they are possible at all.

The need to achieve results in the short-term pushes parties and presidents to put together short-term ad hoc coalitions around specific issues and to assemble broad public support, sustained by rhetoric with wide but shallow and often vague appeal.[64] Although the support engendered by such appeals may be diffuse or ephemeral, it serves immediate political needs.[65] In this context, policies that depend on reforming existing institutions or building new institutional capacity are less attractive than those that funnel distributive benefits through existing institutions, those that bypass existing institutions altogether, or those that rely on private activity, since they can be more easily launched. Reliance on new channels or private actors to implement policy also helps to solve obstacles posed by the federal system. Because there is little incentive to consider the long-range repercussions of policy, tactics useful in passing a particular policy can actually undermine the emergence of the long-term political coalitions and enduring institutions needed to sustain a particular policy direction.

The approach to strategy adopted here is one that is organizationally bounded. Evaluations based on individual beliefs, ethical concerns, and political imperatives are all very much conditioned by organizational settings. Because political actors make choices with less than perfect information about which policies will best meet their goals, the institutional fields within which they operate are crucial in understanding whom they select as their advisers, what choices they perceive as open to them, how they frame problems, and how they devise political strategy. Yet in circumstances when established institutions or intellectual frameworks begin to break down, the scope of choice for political actors may widen. Such instances are often important turning points in the evolution of policy; and precisely because structures are crumbling, strategies may play a far more independent role in determining choices and in charting these sharp departures from the usual contours of policy.

Political Alliances and Policy Packages

Policy ideas may reach the national agenda and even be selected by politicians, but unless they build supportive alliances, they will be vulnerable to political attacks. Such support is often critical in allowing policy administrators to "learn from their mistakes" and modify policy accordingly. It also permits policymakers to redesign policy to respond to new circumstances. How, then, do supportive alliances emerge and endure?

I argue that such alliances are the product of political processes, not preexisting preferences.[66] This view presumes that policy interests can be defined in different ways so that several distinct policies may be compatible with a group's interest: potential group members do not always know their interests in a specific policy area; moreover, existing groups may be divided or ambivalent about their policy interests. This means that the process by which a group forms around support for a specific set of policy preferences cannot be taken for granted; instead, questions must be asked about why one policy is favored over another.[67]

One of the most powerful factors determining how groups define their policy interests and which alliances they enter is the organization of political institutions. The aspects of the political system that aggregate interests, in particular the party system and Congress, are central in this regard. By channeling the way groups interact in politics and policymaking, these institutions greatly affect the possibilities for diverse groups to recognize common interests and construct political alliances and often determine whether such alliances are necessary.

Another factor affecting the way groups define their interests is the way a policy is "packaged." Conceptualizing policy as part of a package helps to locate it within the broader framework of political conflict by identifying its relation to past policies and to other items currently on the national agenda. Thinking about policy in such relational terms helps make sense of patterns of support and opposition, since a single policy is unlikely to be judged simply on its own terms; rather, it will be considered as part of a constellation of policies that seem to be related. Situating policy in this way helps to show how a particular policy may be posed as an alternative to some policies and a complement to others; it also clarifies the trade-offs that are associated with the policy. The way a policy is packaged plays an important role in maintaining the diffuse support or acceptance necessary to protect it from challenge.

Politicians seek to affect these processes of group interest identification and alliance formation, but various strong inertial forces limit what they can do. Interests attached to established policies can obstruct later efforts to reorganize policy along new lines.[68] The political terms on which policies are first introduced may also block later efforts to mobilize political backing. For example, if social support has been initially won on the basis of the effectiveness of the policy, efforts to sustain support on different grounds, such as citizens' rights, will prove difficult. Likewise, initial decisions about implementation may affect later possibilities for sustaining a supportive alliance. Implementation problems can erode support for a policy by giving force to arguments that unwanted side effects outweigh benefits, even if the policy is inherently desirable. At the extreme, poorly implemented policies can undermine support to the extent that the goal is deemed outside the realm of public policy altogether.[69]

Efforts of politicians to create support for policies are also limited by events they cannot control, such as social movements, economic changes, or international political developments. Such events, often only indirectly connected to a particular policy, can nonetheless have important ramifications for the positioning of that policy. By creating a new context for policy, such events can change the meaning of a policy, linking it with a different set of issues and tying its fate to new forces.

Conclusion

In the pages that follow, I track two key episodes in the effort to develop an active employment policy in the United States: Keynesianism and labor market policies. I focus the discussion of each policy on a formative period, when critical decisions about the shape of the policy were made, beginning with Keynesianism in the 1930s and 1940s, and then discussing labor market policies in the 1960s and mid-1970s. I then examine the failure of planning and tripartite policies in the late 1970s. This roughly chronological account allows consideration of the particular factors that shaped each policy domain but also draws attention to the way these policies influenced one another over time. In this way, the study links areas of policy that are often treated separately, showing how these distinct areas influenced one another by institutionalizing particular ideas and creating particular political alliances.

Two

Creating an American Keynesianism

In 1938, the United States embarked on its first experiment with Keynesian-style macroeconomic management. Prodded by a sharp economic downturn that had sent unemployment rates shooting up and production levels plunging, the president announced a new program of government spending that aimed to revive the nation's economy. With congressional approval secured several months later, the United States became one of the first nations in the West to employ Keynesian principles to guide the economy. The influence of these ideas expanded during the war, as economists put them to work in managing the war economy.

When the decades of depression and war drew to a close, however, the United States turned its back on the grand vision of the earliest American Keynesians. The defeat of the Full Employment bill in 1945 signaled the political failure of a "social Keynesianism" that joined economic and social policies by institutionalizing government spending to ensure full employment. The Employment Act that was ultimately enacted in 1946 acknowledged that the federal government should bear some responsibility for the health of the economy, but it embodied an uncertain commitment to government action and provided few tools to facilitate that action. In less than a decade, the United States had moved from a position of international leadership in employment policy innovation to a stance that reflected severe doubts about the desirability of active government measures to reduce unemployment. For two decades after the war, American economic policy reflected the influence of Keynesian ideas, but in a form that relied on the "automatic" effects of spending programs, such as unemployment insurance, that would rise and fall with the business cycle.

This chapter explores this shift in policy. I ask why the United States was an intellectual leader in experimenting with Keynesian ideas and why the early experiments with deficit spending produced only an uncertain commitment to Keynesian macroeconomic management. As I examine the evolution of employment policy during the New Deal, I discuss how Keynesian ideas first reached the national policy agenda and explain why a supportive policy coalition of sufficient strength to sustain this early intervention did not emerge.

I conclude with an analysis of the first Keynesian tax cut, enacted in 1964, evaluating how the new framework for economic policymaking constructed at the end of the war limited the future scope of employment policy in America.

Putting Keynesianism on the Nation's Agenda

Understanding how Keynesian ideas reached the national agenda during the New Deal poses two puzzles. First, why did Roosevelt's initial recovery strategy emphasize planning to lead the nation out of depression even though it launched a panoply of spending programs as well? Second, why did the president ultimately turn to a deliberate spending strategy in 1938?

Planning or Spending? The Early New Deal

In the early 1930s, as the American economy sank into ever-deeper depression, advocates of diverse recovery strategies paraded before Congress and pressed government officials in an effort to influence the national agenda. Of the many policies actively debated, the New Deal initially pinned its hopes on a version of planning to pull the economy out of the doldrums. At the same time, it enacted a variety of emergency relief programs to help the temporarily destitute. To see why this route was chosen, we must examine the influence of past debates about planning and government spending on the president and his brain trusters and weigh the role that social interests played in this initial decision.

In the decades before the Great Depression, planning and government spending were both widely discussed as strategies to cope with economic problems, including unemployment. As the economic turbulence of the 1800s spilled over into the new century, unemployment increasingly came to be seen as "a problem of industry" rather than the product of individual failure.[1] This new interpretation of unemployment spurred investigation into the operation of the economy and, in particular, into the dynamics of business cycles. American social scientists contributed to these new understandings with an empirically focused program of research, which included Wesley C. Mitchell's statistical studies of business cycles and John R. Commons's institutional approach to labor relations.[2] From these new understandings and insights emerged a variety of policy proposals, some calling for legislation at the national and local levels and others urging political executives—including mayors, governors, and the president—to promote private action.

Ideas about planning had been on the national stage in various guises well before the New Deal.[3] The dominant approach to planning in the decades before the New Deal held that the economy could be stabilized and unemployment reduced by decentralized business planning; individual firms could pace production to stabilize their demand for labor. As secretary of commerce during the 1920s, Herbert Hoover embraced this version of planning, envisioning an "associative state" in which government would encourage planning within individual companies and cooperation among business enterprises.[4] In this voluntaristic approach to planning, the federal government's role was limited to disseminating information and promoting business organization.[5]

By the 1920s, there was also broad agreement that spending on public projects should be increased during periods of economic distress. For over a century, urban political machines had inaugurated short-term public projects to provide work during economic depressions.[6] During the severe downturn in the 1890s and those that followed, many localities had increased spending on public projects to provide jobs for those without work. The widely circulated "Proposal to Reduce Unemployment" published by the American Association for Labor Legislation made public works a central part of its program; President Harding's 1921 Conference on Unemployment likewise urged that spending on public works be increased during economic downturns.[7]

Boosting spending on public works was attractive for both political and economic reasons. Politically, it was more desirable to offer the unemployed work than to give them "handouts." And, as the leaders of urban machines had long realized, generous political benefits could be reaped by offering jobs to those out of work. In the early twentieth century, new knowledge about business cycles made public works attractive from an economic perspective as well. By increasing spending during periods of economic distress and decreasing it when the economy was booming, government could act as a balance wheel, helping to stabilize the economy.[8] Some advocates of public works also argued that such spending could actually promote economic recovery by priming the pump of the private economy. Although economic reasoning about the forms of financing and the extent of the priming was unclear, this thinking clearly foreshadowed the policy prescriptions that would emerge from Keynes's *The General Theory*.[9]

Despite the broad support for such a countercyclical public works

policy from business, labor, and political leaders, only limited use
was made of the strategy before the 1930s.[10] Prior to the 1920s, public works had been strictly a local matter. But, galvanized by the Conference on Unemployment of 1921 and the severe slump that had
called it into being, advocates of federal action emerged. In keeping
with Hoover's view that action should be local and voluntary, the
conference restricted the federal role to promoting local initiatives.
The ongoing standing committee of the conference launched an ambitious campaign to get every city with a population over twenty
thousand to set up an emergency unemployment committee to
oversee local activities.[11] But, with the federal role limited to exhortation, the local response was spotty and weak.[12] As the decade wore
on, various proposals for allocating federal money to countercyclical
public works were introduced in Congress and defeated. The only
fruit of this activity was a highway bill that provided federal aid for
road construction.

By the time Roosevelt took office, then, both industrial planning
and countercyclical public works had a rich history of public discussion. Yet industrial planning was the recovery course emphasized in
the early New Deal. The core legislation of the recovery program, the
National Industrial Recovery Act (NIRA), contained provisions for
both industrial planning and public works, but from the start the
Roosevelt administration emphasized industrial planning. The man
Roosevelt appointed to head the new Public Works Administration
(PWA), Harold Ickes, was an old Progressive, whose objective in administering the new program was not to stimulate the economy, but
rather to spend the money in ways that would contribute to the
national good and avoid corruption.[13] Roosevelt applauded such a
"deliberate carrying out of the public works program" because it
"would mean money saved to the Treasury."[14]

Why did the first New Deal not pin its hopes for recovery on
spending? One possibility is that the institutional capacity of the federal government strongly suggested planning over spending. Yet neither route boasted an established institutional framework that
would make it an obvious choice for combating depression. Public
works had been used in earlier economic downturns, but the federal
government had no experience in launching and coordinating a
massive public works program. The institutional supports for industrial planning were even weaker than those for public works. There
was no governmental apparatus to oversee such planning, since
Hoover and his allies had envisioned planning as a voluntary private
activity. The only legacy of the previous decade in this realm was the

sharp increase in the number of trade associations, which provided a forum for interindustry discussion.

A second possible explanation, the advice of experts, also offers little help: both planning and spending found strong supporters among American academics and among those Roosevelt chose to advise him. Some members of Roosevelt's early brains trust, most notably Rexford Guy Tugwell, were deeply interested in the authoritative versions of industrial planning that had grown in popularity under the impact of the Depression. But many policy advisers also supported government spending. As academic economists assimilated the new evidence about business cycles, many had abandoned the old orthodoxy that counseled inaction in favor of government spending to pull the economy out of the Depression.[15] In the early 1930s, voices advocating spending were heard in congressional testimony, in popular publications, and within the ranks of Roosevelt's advisers.[16]

A third explanation, the preferences of social interests, offers more direction but remains insufficient to account for Roosevelt's decision to see industrial planning, not spending, as the key to recovery. Both strategies enjoyed support from organized labor and business, although business clearly preferred planning (as defined by business) to spending. Planning was able to attract broad backing, since its advocates held widely divergent views about what it actually entailed.[17] Labor supported it because the NIRA brought labor into the planning process. Many prominent business leaders, on the other hand, favored planning because they viewed it as an exercise in business self-government in which the federal government would play only a facilitating role, and labor, presumably none.[18]

But, as among experts, enthusiasm for planning did not preclude support for spending. During the 1920s, the Chamber of Commerce joined the American Federation of Labor (AFL) in backing proposals for local public works to "balance" the economy.[19] Organized labor extended this support to endorsing federal spending on public works, a position that business groups were far more reluctant to endorse. In 1932, in fact, the Chamber of Commerce launched a major campaign to counter the growing demands for government spending.[20] Once Roosevelt was in power, however, leading business organizations moderated their opposition to spending. During the congressional hearings on the NIRA, Chamber of Commerce head Henry Harriman backed public works as part of an overall program that highlighted planning and regulatory measures.[21] Business had not changed its views about the undesirability of deficits but was willing to tolerate them until the economy recovered. Moreover, with a broad range of policies on the national agenda, attention to deficits wavered: businesses were far more concerned about policies that might affect them directly than with general fiscal policy.[22]

Roosevelt's failure to take advantage of this new business tolerance to highlight a spending strategy suggests that social interests were not the only factor governing policy choice. Strong pressures in favor of federal spending make the president's reluctance to embrace spending all the more puzzling. By 1933, local political jurisdictions had shed their former mistrust of federal aid and were clamoring for financial help from the federal government.[23] They were far more interested in spending on public works, which addressed their immediate concerns in a way that planning did not.

Thus, Roosevelt faced significant pressure in favor of spending and little strong opposition in the first year of his administration. Why, then, did he shy away from spending? To understand why the New Deal produced a welter of early initiatives but emphasized planning as the permanent recovery program, we need to go beyond social interests to consider other factors that influenced the president's policy preferences. In the contest between spending and planning, both the president's beliefs about economic policy and his electoral strategy pointed to a recovery program that emphasized planning over spending.

The striking feature of American political institutions when Roosevelt took office was the enormous discretion available to the president. The typical pattern of policymaking from the Progressive era on was one in which Congress and the executive branch struggled to define policy, each relying on competing sets of institutions.[24] However, the sense of emergency created by the Depression helped to alter this pattern, as did the election of the first Democratic administration in twelve years. A cooperative Congress, hungry for initiatives to alleviate the Depression, focused unprecedented attention on the executive for policy direction.[25] But the executive branch was poorly equipped to fulfill this role. There was no single authoritative source for policy advice on economic issues within the American state, nor was there any well-established bureaucracy responsible for economic matters. This vacuum meant that Roosevelt as president enjoyed substantial discretion in charting the early course of the New Deal.

Because of the importance of presidential action in the early New Deal, understanding Roosevelt's orientations (and those of the advisers he selected) toward different policy routes is critical for making sense of the choices that were made. Experience with past policies offers the best clue to what these orientations were. Although the federal government had no experience with public works programs or with industrial planning per se, past experience with *similar* policies did influence thinking about planning and spending. And planning appeared far more desirable than spending to Roosevelt.

Planning was advantaged by its association with the regulatory measures championed by Progressives in the early twentieth century. Calling on the federal government to help create more efficient forms of business interaction through the use of administrative authority, as the NIRA did, was wholly consistent with the purposes of government envisioned by Progressives. Spending, on the other hand, had far fewer positive associations for politicians who, like Roosevelt, had cut their teeth during the heyday of Progressivism. Public spending in America was tied to a system of party rule, "bossism," and political patronage, which the Progressives hoped to supplant with norms of administrative rationality and efficiency. It was also inevitably associated with the political corruption that the Progressives fought so assiduously to eliminate.[26] Spending that threatened to create unbalanced budgets was particularly noisome; one of the central aims of Progressive reformers since the turn of the century had been to institute new budgetary processes that would enhance the federal government's accountability, efficiency, and economy in fiscal matters.[27]

Thus, Roosevelt's own political background disposed him more favorably to regulatory planning as a recovery strategy than to spending. As a permanent addition to the role of the federal government, planning (ill defined as it was) appeared far more compatible with legitimate functions of government than did spending. Reinforcing these antispending proclivities was the rhetoric of the 1932 presidential contest, in which Roosevelt repeatedly turned Hoover's own argument against him, singling out the deficit as a cause of economic distress.[28]

However, the fragmented nature of the national administration combined with Roosevelt's strategic interests as a politician to produce a jumble of policy initiatives in 1933. Central among these were spending programs that aimed to alleviate the misery created by the Depression. Roosevelt sought to reap political benefits by rescuing local economies with federal funds at the same time that he maintained a reputation for fiscal probity by making his spending a temporary expedient necessitated by the economic emergency. Thus, although the federal government pumped unprecedented amounts

of money into relief efforts in 1933, the president steadfastly reiter-
ated his opposition to deficits and his view that public spending
must be carefully monitored to make sure it was spent in useful and
necessary ways. "Spending was," in Herbert Stein's words, "the ugly
duckling of Roosevelt's 1933 barnyard...."[29]

The two-track strategy of the early New Deal won the Roosevelt
administration broad political support, but the attempt to put the
ill-defined planning strategy into practice proved untenable. Not
only did the NIRA have little impact on the economy; it also set off
massive disputes among businesses, between business and labor,
and between government and business.[30] When the Supreme Court
declared the NIRA illegal in 1935, it only confirmed the fate that the
political strife over planning had made inevitable. If New Dealers
wanted to spur economic recovery, they would need a new strategy.

The Emergence of Keynesianism within
the Federal Government

Despite Roosevelt's distaste for a deliberate policy of government
spending and, particularly, for deficits, that is the route he embraced
in 1938 when confronted with a new economic downturn that cut
industrial production by one-third. To understand how spending
was transformed from the administration's ugly duckling into the
strategy of choice, we need to examine how support for spending
crystallized within the Roosevelt administration and how spending
was related to the president's political ambitions.

The fragmented nature of the American national bureaucracy and
the pattern of recruitment into government during the New Deal are
the keys to understanding how a strong prospending network
emerged within the Roosevelt administration. When Roosevelt assumed the presidency, executive authority to control finances was
housed in the Bureau of the Budget, a small, ineffectual agency established only a decade earlier.[31] The only overarching authority
within the executive branch was the president, but he did not have
the means to impose a single viewpoint on the federal bureaucracy,
and Roosevelt, in any case, preferred a rather freewheeling competition of ideas within his own administration.[32] In fact, he exacerbated
the fragmentation by setting up a wide variety of ad hoc advisory
groups and emergency agencies with little reference to the existing
structure of public administration.

Fragmentation encouraged diverse policy views within the executive branch, and the lack of centralized authority within the federal

bureaucracy allowed like-minded policy advocates to create niches within the federal government and build networks across agency lines. Their ability to construct such niches was enhanced by a system of departmental recruitment and advancement that allowed agency heads considerable room to select and mold their staffs as they saw fit. The American civil service posed little obstacle to this style of recruitment: although long-fought-for reform had been enacted a decade earlier, the American civil service was a relatively weak system, regularly bypassed by New Deal agencies.[33]

Advocates of spending as a recovery strategy were able to use these administrative structures and recruitment practices to gain strength within the executive branch. The pivotal figure in creating a core of spending advocates was Marriner Eccles, a Utah banker appointed to head the Federal Reserve in 1934. Eccles brought with him to Washington a set of highly unorthodox perspectives about economic recovery; unlike the mainstream of the banking and financial community, whose views reflected Eastern interests, Eccles had little attachment to the sanctity of balanced budgets. Instead, he argued that public deficits, deliberately incurred by government spending, would promote economic recovery by increasing purchasing power.[34]

Eccles pierced the conservative orientation of the Federal Reserve by bringing intellectual allies into the bureaucracy and bypassing the established hierarchy.[35] He recruited as his assistant Lauchlin Currie, a former economics instructor at Harvard, who had been formulating proto-Keynesian ideas about deficits since 1930.[36] First at the Treasury and later at the Federal Reserve, Currie developed a statistical series, initially called the pump priming deficit, that sought to provide intellectual support for a policy of deficit spending.[37] Eccles's advocacy of unorthodox economic views also began to attract allies from other government agencies, most notably Henry Wallace, the secretary of agriculture, and Harry Hopkins, the administrator of the Works Progress Administration (WPA) and Roosevelt's confidant.

As head of the WPA, Hopkins's support for spending could easily be dismissed as agency bias, but his arguments that the United States now was capable of channeling any spending it might want to undertake would be harder to contradict. The various spending programs launched as "temporary" expedients had created new links between Washington and local governments that would allow the federal government to pump money into the economy if it chose to do so. Beginning in 1935, the WPA oversaw projects that put citizens to work in a wide range of public jobs. Although WPA projects were

initiated locally, Washington approved all proposals and set employment quotas and monthly program budgets for each state.[38] National control over the program increased each year, as Hopkins
strengthened the capacities of the central administration. The PWA,
under Ickes, had also geared up, offering a second—although still
slower—way to channel money into the economy. After 1935, Ickes
added his voice to those endorsing spending as a way to revitalize
the economy.

Thus, even as the NIRA was disintegrating administratively and
politically, a network of support for an alternative recovery policy
was growing within the executive branch. The discretion that agency
heads had in recruiting staff and their relative autonomy within the
administration were critical in allowing the spending strategy to
emerge. Over time, the scattered advocates of spending made con-
tact with one another, brought in like-minded allies, and converted
those likely to be sympathetic to their arguments. As these networks
grew stronger, so did the intellectual and practical arguments favoring their policy proposals.

But, even with a strong network arguing in favor of spending,
Roosevelt probably would not have turned to a course he perceived
as politically damaging. In fact, spending had won Roosevelt spec-
tacular political rewards. Dramatic gains for congressional Democrats in 1934 were followed by Roosevelt's landslide reelection two
years later. In each case, the outpouring of popular support owed
much to the New Deal spending programs, which made the federal—and particularly the presidential—presence felt more deeply
in citizens' lives than ever before.

The political drawbacks of spending were less compelling. Neither
of the two major interests that might have opposed spending strategies—business and conservative southern agricultural interests—
was well-positioned to block a new program of spending. The over-
whelming majority of the business and banking communities
continued to oppose budget deficits. As the New Deal swung left in
1935–1936, mainstream business organizations grew increasingly
hostile to Roosevelt, and their tolerance for budgets deficits sharply
diminished.[39] But the rift between the administration and the bulk of
the business community was so deep by this point that business opposition to spending and deficits could not by itself prevent action
along these lines.

A second political problem was the increasing wariness of many
southerners toward social spending, which they feared was slipping
out of their control.[40] Opposition from southern Democrats was a
more serious obstacle, since they were in a position to block spend-

ing proposals in Congress. But in the late 1930s, these Democrats had limited leverage because they depended on northern urban interests to support the parity payments for their agricultural constituents. The Supreme Court's invalidation of the first Agricultural Adjustment Act deprived farm programs of the processing tax on which they had relied for funding; they were thus forced to secure their funds by annual appropriations in Congress. Cooperation on spending with northern labor was the price they paid.[41]

Thus, when the recession of 1937 showed no signs of abating, Roosevelt ultimately heeded the advice of the spenders in his administration. In late March of 1938, while the president was resting at Warm Springs, Georgia, spending advocates converged, under the direction of Hopkins, to persuade the president to shift course. Ensconced in nearby Pine Mountain Valley, Leon Henderson, an administration economist, Aubrey Williams, the WPA deputy administrator, and Beardsley Ruml, a prominent business adviser and currently treasurer of Macy's (who had been on his way to a Macy's department store in Atlanta when he met up with Henderson and Williams on the train south) worked up a series of memoranda that Hopkins deployed in his conversations with the president.[42] Within a matter of days, the president had decided to endorse a spending program to pull the nation out of the recession.

Despite the strenuous objections of Treasury Secretary Henry Morgenthau, who complained that the spenders had "stampeded [the president] like cattle," Roosevelt stuck with his decision to support spending.[43] The program he proposed would release $6.5 billion in federal funds: over $2 billion to come from monetary measures, $1.5 billion in Reconstruction Finance Corporation loans, and about $3 billion in congressional appropriations, mostly for WPA and PWA projects.[44] After some debate over how the money would be spent, Congress approved the entire package, and actually increased its size by adding on a parity payment. Figure 2.1 shows New Deal spending on public assistance and federal work programs; for the economic context in which these and subsequent spending decisions were made, see Figures 2.2 and 2.3.

The decision to endorse spending as a recovery strategy in 1938 was the product of a movement from within the administration that accorded well with the sources of the president's political successes of the past four years. Ideas about spending that had previously enjoyed broad but inchoate support now had the active backing of a well-articulated network within the Roosevelt administration. The campaign to win the president over to spending was orchestrated by members of this network, with Hopkins playing a central role. To

Figure 2.1
Public Assistance and Earnings of Persons Employed under Federal Work
Programs, 1933–1939. Reprinted from Advisory Commission on Intergov-
ernmental Relations, *The Federal Role in the Federal System: The Dynamics
of Growth: Reducing Unemployment: Intergovernmental Dimensions of a
National Problem* (Washington, D.C.: Government Printing Office, 1982), 15.

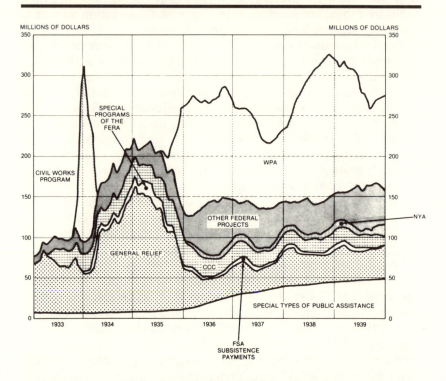

make their case, they relied mainly on allies within the administration, but they also drew in some friends from the outside. Foremost
among these was the brilliant business adviser and "policy entrepreneur" Ruml. Although Ruml played a key role in drafting the
memos that persuaded the president to endorse a spending program, there is no evidence that he was acting at the behest of business. Every account of the 1938 decision places the initiative with
figures within the Roosevelt administration, whose motivations are
not easily attributed to business.[45]

A handful of businesspeople did favor deficit spending, but they
saw their task as that of persuading other business leaders, not the
administration. These forward-looking business leaders, including
Ralph Flanders, from Springfield, Massachusetts, Lincoln Filene, the

Figure 2.2
Gross National Product—Percentage of Change from Preceding Year, 1930–1950. *Source:* U.S. Department of Commerce, *Historical Statistics of the United States, Colonial Times to 1970,* Part 1 (Washington, D.C.: Government Printing Office, 1975), 226–27. *Note:* GNP is measured in 1958 dollars.

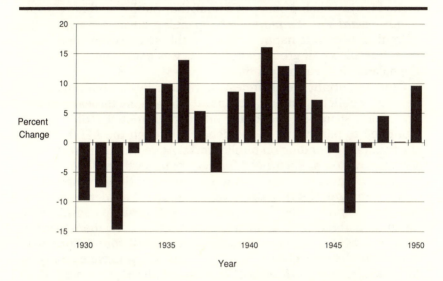

Figure 2.3
Unemployment Rate of the Civilian Population, 1930–1950. *Source:* U.S. Department of Commerce, *Historical Statistics of the United States, Colonial Times to 1970,* Part 1 (Washington, D.C.: Government Printing Office, 1975), 135.

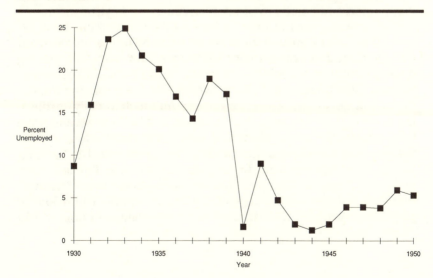

Boston department store chairman, and Henry Dennison, a paper goods manufacturer, were all members of the Business Advisory Council (BAC), a body created by the Commerce Department in 1933. Although the BAC, like every other major business organization, condemned the 1938 decision, Dennison and his allies had argued for just such a policy in a book they published that year, entitled *Toward Full Employment*.[46] Spending advocates within the administration were happy to point to this source of business support, but this small group of mavericks was hardly sufficient to tilt the balance in favor of spending.

Other important social interests were virtually absent from the debates over deficit spending. Organized labor, in the throes of violent organizing struggles and bitter interorganizational strife, was ill equipped to participate in the debate, although the AFL had routinely backed spending on public works. Agricultural interests were too constrained by their need for help from northern labor Democrats in Congress to stake out a more general position on spending.

Not until after the 1938 decision did groups of academics and associations representing major social interests begin to construct the channels and forms of organization that would allow them to influence federal fiscal policy. The earliest and easiest connections were made with the new advocates of Keynesianism, who were springing up in academic departments of economics. Although Keynes's *General Theory* was published in 1936, it had little direct influence on Roosevelt's 1938 decision. Spenders within the administration had been working on their arguments quite independently for years. But by the late 1930s, Keynesian ideas had slowly won acceptance among some professional economists, many of whom were drawn to Washington and helped to develop an American Keynesianism.

The earliest school of American Keynesianism and the most important recruiting ground for bringing economists into government was the economics department of Harvard University. The leading figure in creating this school and its distinctive brand of Keynesianism was Alvin Hansen, a professor who had arrived from the University of Minnesota only a few years earlier. Although initially hostile to the ideas of *The General Theory*, Hansen had by 1938 accepted the basic tenets of Keynesianism and was developing a more radical analysis to make sense of the Depression in America. The "stagnationist" theory that became the hallmark of American Keynesianism in the 1930s and 1940s argued that the United States was a "mature" economy, tending toward stagnation without increasing infusions of public investment.[47] It envisioned major programs of public works and social spending that would pump money into the economy as needed. And, as Hansen recognized, such an investment program would have to be planned and organized (although not necessarily implemented) by the federal government. In this way, Keynesianism would fuse economic objectives and social goals in a planned process overseen by the federal government.[48]

The administrative openness of the New Deal facilitated the initial links between this emerging school of Keynesianism and policymaking agencies in the executive branch. Spending advocates already in the administration could now turn to the university as a recruiting ground, a path well worn by the lawyers recruited into government during the early New Deal.[49] The task was made easier by the explicit policy orientation of Hansen and his followers; the fiscal policy seminar that Hansen conducted and the newly established Littauer School of Public Administration in which he taught aimed to develop economic thinking in the context of current economic problems.[50] With many of Hansen's students moving into important executive branch positions by 1939, and Hansen himself involved in several advisory posts, the ties between the academy and government strengthened.

Despite the inroads Keynesians were making, however, their ties to government were essentially ad hoc. The future of this new relationship between economists and government would depend on how Keynesianism became institutionalized in the United States. The program envisioned by the stagnationists required the creation of new federal authorities and the recasting of relationships between Congress and the executive branch and between the federal government and the states. The ability to construct these new institutions and relationships would thus be central to the fate of Keynesianism in the United States.

The Retreat from Social Keynesianism

American participation in World War II required an unprecedented mobilization of national resources to boost economic production. This presented an excellent opportunity for extending and consolidating the influence of Keynesian principles. Building on the networks that had been established before the war, a large number of Keynesian economists were recruited to Washington to direct the war effort. As they put their ideas into use, they made important advances in collecting and analyzing data needed for a Keynesian economic policy.[51] Moreover, the reaction of the economy to the stimulus of war production seemed to confirm Keynesian predictions: as the federal government pumped money into the economy to support the war, unemployment melted away.

These favorable developments, however, did not lead to a smooth acceptance of Keynesian principles in the United States after the war. Instead, an intense battle over the framework for postwar economic policy erupted and the supporters of deficit spending—the great majority of Keynesians—were unable to institutionalize their version of Keynesianism. Their failure left American economic policy in an uneasy limbo until the 1960s. Although the orthodoxy of annually balanced budgets had been broken, active use of Keynesian principles was still in doubt. The combination of political resistance to institutional reform and powerful social interests opposed to spending worked together to block the acceptance of social Keynesianism. Understanding the bounds of employment policy after the war thus requires an explanation of the political factors that stood in the way of institutional reform, the reasons important socioeconomic groups defined spending as antagonistic to their interests, and the way the political system facilitated the emergence and maintenance of an alliance opposed to spending.

The Politics of Institutional Reform and Public Spending

Central to the fate of Keynesianism after the war was the fact that the systematic public spending advocated by most Keynesians could not be implemented through the existing institutional structure of the American government. The fragmentation of the executive branch would make it difficult for an administration to formulate and present to Congress a package of spending programs keyed to macroeconomic objectives. Such fragmentation weakened the executive in its interactions with Congress and exacerbated problems the executive might have in securing congressional approval in any case. Because institutional reform was a prerequisite to institutionalizing Keynesianism, the struggle over Keynesianism in the United States became a contest about institutional reform, and in particular about innovations that would create more hierarchical lines of authority within the executive branch and strengthen the executive vis-à-vis Congress. Because such reform required congressional approval, policy coalitions organized through Congress would play a central role in determining the fate of Keynesianism.

Understanding the pattern of support and opposition in these conflicts, particularly the relative roles of social and political interests in determining the outcome, is thus the first step in understanding why the early experimentation with Keynesianism in the United States did not lead to its swift acceptance. The central battle in the struggle to institutionalize a policy of deficit spending was waged in the 1945 debate over the Full Employment bill. But earlier conflicts had set the stage. The defeat of Roosevelt's 1937 executive reorganization plan had underscored the difficulty of augmenting executive power by legislation. The debates over the "spend-lend bill" in 1939 and the National Resources Planning Board (NRPB) in 1943 had both previewed the outcome of the later fight.

The aims of the executive reorganization plan and the reforms it proposed reflected the Progressive roots of its authors. The three men Roosevelt tapped to direct the study in 1936 had long been active in the Progressive movement for administrative reform.[52] They believed that government should be organized to reflect administrative criteria of efficiency and rationality instead of political considerations, and they saw the executive, not the legislature, as the focal point of policymaking and problem solving.

The plan that they devised aimed to enhance the power of the president and increase accountability and coordination within the executive branch by consolidating independent agencies into cabinet departments. It also proposed three new departments—Conservation, Social Welfare, and Public Works—reflecting the broadened scope of federal activity during the New Deal. The ability to plan future public initiatives would be increased by strengthening the National Resources Planning Board and the Bureau of the Budget and placing them under the control of the president. The president's power would also be augmented by six new assistants, who the president could direct as he wished.[53]

Although the plan was not initiated with the policy of deficit spending in mind, it had important implications for the conduct of economic policy.[54] The plan effectively institutionalized the increased power that the president had assumed during the Depression; it also enhanced federal authority by consolidating and centralizing control over federal agencies, which had been multiplying helter-skelter. These centralizations of authority, together with the new departments of public works and social welfare, would greatly facilitate the implementation of a social Keynesian policy. Plans for countercyclical spending could be drawn up far more easily and swiftly within this framework. And the public works department would provide ongoing pressure for a permanent program of public investment, much as Hopkins and Ickes had throughout the New Deal.

The potential ramifications of the reorganization plan for congressional-executive power relations were not lost on Congress, which soundly rejected the proposal in 1938. Much of the heated rhetoric about a presidential power grab that surrounded reorganization was fueled by Roosevelt's unsuccessful court-packing attempt, which was being debated at the same time. Despite the shrill tone and often far-fetched claims of the groups that mobilized to oppose reorganization, members of Congress of diverse persuasions added their voices to the opposition.[55] The final vote did not reveal a pronounced regional split or urban-rural divisions. The ease with which many congressional representatives normally sympathetic to the New Deal were won over to the opposition indicated that the enhancement of executive capacities did not rank high among the priorities of even liberal members of Congress.

In 1939 Congress did ultimately approve a reorganization act that included some of the provisions of the original bill. It created the Executive Office of the President, in which the Bureau of the Budget would be placed. And it gave the president his executive assistants. But it created no new departments, nor did it disrupt the status of existing federal agencies. As approved, reorganization would improve the president's ability to manage the government, but it did not create the planning and coordination capacities that would have facilitated a Keynesian spending policy.

More surprising than the defeat of the reorganization plan was the rejection of a major spending proposal in 1939. When New Deal reform efforts began to bog down in the late 1930s, spending initiatives proved happy exceptions for Roosevelt. The 1938 fiscal stimulus package had handily won approval from the same Congress that had defied the administration on reorganization, the court-packing plan, and tax revision.[56] But in 1939, spending, too, became vulnerable; Congress rejected the "spend-lend bill," a fiscal stimulus package the administration had proposed as an economic recovery measure. The opposing coalition took a form that would become increasingly familiar. A bloc of southern Democrats joined with Republicans, whose ranks had grown after the 1938 election, to defeat the measure.[57]

This same coalition, much strengthened by congressional elections in 1942, was instrumental in cutting off funding for the National Resources Planning Board in 1943, effectively forcing the agency to disband. The abolition of the NRPB was an ominous event for social Keynesians hoping to institutionalize their ideas because the agency was the most likely candidate for developing the capacity to plan compensatory spending projects. Moreover, for the past five years the NRPB had served as a base within the federal government for prominent Keynesian economists, most notably Alvin Hansen.

Existing in various guises since 1933, the NRPB was by 1943 a small agency in the Executive Office of the President with a broad mandate to consider the problems of postwar adjustment. It had no power to translate its ideas into policy, but opponents rightly saw it as a potentially influential platform for those advocating deficit spending and extensions of federal power. Hansen saw the board's mandate as an opportunity to launch a public education campaign to seeing the public deficit as an "instrument of public policy."[58] In the early 1940s, the NRPB articulated its vision for postwar America in a series of reports that called for large-scale public investment and substantial increases in public spending on social welfare.[59]

The congressional coalition that abolished the NRPB in 1943 was similar to one that opposed spending in 1939. Once again, Democrats joined forces with a united bloc of Republicans to deny the NRPB sufficient funds to continue operating. The debate over the NRPB also echoed aspects of the controversy over the reorganization plan; in both cases, even liberal allies of the New Deal exhibited only a weak commitment to these measures. The chief defender of the NRPB in the Senate, Senator Kenneth McKellar (D. Tenn.), for example, was shocked when he was informed during congressional debate that the NRPB endorsed deficit spending.[60]

Each of these defeats bode ill for the fate of the Full Employment bill introduced in the Senate in 1945; the bill was based on the same Keynesian principles that underlay the 1939 spending initiative, and it called for organizational innovations that resembled those of the reorganization act and the NRPB. But, unlike the earlier initiatives, the Full Employment bill declared a right to employment for all Americans who sought work and committed the federal government to securing that right. Reflecting the influence of the stagnationist Keynesian analysis, the bill envisioned a permanent federal role in regulating the economy.[61] It created a National Production and Employment Budget, which the president would use to anticipate shortfalls in private investment, and it charged the government with undertaking the compensatory investment needed to reach full employment. Thus, without creating new agencies, the bill sought to centralize authority within the federal executive and enhance the executive's coordination capacities. At the same time, it committed the federal government to an essentially open-ended program of public spending.

The bill grew out of the old network of Keynesian advocates in the executive branch and their congressional and interest group allies.[62] In contrast to the reorganization plan or the NRPB, the Full Employment bill was attentive to the congressional role; unlike these earlier initiatives, it included Congress in its planning process by setting up a Joint Committee on the Budget.[63] Recognition of Congress helped mitigate charges of presidential power grabbing, but it could not quell interest group and regional discomfort over the provisions of the Full Employment bill. The structure of the coalitions opposing and supporting the bill reflected a clear division of interests along social interest lines, with important regional dimensions as well.

Most congressional support was drawn from representatives of northern urban areas, but a scattering of western progressives also backed the bill. Organized labor became the most important interest group defending the Full Employment bill, although it was not involved in initiating the legislation.[64] The core of the opposition was composed of business interests and large-scale agricultural concerns. Representatives of the Chamber of Commerce, the National Association of Manufacturers, and the American Farm Bureau Federation worked with sympathetic members of Congress to defeat the bill.[65] Their congressional allies were disproportionately drawn from the ranks of midwestern Republicans and southern Democrats.

When the Full Employment bill was first introduced in the Senate, it was helped by that chamber's more liberal cast and by the failure of opposing interest groups to mobilize quickly. But with the bill's passage in the Senate, opponents were galvanized into action and successfully blocked it in the House. The policy coalition of southern Democrats and midwestern Republicans in Congress and their interest group allies in business and agriculture had managed to circumscribe sharply the reach of the 1946 Employment Act ultimately enacted.

The new act eliminated the National Production and Employment Budget, along with its bias toward spending. Instead it created a small Council of Economic Advisers (CEA), a nonoperational body charged only with advising the president about economic matters. It preserved the joint congressional committee on economic affairs called for in the earliest versions of the measure. The Employment Act revealed broad support for a federal framework to monitor the economy, but it did not create institutional reform that would facilitate social Keynesian economic policy. It shied away from making specific commitments about future government action, and it did little to aid in planning public investment or to address problems of centralization and coordination within the executive.

These conflicts over institutional reform revealed a distinctly political dynamic, in which even liberal members of Congress opposed or only lukewarmly supported measures that would strengthen the hand of the president. The more obviously institutional reforms would disrupt existing arrangements for spending and increase executive control, the less likely that they would be supported. But more persistent than the opposition stemming from presidential-congressional tensions were underlying social cleavages in which agricultural interests represented by southern Democrats and business interests with close ties to Republican congressional representatives joined together to block the combination of spending and institutional reform.

Policy Packages and the Definition of Interests

To understand the defeat of social Keynesianism, then, we need to clarify why most influential business and agricultural organizations lined up against spending and institutional reform policies. Why did they define social Keynesianism as inimical to their interests? Much of the answer has to do with their experiences with earlier New Deal policies and with the relationship of Keynesian policy to other items concurrently on the national agenda. For both business and agricultural organizations, Keynesianism was part of a broader political package that made it unattractive to these groups.

The strong opposition of agriculture and business to Keynesianism and to the Full Employment bill in particular calls for explanation because Keynesian economic policy was not necessarily at odds with the interests of either group. In fact, in some ways, it could be seen as supportive of their interests.[66] Stabilizing the purchasing power of domestic consumers would benefit producers oriented to national markets by ensuring an outlet for their products. Moreover, Keynesian economic policies promised to stabilize the economy without the micro-level intervention of sector-specific planning. Yet the initial evaluation of Keynesianism by most business and agricultural interests did not focus on these beneficial features. Instead, the vast majority in both groups assailed Keynesianism as an interference in the free market and the opening wedge for permanent state intrusion into the economy.

The effects of past policies and the way Keynesianism was "packaged" with other policies in the United States offer important insights into why agriculture and business defined Keynesianism as hostile to their interests. Particularly important is the way early New Deal measures affected later policy orientations. In the early 1930s broad segments of business and agriculture agreed about the need to reorganize their relationships with each other and with the federal government in order to create predictable and profitable market conditions. The Agricultural Adjustment Act of 1933 sought to regulate farm production by setting restrictions on output; business practices were to be reorganized by the price codes set under the auspices of the National Recovery Administration (NRA). Both the NRA and the Agricultural Adjustment Administration (AAA) had repercussions that affected business's and agriculture's assessments of later policy innovations.

The AAA affected farm interests by strengthening the ties between large commercial farmers from the South and the Midwest, bringing them together into an increasingly effective organization, the American Farm Bureau Federation. In order to administer the new production controls, the AAA had worked with the Extension Service to build up the Farm Bureau, particularly in the South where it had traditionally been weak. This cross-regional union provided large commercial farmers—the chief beneficiaries of New Deal farm policy—a powerful organizational tool for influencing congressional politics.[67]

The legacy of the AAA helps explain why political unity and organizational cohesion emerged among large commercial farmers, but to understand why they assumed leadership in the fight against Keynesianism we need to look at how Keynesianism was associated with other policies. Not only was Keynesianism tied to the entire New Deal agenda; it was identified with the most liberal elements of the New Deal. The WPA, which provided temporary work to the unemployed, and the Farm Security Administration, which aided poor farmers and sharecroppers, had shown the potentially disruptive effects that federal programs could have on local political and economic relationships.[68] Southern agricultural elites in particular feared that federal spending programs would undermine their control over farm labor and raise wage rates in the process.[69]

The fusion of economic and political power in the South meant that the repercussions of losing control over labor were political as well as economic. Keynesianism, associated as it was with social welfare benefits and increased federal oversight of local activities, thus seemed to threaten an entire way of life. Central to that way of life was a racial caste system that rested on the social, political, and economic subordination of African-Americans. Although Roosevelt had carefully avoided directly confronting racial issues, New Deal measures, such as the WPA and the Farm Security Administration, had supplied black Americans with outside resources that could undermine the control of southern white elites.[70] These leaders accordingly viewed the defeat of measures that supported spending and federal control as essential to preserve the system of political exclusion and social control that had organized southern life for over half a century.

The National Recovery Administration left no organizational legacy comparable to the strengthened Farm Bureau. But the chaotic administration of the NRA engendered an enduring bitterness in the business community, which reinforced pre–New Deal antipathy to government involvement in the economy.[71] Although business's initial enthusiasm for the NRA had not reflected any broad sentiment in favor of government intervention, it did express a new openness about what the federal role might be. With the failure of the NRA, this more flexible attitude evaporated, and most business groups returned to earlier, strongly negative views about government involvement in the economy.[72]

Three aspects of Keynesianism resonated with the NRA experience and set business against the Full Employment bill. The first were the provisions for deficit spending. Deficits had never been popular with business, but in the early part of the New Deal they had been tolerated. Once the bulk of business organizations had concluded that the drawbacks of government involvement outweighed its benefits, tolerance for deficits disappeared. From the mid-1930s on, business groups denounced deficit spending, charging that it would lead to a stronger federal government, increasingly able and willing to intrude on private affairs.[73]

The second aspect of Keynesianism that provoked business opposition was its association with planning. Although the stagnationist Keynesians advocated a version of planning that differed greatly from NRA-style industrial planning, business rarely distinguished between the two in its denunciation of Keynesianism. Business opponents of the Full Employment bill invoked the specter of federal domination of the economy and the end of market freedom as they denounced the bill.[74] Advocates of Keynesianism could do little to break the association with planning because Keynesianism had entered the American context in a way that entangled it both institutionally and intellectually with a notion of planning. By the late 1930s, the National Resources Planning Board, long identified with "planners," provided a central base for Keynesians in the federal government. Moreover, leading Keynesians, such as Alvin Hansen, borrowed from planners' language and supported the setting up of planning facilities within the federal government.[75] Although they aimed to plan public investment, not private activity, business feared that the creation of any planning capacity would only lead to greater government control.

The third fear that business organizations had was that social Keynesianism would strengthen organized labor. Although business leaders rarely voiced their opposition to Keynesianism in these terms, experience with the NRA, and with a strengthened federal government more generally, had alerted them to the ways that government power could be used to secure unions. Thus, business's opposition to the Full Employment bill was a part of its more general campaign to contain the spread of unionism and curb the political power of organized labor after the war.[76]

Agricultural interests and businesses each had prior experiences with New Deal policies that led them to similar conclusions about social Keynesianism. These similarities in viewpoint were reinforced by the close links between political and economic elites in the South, which disposed southern conservatives to align with business and facilitated the cooperation between these groups in Congress. After the Full Employment bill was defeated, the Chamber of Commerce worked closely with southern congressional conservatives in crafting the substitute bill that posed little threat to either of their interests.[77]

Constructing the Alliance against Social Keynesianism

The alliance of business and agriculture was facilitated and rendered particularly potent by several features of the American political system that organized relationships among social interests, policy, and government. The limits on democracy in the South, the rural bias of Congress, and the loose organization of American political parties all strengthened the coalition that opposed social Keynesianism. These institutional characteristics interacted with two less predictable factors: the buoyant economic climate after the war and America's new position on the international stage. Both of these changes had implications for the resources and motivations of actors who had pressed for strong employment measures during the previous two decades.

The antidemocratic character of southern political institutions amplified the power of the South in Congress.[78] The sharply restricted scope of democracy in southern states prevented blacks and, in many cases, poor whites from voting. The vacuum allowed organized groups of elites, such as the Farm Bureau, to dominate the political life of many southern congressional districts, so that the interests of the rural poor were vastly underrepresented. Limited democracy meant that congressional representatives from these areas faced few political challenges and consequently built up seniority in Congress. In the debate over the Full Employment bill, southern members of Congress, such as Carter Manasco (D. Ala.), chair of the House Expenditures Committee that handled the bill, were able to use their strategic positions as committee chairs to derail it. The power of conservative southerners representing agriculture was further strengthened by systems of congressional representation biased in favor of rural areas.[79]

Although business did not share comparable institutional advantages in Congress, the close ties between business and agriculture in many localities worked to increase business influence over legislation. Moreover, the conduct of World War II served to rehabilitate business politically and open new channels of influence within government. Reliance on business expertise to oversee the war mobilization meant that business interests were well positioned to make their voices heard after the war. The war had a much less salutary effect on the political influence of organized labor, the main social group supporting social Keynesian measures. Although union membership had grown during the war, labor's influence in conducting the war effort was sharply confined; labor energies after the war were diverted into strikes aimed at making up for wage sacrifices agreed to in wartime.[80]

Interests supporting social Keynesian measures in general and the Full Employment bill in particular were also handicapped by the organization of political parties. The decentralized and nonprogrammatic nature of American parties gave Democratic supporters of the bill little leverage over opponents in the party. Southern Democrats could desert their party with little fear of reprisal. Late in the 1930s, Roosevelt had realized the problems that such intraparty dissension posed for extending the New Deal and sought to replace southern opponents in Congress with New Deal allies. The failure of this 1938 "purge" indicated the continuing strength of local party organizations and the elites that controlled them.[81] It also meant that political parties could not easily serve as sites for reformulating policy interests or enforcing compromises around policy.

The political weakness of those favoring full employment legislation was exacerbated by the prosperous economic conditions after the end of the war. Although wartime public opinion polls had regis-

Table 2.1
Public Attitudes toward Government Action to Ensure Full Employment,
1935–1944

Question: 1935—"Do you believe that government should see to it that every
man who wants to work has a job?" 1939—"Do you think our government
should or should not be responsible for seeing to it that everyone who
wants to work has a job?" 1944—"Do you think the federal government
should provide jobs for every one able and willing to work but who cannot
get a job in private employment?"

	% Replying		
Year	Yes/Should	No/Should Not	Don't Know
1935	77	20	3
1939	61	32	7
1944	68	25	7

Source: Based on data reported in Hadley Cantril, *Public Opinion, 1935–46* (Princeton, N.J.: Princeton University Press, 1951), 893, 897, 901. See also Robert Shapiro and
Kelly D. Patterson, "The Dynamics of Public Opinion toward Social Welfare Policy"
(paper presented at the 1986 Annual Meeting of the American Political Science Association, Washington, D.C.), tab. supp., p. 41, tab. 51.
Note: Numbers are rounded to the nearest percentage.

Table 2.2
Public Attitudes toward Government Planning to Prevent Unemployment,
1943

Question: "For handling domestic problems like unemployment, the con-
verting of war plants to peacetime use, or the demobilization of soldiers—
do you think the Government should set up a central agency now with full
authority to make plans and with full authority to carry out these plans as
soon as the war is over?"

	% of Respondents
Favor central planning agency	75
Oppose central planning agency	14
No opinion	11

Source: Office of Public Opinion Research, Princeton University, reported in Jerome Bruner, *Mandate from the People* (New York: Duell, Sloan and Pearce, 1944), 175.

tered strong support for government action to ensure full employment (see Tables 2.1 and 2.2), the economic boom stripped the employment issue of the urgency it had previously enjoyed.[82] As unemployment dissolved on its own, legislation seemed less pressing
to most Americans. President Truman came out strongly in favor of
the Full Employment bill soon after he assumed the presidency in

1945, but he had few resources with which to back up his support.[83] Unable to command party loyalty, the president was also unable to rely on the impetus that strong public pressure would have created for passing legislation.

Full employment legislation was further hampered by the leading position that the United States assumed in international politics during and after the war. One of the key ways that America's new geopolitical role influenced the possibilities for employment policy was by the way it set up a new, and often competing, set of incentives for the president. Although Roosevelt declared a bold "Economic Bill of Rights" in 1944, he did little to promote passage of its objectives. During the war, Roosevelt's inattention to domestic issues and his outright sacrifice of some domestic policies related to employment offered early indications of what was to be a continuing pattern in postwar politics.[84] As international policy objectives grew in political importance, the president's role as overseer and energizer of domestic policy innovation—a role forged in large part by Roosevelt himself—would be jeopardized.

Although the United States had been a pioneer in experimenting with economic policies that sought also to meet social objectives, the organization of politics and the sequence of policy innovation during the New Deal facilitated the emergence of a powerful opposition, which blocked the institutionalization of social Keynesianism after the war. But Keynesianism did not disappear from the national agenda with the defeat of the Full Employment bill; instead, its meaning and the institutional framework for implementing it had to be reworked in ways that did not transgress the new boundaries of politics in postwar America.

The Boundaries of Employment Policy in America

The most visible difference between the 1946 Employment Act and the bill that had been originally proposed was the omission of the slogan "full employment." Behind the change in language lay a quite distinct vision of the goals and conduct of economic policy. At the heart of the new conception was a much weaker public role than that envisioned by the New Deal's social Keynesians. In postwar America, Keynesianism was refashioned in ways that severed economic goals from social welfare provision and sharply curbed the authoritative role of the federal executive. Moreover, the acceptance of even this limited version of Keynesianism was uncertain for many years after the war. Despite considerable innovation during the New

Deal and the war, the United States was left with a set of economic policymaking institutions that would make acceptance of Keynesian principles provisional and restricted even in the period of their greatest influence.

Remaking American Keynesianism

In the years after 1946, Keynesian ideas were reworked and disseminated in a prolonged process of "social learning." Conducted within the framework left by the Employment Act, the striking feature of this process was the limited role that public institutions were able to play. As a consequence, the new versions of Keynesianism de-emphasized government activity, as technical advances quickly outstripped administrative and political changes. Even in this much less intrusive form, the acceptance of Keynesian ideas was slow and uneven.

Much of the process by which Keynesianism was reworked can be understood by examining the framework of the Employment Act. The act did not write Keynesian principles into government activity the way the Full Employment bill had. Instead, systematic attention to economic matters would be ensured by an annual presidential report to the Congress on the state of the economy. Presidential capacities to analyze the economy were enhanced by the establishment of the Council of Economic Advisers, a small body of advisers appointed by the president and mandated to serve him in an advisory capacity only. A companion body in Congress, the Joint Committee on the Economic Report of the President (later the Joint Economic Committee) would ensure congressional consideration of economic conditions.

This set of institutions and mechanisms gave Keynesian ideas a tenuous foothold in the federal government. They enhanced the federal capacity for monitoring the economy and encouraged (although they did not guarantee) the collection of economic data that would make it possible to guide the economy according to Keynesian principles.[85] But the Employment Act did not direct policymakers toward any particular principles of economic policymaking, nor did it provide institutions or mechanisms to facilitate active use of Keynesian policies. The CEA could act as an advocate for Keynesian ideas only if the president allowed it to play that role and if he appointed Keynesians to the council. Even then, the council would need substantial authority and influence within the executive branch if discretionary action, such as tax cuts, were to be accepted. The experience of the CEA under Truman and Eisenhower demonstrated that it would take time to build such influence. In the interim, the willingness of postwar administrations to tolerate unbalanced budgets during recessions indicated that pure orthodoxy had lost its hold on the economic thinking of both parties even if active fiscal policy was not yet accepted.

Truman's appointees to the CEA were sympathetic to Keynesian ideas and made significant contributions to their development by tying them to growth theory for the first time.[86] Nevertheless, their impact on policy was small. As a new agency that had to compete with large, well-established departments including the Treasury, the Federal Reserve, and the Budget Bureau, the CEA had neither the authoritative position nor the institutional strength to control policy. According to Eisenhower's first CEA chairman, Arthur F. Burns, the council "did not have systematic links to the rest of the government and therefore had frequently resorted to the grapevine."[87] The CEA's early years were thus spent trying to sort out its status: the relationship among the three members of the council had to be thrashed out, as did the council's relationship to the president.[88]

The CEA's inability to direct economic policy had few visible repercussions during the Truman administration. Buoyed by a decade and a half of pent-up demand, the American economy exhibited unanticipated vigor, to which the federal government contributed with a generous program of veterans' benefits and a military budget swollen by the Korean war and later by cold war expenses. Underlying this path to economic growth was America's preeminent position in the international economy. Not only did the United States face little competition on world markets; it also underwrote the reconstruction of Europe.[89] Such federal spending contributed to postwar economic prosperity, but because it was keyed to foreign policy objectives, it could not easily be varied in accordance with macroeconomic goals.

Further doubts about the future of Keynesian-inspired macroeconomic management emerged in 1953, when for a brief period it was unclear whether Congress would appropriate sufficient funds for the council to continue operating.[90] The council's survival and Eisenhower's appointments to it signaled that there would be no return to pre–New Deal economic orthodoxy. Yet the council was limited as a purveyor of Keynesian ideas. Although it accepted some aspects of macroeconomic management, Eisenhower's appointees did not identify themselves as Keynesians and were reluctant to embrace active government measures, such as spending increases or tax cuts, to manage the economy. In any case, the council was only one voice among many advising the president. Throughout Eisenhower's administration, the CEA had to compete with more conservative economic policy recommendations emanating from the Treasury.[91] Moreover, Eisenhower's council was a poor vehicle for building policy coalitions around Keynesian principles. It had limited resources and little disposition to reach outside the purview of the federal government.

The other major innovation of the 1946 Employment Act was more successful in building support for Keynesian ideas. In the latter half of the 1950s, the Joint Economic Committee in Congress played a key role in bringing liberal Democrats, organized labor, and liberal economists together around a Keynesian economic agenda.[92] Because the committee's Democratic majority was dominated by liberals, it could function with a set of shared understandings about economic goals and government action that were absent from the Democratic party as a whole. But the Joint Economic Committee could not disseminate and organize broad support for Keynesian ideas. It did schedule hearings to publicize particular perspectives, but its lack of legislative function and staffing limitations restricted its reach.

Apart from the CEA and the Joint Economic Committee, there were few other public agencies well situated to promote Keynesian ideas. In the late 1930s and into the war, the newly created Fiscal Division of the Bureau of the Budget served as a high-level gathering point for Keynesian economists in government. But after 1952, when the division was abolished, the Budget Bureau lost its capacity to do much more than short-range routine budget preparation.[93]

The inadequacies of public vehicles for advancing and adapting Keynesian ideas allowed private groups to play a particularly important role in reshaping and winning acceptance for Keynesian principles of economic management. The model for this type of activity and a key actor in the development of Keynesian ideas was the Committee for Economic Development (CED). Launched in 1942 by forward-looking business leaders concerned that business be prepared to help shape postwar policy, the CED was a small research organization that brought together social scientists and members of the business community. Even before the war was over, the CED began to rework Keynesianism so that its most objectionable features—especially fear of capricious action on the part of the federal government and out-of-control spending policies—were removed. In place of spending and the larger public sector it entailed, the CED advocated reliance on automatic stabilizers—variations in government revenues and expenditures that occurred in response to economic conditions without any deliberate government action. If discretionary action was to be undertaken, tax cuts, not spending, was the method advocated by the CED.[94]

The committee's organizational form, a small, well-funded group of economists working with liberal business leaders, was an ideal setting for advocacy and development of innovative economic ideas. This type of forum was far more insulated from outside pressure and from shifts in the political winds than were the public institutions responsible for economic policymaking. Because it was not immediately answerable to a broad business constituency, the committee could advocate policies that the majority of the business community opposed. Yet, the committee's undisputed expertise in economic matters and its ties to important business interests allowed it to play an important educational function. Through its vigorous educational campaign, the CED helped business to reinterpret its economic policy interests in ways that embraced Keynesian principles of demand management at the same time that it made Keynesian policies more palatable to business.[95]

Other private organizations, less directly tied to business, also sought to develop and influence policy, using the CED model. The National Planning Association, for example, brought together representatives of labor, business, agriculture, and the economics profession sympathetic to Keynesian ideas.[96] Like the CED, it issued pamphlets and testified in Congress to publicize its ideas, but more modest resources made it a less visible presence in the diffusion of Keynesian ideas in the 1950s.

If in private organizations Keynesian ideas were being reworked to make them more acceptable to business, within the academic discipline of economics, they were being transformed into technical and theoretical problems. Within the academy, economics sought to model itself on the natural sciences, with a considerably narrowed agenda that excluded concerns not readily handled by prevailing models of economic behavior.[97] Increasingly, economic questions were severed from the institutional considerations that had been present in the era of institutional economics before the New Deal and in the 1930s and 1940s, when economists worked with government administrators on administrative and political innovations relevant to policy. In William Parker's words, "Keynesian political economists took over the income and product measurements of the National Bureau [of Economic Research], and resolving all economic problems into that of providing full employment, they produced a universal remedy through manipulation of the federal budget."[98]

The dominant economic ideas about employment issues contracted and became more technical in response to the political barriers that diverted further development of the social Keynesian track. The definition of the problem narrowed to concern about a single (albeit flexible) goal—balancing the budget at full employment—as the broader social vision that had animated Keynesians during the New Deal receded. The importance of private groups in reworking Keynesian ideas helped skew thinking about economic policy away from embracing a significant public role. Even in organizations not dominated by business, the proclivity of the economics profession to favor markets over public authority was far more likely to win out when public authorities were not significantly involved in defining the problem and framing policy choices.[99]

Economic policymaking in the Eisenhower administration underscored the difficulties of effecting any smooth progression in the development and application of Keynesian ideas from within the federal executive. During the 1950s, the resources available to the CEA were too meager, its membership too uncertain, and its influence too fragile for it to elaborate Keynesian policy options and mobilize support for them. Not until the Kennedy administration would support for active use of fiscal policy triumph within the executive branch; the conditions of its triumph would underscore the limits of making economic policy within the inherited framework.

Kennedy's Keynesian Tax Cut

Although Kennedy did not endorse Keynesian ideas in his presidential campaign, and opposed cutting taxes, his appointees to the CEA were drawn from the leading liberal Keynesian economists in the nation. His choice reflected the available pool of expertise: in 1960 economists who aligned with liberal Democrats were likely to be thoroughly steeped in Keynesian ideas.[100] The selection of CEA members also reflected the emergence of a consensus among liberal economists about the relationship among economic policy, social welfare goals, and expansion of the public sector. While it might be desirable to promote certain social policies and enhance public capacities, economic policies should not be held captive to such goals. Thus, the closest "ideological heir" of Alvin Hansen and the most eloquent proponent of linking Keynesianism with expanding the public sector and social policies, John Kenneth Galbraith, was not named to Kennedy's council.[101]

Led by the energetic and persuasive Walter Heller, the CEA played the role of economic educator and advocate within and outside the Kennedy administration. The council enjoyed unprecedented influence under Kennedy because of the substantial access that the president granted it and the encouragement he gave it to publicize its analysis through congressional testimony and public speeches.[102] It was also helped by the strength of the Keynesian consensus within the economics profession at the time. Heller could—and did—call upon a range of prominent economists from prestigious universities to reinforce his message.[103] His efforts ultimately paid off in 1962, when the president acknowledged the need for fiscal stimulus in the midst of an economic recession that appeared impervious to the operation of automatic stabilizers.

Tax cuts were the route selected. This choice reflected the doubts about the administration's ability to secure congressional approval for spending increases. From the beginning, the council had supported a temporary tax cut as the more efficient means of generating the necessary deficits, but it had not ruled out expenditure increases.[104] The cumbersome process of enacting the few spending measures that did pass in the first year of Kennedy's administration convinced Heller and his colleagues that tax cuts were the only realistic means of achieving their aggregate objectives. Given the limits of established channels for funneling public spending, the prospects for reaching agreement on large new spending programs were dim. Pointing out that the $9 billion increase necessary would mean a 40 percent boost in nondefense expenditures from fiscal year 1963, the council maintained that such spending could not be accomplished rapidly without "serious risks of inefficiency and profiteering." Moreover, it noted that spending proposals, unlike tax cuts, were subject to opposition as a power grab by the federal government.[105]

The president received further encouragement to go with the tax cut strategy. The long educational project of the CED had paid off by the early 1960s in widespread business acceptance of federal deficits as a means of economic stimulus, although not all major business organizations supported cutting taxes to create those deficits. But for a president who worried about being branded antibusiness, this broad approval likely helped to tip the balance in favor of the decision to act.[106]

However, direct business pressure had not eliminated the spending alternative; this route had already been ruled out by the political configuration in Congress. The long-standing divisions between southern Democrats and the rest of the party about spending on social welfare measures and extensions of federal power continued to block agreement on spending proposals. The 1946 Employment Act was a product of that division, and it did nothing to help reconcile the interests of these two wings of the Democratic party. Although the undemocratic political system of the South had been under challenge by the civil rights movement for nearly a decade, a sharply restricted electorate was still the order of the day throughout much of the South. While they supported spending for agricultural subsidies and defense, many southern representatives in Congress continued to find proposals for social spending suspect. Such spending would threaten southern economic, political, and race relations, especially if the federal government were to come to control it.[107]

These entrenched divisions in the Democratic party, inherited from the New Deal, were also reflected in presidential strategy. Although he came from the northern liberal wing of the Democratic party, Kennedy was neither disposed nor positioned to launch a major challenge to the existing framework of political relationships within the Democratic party. Elected by a slim margin and facing a Congress in which southern Democrats and Republicans together accounted for 59 percent of the vote in the Senate and 65 percent in the House, Kennedy had few political resources with which to press for reorganizing politics.[108] Nor could he claim any public opinion mandate for bold moves in economic policy; although unemployment had been drifting upward, its magnitude and its regional concentration did not make it a subject of broad public concern.[109] Kennedy's policies, not surprisingly, sought to accommodate the divisions within his party rather than to change to them.[110]

Even so, there was considerable congressional resistance to enacting a tax cut in a period of rising deficits. The intensive educational activities of the CED and later of Kennedy's CEA had swayed opinion at the elite level, but had not conquered the realm of popular economic discourse to which Congress was more closely attuned.[111] Not just southern conservatives but many moderate Democrats as well worried that cutting taxes would be economically irresponsible. In fact, congressional approval of the tax cut was not assured until after President Johnson had agreed to trim his 1965 budget request.[112] During the Kennedy administration, Democratic economists had created a new language with which to justify deficits; by promoting such concepts as the "full employment budget," they succeeded in blunting the influence of the balanced budget ideology.[113] But continued congressional wariness raised questions about the depth of the nation's conversion.

Working with the institutional framework and the configuration of interests left by the Employment Act of 1946, Democratic politicians and their economic advisers had finally launched an activist fiscal policy twenty-six years after Roosevelt first proposed spending to stimulate the economy. In Andrew Shonfield's words, Americans had been the "intellectual leaders" and the "institutional laggards" in actively deploying Keynesian principles.[114] The institutional fragmentation that had allowed experimentation with Keynesian ideas during the Depression later prevented those same ideas from being accepted as government policy for many years. Only after a reworking of the ideas, the emergence of a strong consensus in the economics profession, and a long process of education did an administration propose deliberately to increase the deficit in order to stimulate the economy.

Conclusion

American politics and policymaking were transformed during the 1930s and 1940s; expectations about the responsibilities of the national government escalated, as did its size and administrative capacities. Yet the boldest impulses for transforming politics and ensuring social and economic security met with defeat. The sequence of policies enacted during the New Deal and the organization of American representative institutions strengthened the opponents of social Keynesianism, who objected more to reorganizing institutional power than to increasing spending.

The peculiar features of the governmental framework that had emerged by midcentury would channel and limit later initiatives by the way it linked—or failed to link—administration, politics, and policy ideas. In the realm of employment policy, the meager institutional legacy of the Employment Act would facilitate conceptions of policy that sharply differentiated between the "economic" and the "social" and would fix concern about employment on a single focus, the rate of unemployment. The negative political consequences of this version of Keynesianism would begin to unfold even as its limits as an economic strategy became apparent.

Three

Race and the Politics of Poverty

DURING the 1960s, a multitude of social experiments sought to transform the aims and activities of the American government. The area of employment policy was no exception. Against a backdrop of economic prosperity and political upheaval, Democratic policy-makers raised new questions about employment and unemploy-ment, bringing fresh perspectives to old problems and, in key ways, redefining the problems that needed solving. In employment policy, the most intensive experimentation and innovation occurred in labor market policy. Pressures for expanding labor market policy hinged on a variety of arguments, which developed over the course of the decade: department of Labor officials sought to establish job training as an essential complement to macroeconomic policy; con-gressional supporters of public employment maintained that public jobs were needed to supplement private economic activity. Secre-tary of Labor Willard Wirtz sought to expand the definition of the employment problem to include attention to subemployment, while President Lyndon Johnson attempted to secure private sector coop-eration with public training goals.

This decade of intellectual ferment and policy experimentation left a surprisingly meager legacy for employment policy. Labor mar-ket policy became subsumed into the poverty program, offering job preparation to those on the fringes of the labor market, and to the black poor in particular. Consequently, these policies performed re-medial functions, with little significance for the private economy. Although many new programs were created, little in the way of in-stitution building or even substantial institutional reform was achieved. Nor did these new measures attract enduring political support for labor market policy. Labor market policy became politi-cally identified as a "social" policy that offered assistance to needy individuals; it was rarely defended or promoted as a corrective to deficiencies in the private economy or as a potential contributor to broad economic goals.

Why did the various impulses to define, expand, and institutional-ize a role for labor market policy amount to so little during the 1960s? This chapter takes up this question, showing how ideas about employment and poverty intersected with the upheavals in racial politics. I argue that the organization of expertise and presidential strategies in the early 1960s combined with the existing framework of interests to create the poverty approach, limiting the purview of labor market policy and stymieing the construction of enduring institutions, despite considerable innovation. By the mid-1960s, the national prominence of the civil rights movement and the onset of northern urban riots drove policymakers and politicians to make poverty programs more responsive to the needs of the African-American poor. Identifying the poverty programs with African-Americans narrowed support for the programs and at the same time constricted public understanding of the causes of black poverty. By the late 1960s, labor market policies had become politically identified as income maintenance policies not much different from welfare. In this context, they were highly vulnerable to political attacks, and poorly positioned to benefit from the new insights into poverty and employment gleaned during this decade of policy experimentation.

Throughout this chapter, I shall argue that political and institutional tensions inherent in the organization of labor market policies during the 1960s led to their downfall. This view contrasts with that of those who contend that the poverty programs of that decade unraveled because of the economic and political disruptions engendered by the Vietnam War.[1] The war exacerbated the problems of poverty programs by depriving them of funds and presidential attention at a critical time, but I argue that emphasis on the war has led analysts to understate the political tensions inherent in the organization of these policies. At the same time, however, I reject the view that these policy experiences prove that labor market policies are intrinsically flawed or impossible to implement in the United States; by stressing the choices to organize policy in some ways rather than others, and the specific historical circumstances surrounding labor market policy in the 1960s, I hope to suggest that an alternative organization of policy in different political circumstances could lead to different outcomes.[2]

Defining the Problem: Poverty and Employment

The initial decision to launch a war on poverty and the subsequent design of the program pose two related questions. First, why did the poverty idea reach the national agenda in the early 1960s? Second, how did the new thinking about poverty intersect with arguments about employment policy?

The poverty policies of the 1960s incorporated two decisions about the proper focus of labor market policies: such policies should be remedial measures targeted on the lowest end of the labor market, and they should aim to alter the supply of labor by modifying workers' characteristics rather than seeking to change the demand for labor. This outcome can be explained by examining how the organization of expertise in the federal executive interacted with the strategic perspective of the president to advantage a remedial, supply-oriented policy. In this section I examine how growing interest in broader labor market policies was displaced by the poverty perspective, describing the initial emergence of interest in broader policies and analyzing the reasons for their limited impact on the design of the War on Poverty.

The Labor Market Policy Network Emerges

Prior to the declaration of the War on Poverty, a nascent issue network had begun to formulate a rationale for labor market policies and to sketch out the form such policies would take in the United States. During the 1950s, Department of Labor officials, a few empirically oriented labor market economists, and congressional representatives from "depressed areas" began to support a range of labor market policies, including skill training, job placement, measures to aid mobility, and public employment. Their reasoning was loosely based on a structural interpretation of unemployment, which, in contrast to the Keynesian analysis, argued that labor markets would not by themselves adequately adjust to industrial change. Accordingly, they argued, a range of new measures was required to increase the efficiency of the labor market, provide an adequately skilled labor force, and reduce unemployment.

The structural interpretation was intuitively appealing because unemployment and poverty in the late 1950s and 1960s were so concentrated in particular groups and geographical locations.[3] In contrast to the widespread deprivation caused by the Great Depression, economic distress in the 1950s could be pinpointed. The rural poor of Appalachia, unemployed miners from the bituminous coalfields, and laid-off autoworkers and aircraft workers provided conspicuous examples.[4] The economic problems of these groups were often a direct result of automation and technical change, bolstering arguments for special structural measures. Added to these worries about structural unemployment was the related concern that the United

States needed an adequately skilled labor force in the event that the cold war turned hot.

The supporters of structural measures had few precedents on which to build a new set of policies. The various public jobs programs that had been set up during the Depression had included little training and, in any event, had been abandoned during the war. The Fitzgerald Act of 1937 had established an apprenticeship program under the auspices of the Bureau of Apprenticeship and Training (BAT) in the Department of Labor, but the program had remained small and the federal role confined to setting standards, approving programs, and encouraging private action. Most training and job placement was firmly in the hands of the private sector, which evinced little interest in government help.[5]

The initial impulse of those concerned with labor market policy was to encourage private efforts. In the area of skilled labor, the National Manpower Council, a private group of educators, business leaders, and representatives of organized labor, funded by the Ford Foundation, took the lead. Established in the heat of the Korean War, the council believed that long-term planning was needed if the nation were to utilize its labor force effectively. It urged that both private industry and government be engaged in the development of an appropriately trained work force.[6] The council was particularly concerned with the supply of skilled labor, especially scientific and professional workers. Throughout the 1950s, the organization held numerous regional and national conferences, producing published accounts of these proceedings and other studies to disseminate its policy recommendations.

The council established close ties with the Department of Labor in the 1950s.[7] Secretary of Labor James A. Mitchell sympathized with arguments about the need for developing human resources and in 1954 set up an Office of Manpower Administration to plan for labor needs created by the cold war.[8] Within the department, program planners urged the secretary to design a comprehensive manpower policy for skilled labor, drawing on existing agencies and bureaus. Mitchell agreed to this plan, which called on the department to distribute information and encourage private and local actors to adopt training programs.[9]

As the decade wore on, the Department of Labor moved beyond simply encouraging private action. Department officials took a closer look at programs supervised by the department and began to consider manpower policy as a means of addressing unemployment. Prodded by National Manpower Council Research Director Eli

Ginzberg, the department vowed to improve apprenticeship training, for which it had oversight through the Bureau of Apprenticeship and Training. By the end of the Eisenhower administration, a substantial group within the Department of Labor had become supporters of manpower training, convinced that a better match between workers and available jobs would help to reduce the rising unemployment rate.[10]

The real push for legislation to affect the labor market, however, came from Congress. Representatives of "depressed areas"—areas with high rates of unemployment and declining industrial bases—backed proposals for targeting federal aid to such regions.[11] Spearheaded by Senator Paul Douglas (D. Ill.) in 1955, an initially small band of congressional liberals and representatives of declining areas began to fashion a package of proposals for area redevelopment that included public works, extension of unemployment insurance, credit to industries locating in such areas, and retraining programs and subsistence allowances for unemployed workers. They drew up bills that passed both houses of Congress in 1958 and in 1960, only to be vetoed by President Eisenhower.

The recession of 1957–1958 and the increase in Democratic strength that it brought to both houses of Congress made unemployment an area of continuing congressional action and initiative. The measures they supported were a blend of Keynesian macroeconomic stimulus and labor market policies. Responding to the AFL-CIO's Unemployment March on Washington in 1959, Senate Majority Leader Lyndon Johnson appointed a special Senate committee to study unemployment. The committee launched an extensive schedule of hearings around the country that fixed attention on unemployment and underemployment. The graphic testimony of the unemployed highlighted the distress accompanying technical change, inadequate training opportunities, and insufficient jobs.[12] The committee's final recommendations endorsed tax cuts to stimulate economic growth but highlighted measures including aid to depressed areas, a national vocational training program of grants-in-aid to the states, a shelf of standby public works, and upgrading of the Employment Service and social insurance programs.[13]

After the committee's report was issued in March 1960, several key committee members sought to implement its recommendations with a variety of proposals. Most easily accomplished was the creation of a permanent Senate subcommittee, the Subcommittee on Employment and Manpower under the Labor and Public Welfare Committee, made responsible for a wide range of concerns associated with manpower utilization.[14] Efforts to change substantive policy made little headway until Kennedy's election. The Area Redevelopment Act was the first piece of legislation approved. With the new president's backing buttressed by strong congressional support, the bill passed quickly.[15] Manpower training experienced more resistance. First introduced by Joseph S. Clark (D. Pa.) in 1960, training legislation did not become law until early 1962, with the passage of the Manpower Development and Training Act (MDTA). The new act defined its mission as that of retraining skilled males who had lost their jobs as a result of automation.

This legislative activity was complemented by an upsurge of intellectual interest in labor market policy. In 1962, the Ford Foundation announced a major grant program for research directed at manpower and structural unemployment problems.[16] Open for consideration were questions about what labor market policy should do, whom it should serve, how it should be administered and what its relationship to macropolicy should be. The boldest arguments for a national positive labor market policy came from Yale economist E. Wight Bakke, who advocated a national policy modeled after that of Sweden, where job training and placement activities at all levels of the labor market played a central part in the national approach to unemployment.[17] Bakke argued that the United States needed an integrated set of policies coordinated at the national level to affect both the supply and the demand for labor.

The Department of Labor, which had an obvious bureaucratic stake in a national labor market policy, was the key government agency grappling with the question of how an American labor market policy would be designed and what it would do. The interest in the issue that had begun during the Eisenhower administration intensified under the Kennedy administration. Particularly after Willard Wirtz took over as Secretary of Labor in 1962, the department began to view the recent legislation as the basis for an active manpower policy that would be a vital complement to macropolicy and devoted considerable attention to thinking about how this policy should relate to other national policies.[18]

The Poverty Perspective

The War on Poverty disrupted and redirected thinking about labor market policy by establishing a set of de facto responses to questions about what such policy should do in the United States. The answer implicit in the policies initiated by the War on Poverty was that labor market policy should target the poor and that it should focus on labor supply, particularly on changing the characteristics of workers. Underpinning this strategy was the belief that macroeconomic measures would produce ample opportunities for all who were prepared to take advantage of them.

The idea for a federal policy addressing poverty was first suggested by President Kennedy, who in 1962 requested his Council of Economic Advisers (CEA) chairman Walter Heller to "give him some facts and figures on the things we still have to do" and went on to ask about "the poverty problem in the United States."[19] Although several books and articles—most notably Michael Harrington's *The Other America*, published in 1962—had brought poverty to the public's attention, there was no significant pressure from social or political interests to launch such an initiative.[20] Nor is there evidence that an attack on poverty was conceived as political strategy for strengthening black loyalty to the Democratic party or that it was even initially intended to focus on African-Americans.[21] Instead, the president's vague request to the CEA appears to have been motivated by a more general desire to devise some policies that would give his administration a stamp of originality and energy.[22]

If there was little presidential direction about what an attack on poverty would look like, neither was there a substantial body of literature to serve as guide or even to provide a starting point for designing policy. As James Sundquist has noted, "the word 'poverty' did not appear as a heading in the index of either the *Congressional Record* or the *Public Papers of the Presidents*" until 1964.[23] Nor was poverty a focus of academic concern: those involved in planning the new program had a bibliography of less than two pages to inform their deliberations.[24]

The vagueness of the presidential directive and the dearth of academic material about poverty gave the Council of Economic Advisers considerable latitude in setting the terms for considering the new poverty program. Their deliberations were bounded by two factors. The first was political: simply increasing the income of the poor by creating new income support programs or boosting Aid to Families with Dependent Children (AFDC) payments was off the agenda because of the difficulty of securing congressional approval.[25] The second guideline shaping the CEA's discussions was the conviction that macroeconomic stimulation would reduce joblessness to an interim target rate of 4 percent by opening a range of new employment opportunities. Contrary to the structuralists, the council believed that the private labor market would, on the whole, make the adjustments in skill levels and labor supply needed to accommodate this higher level of economic activity.[26] The council had supported the MDTA but did not see any reason for expanding job training efforts.

As the council grappled with designing the poverty program, it assumed that tax cuts, the training programs operated by the MDTA, and the 1962 Public Welfare Amendments were already successfully alleviating the problems toward which they were addressed and that the remaining poverty was the product of different sources.[27] One source was racial discrimination, and the council repeatedly urged broad support for the antidiscrimination activities of various government agencies. But the council's central view of poverty was that it was a problem of individuals who lacked the necessary motivation or skills to benefit from the opportunities open to them. The objective of a government poverty program, then, would be to prepare poor individuals to take advantage of such opportunities. Accordingly, the council adopted a focus on youth, and an emphasis on motivations and attitudes as strong or stronger than the emphasis on skills training.[28] Undergirding its approach was the notion of a cycle of poverty, in which "cultural and environmental obstacles to motivation," along with "poor health, and inadequate education, and low mobility limiting earning potential," led to "limited income opportunities," trapping the individual within the cycle.[29]

Although the economists who conceived the War on Poverty put little stock in cultural explanations of poverty, focusing instead on income factors, their explanations tended to stress the "social" origins of low income.[30] They devoted little attention to the relationship between poverty and underemployment, and directed thinking away from the relationship between poverty and the structure and operation of labor markets, and toward the problems of individuals. As Henry Aaron has noted, "Perhaps the most striking characteristic of this view of the poverty cycle is the absence of any mention of the economic system within which it operates."[31] This approach would negatively affect the possibilities for changing policy to accommodate new understandings of poverty later in the decade, when poverty had become a deeply politicized, highly charged racial issue.

Ideas and Presidential Politics

These assumptions and the approach to poverty that grew out of them were challenged at various points by supporters of a broader role for labor market policies. The Department of Labor was the most consistent advocate of alternative policies, although it was joined at various points by other executive actors and members of Congress. In communications with the CEA over the design of the poverty program, Department of Labor officials argued for the centrality of employment in any attack on poverty, and questioned the ability of the tax cut alone to solve the employment problem. The department argued that the most important contribution to eliminating poverty would be "to provide the family head with a regular, decently paid job."[32] It disputed the CEA's conclusion that youth was the place to break the poverty cycle, maintaining instead that stable employment for male heads of households was the optimal route.

Calling the tax bill "probably the principal [antipoverty] weapon we have," Secretary of Labor Wirtz acknowledged the importance of aggregate economic stimulation, but he also called for "special programs to create useful jobs" for the unemployed.[33] Although it stopped short of recommending a major program of public works, the Department of Labor's proposal to the CEA for a war on poverty contained several provisions for creating jobs in areas of high unemployment and for redirecting government contracts to such regions. Only if all other efforts to increase employment failed should a public works strategy be used. The argument for an employment strategy was presented in the Senate by Gaylord Nelson (D. Wisc.) in January of 1964 during a speech proposing a ten-year, ten-billion-dollar fund for the antipoverty program, along with a five-cent federal tax on cigarettes to fund a public employment program.[34] Neither of these proposals made headway with Budget Bureau and CEA officials, who continued to direct the policy discussions.

The prospects for the employment strategy improved when former Peace Corps director Sargent Shriver took over coordination of executive branch deliberations on the poverty program at the president's request. Shriver was sympathetic to public jobs; in fact, at a cabinet meeting, he presented the proposal for a jobs program for the adult unemployed, to be financed by the cigarette tax. The president rejected the proposal on the ground that it made no sense to impose a new tax when the administration was in the process of cutting taxes.[35]

Support for more encompassing labor market policies, and for public employment in particular, continued to emerge in Congress. In April of 1964, the recommendations of a year-long inquiry by the Senate Subcommittee on Employment and Manpower, chaired by Senator Clark, were issued.[36] The report called for setting a goal of 3 percent unemployment to be reached by 1968. In order to reach this objective, it advocated considerable expansion of public spending—increases of at least $5 billion annually.[37] The report also noted that some unemployment would be unreachable by aggregate measures alone and recommended joint federal, state, and local programs to provide employment to the hard-core unemployed. It envisioned projects that undertook infrastructure repair and other community betterment tasks. In making this proposal, the committee challenged the practice of adjusting the supply of labor to meet demand, arguing instead that "sensible policy requires that we seek to create some jobs which fit the more disadvantaged portions of the labor force."[38]

None of these proposals was able to alter in any fundamental way the framework and focus of policy originally laid out by the CEA. The Economic Opportunity Act of 1964, the charter legislation of the War on Poverty, did incorporate a youth employment bill pending before Congress that the Department of Labor had supported, which became the Jobs Corps and the Neighborhood Youth Corps. But the act that was passed continued to emphasize "employment readiness" for young people. The bulk of funds that the new Office of Economic Opportunity (OEO) authorized were for youth programs—largely designed as educational enrichment and work preparatory programs.[39]

How can we explain the inability of the more comprehensive view of labor market policies to have any appreciable influence on the design of the poverty program? The institutional dominance and coherence of the CEA's approach compared with that of the Department of Labor and its allies offers part of the answer. President Johnson's strategic interests in the attack on poverty provide the second part of the answer: the president reinforced the direction mapped out by the CEA, even as he distorted the cautious program that the council initially presented.

In what sense was the CEA advantaged in the discussions about what shape the War on Poverty should take? After all, the council was a small body with no constituency other than the president, and its official capacity was only that of adviser. Nonetheless, it had several important advantages over the advocates of a broader labor market strategy.

The first was the CEA's ability to dominate arguments about unemployment because of its superior capacity to supply and analyze data. Roger Porter quotes a senior administration official in the 1970s recalling the dominance of the CEA in this regard during the 1960s. The official noted that during the early 1960s, the CEA, "along with a few people at the Treasury," had a "monopoly" on economic support staff in the federal government. In his view, this had allowed the CEA to "blow people out of the water with the depths of its analysis. . . ." He went on, "Few people understood what the term 'multiplier' meant in the 1960s much less were able to argue with CEA's arguments about a tax policy to stimulate the economy. When CEA said the effect of a specific tax action on investment was such-and-such there wasn't any other agency doing its own empirical work to argue with it."[40]

The department was particularly disadvantaged in this kind of argument since it had barely begun to assemble the staff needed to participate in economic policy discussions. The MDTA had provided research funds for manpower issues, and in 1962 the department had established an Office of Policy Planning and Development.[41] But these activities were scarcely under way when the critical discussions about the poverty program were being conducted.

A second intellectual advantage enjoyed by the CEA was the clarity of its arguments and the wide support they claimed within the profession of economics. We have already seen the consensus that had emerged around a revised version of Keynes's ideas within the American economics profession by the early 1960s. There was no such intellectual coherence or professional support for labor market policies. The Department of Labor was only beginning to grapple with the role that such policies might play; it did not make consistent arguments about what policy priorities should be or how institutions should be changed, and its views were not always in line with those of its congressional allies. Moreover there was no comparable pool of policy-oriented experts in the area of labor market policy. The passage of the MDTA and the research moneys it distributed eventually did help to build a community of expertise around manpower policies, but little support of this sort was available in the early 1960s.[42] The Department of Labor's lack of clarity about the purposes of labor market legislation and its failure to rally comparable consensus among prestigious members of the economics profession made it easy to dismiss its proposals as ploys for departmental aggrandizement.

This vulnerability of the Department of Labor to charges of agency or constituency bias further benefited the CEA. Since its establishment, the Department of Labor had been seen as the mouthpiece and advocate of organized labor within the federal government. As it struggled to formulate a rationale and design for labor market policy, the department also had to continue its advocacy role on behalf of organized labor. Labor market policies that sought to fulfill both objectives—such as proposals for public works—were particularly vulnerable to being dismissed as constituency measures.[43] In contrast, the CEA was an impartial group of experts with no constituency. Its policy positions could not be dismissed in the same way.

The visibility of the CEA and its proximity to the president further enhanced its access and credibility. The CEA was created as the president's personal advisory group on economic policy and was located in the Executive Office of the President. Manpower issues had no such prominence. In its 1960 report, the Senate Special Committee on Unemployment Problems had urged the creation of a National Manpower Planning Commission in the Office of the President.[44] A proposal for the new commission was introduced in Congress in 1960, along with other recommendations from the Senate Report. Meant to be equal in status to the Council of Economic Advisers, the manpower commission would have charge of policy and program development for work force training and utilization. Its sponsor, Senator Clark, argued that it was vital that concern for manpower policy be institutionalized at the highest levels of the government if the work of manpower experts in the cabinet departments were to be effective.[45] The failure of this proposal and the emphasis of the CEA on macropolicy meant that the voice for manpower policy remained faint and scattered in the executive bureaucracy.[46]

A final advantage that the CEA enjoyed was the way its views about poverty fit with prior policy commitments. The most important commitment in this regard was Kennedy's decision to endorse a Keynesian tax cut in 1962. The tax cut not only influenced the intellectual discussion about policy; it also affected the political prospects for many kinds of labor market policy. In particular it meant that programs requiring significant expenditures, such as public employment, were off the agenda. Although the election of a far more liberal Congress in 1964 had improved the prospects for spending that existed in 1961, the political deal struck to secure support for the tax cut from a Congress still skeptical about Keynesian ideas required holding down expenditures. As an explicit trade-off for congressional support for the tax cut, Johnson had promised to turn in a 1965 budget request of under $100 million.[47] These budgetary constraints effectively precluded public job creation in 1965. Moreover, the decision to cut taxes handicapped Senator Nelson's proposal for a cigarette tax. As the council and the president noted, it made no sense to impose a new tax when the administration was in the process of cutting taxes.[48]

All of these advantages enjoyed by the Council of Economic Advisers' perspective on the poverty program were reinforced by the president's interest in launching the War on Poverty. The president wanted a splashy, visible project that would distinguish his administration. With large-scale spending off the agenda, labor market policy had little to offer. The kind of slow institution building necessary to create job training programs and improve placement systems was not only unglamorous; it was also politically unattractive. Building administrative capacity in the area of labor market policy would require challenging some existing institutions and the groups attached to them. The War on Poverty, on the other hand, seemed to be free from such costs, since it involved a whole new area of activity for the federal government.

Moreover, the attack on poverty lent itself to grand and encompassing rhetoric that invoked idealism and an affirmation of national purpose. Against the advice of Budget Bureau officials, who tried to dissuade the president from using the "War on Poverty" rhetoric, Johnson embraced the dramatic language as an essential part of the endeavor.[49] The president took the cautious proposal first presented to him by the Council of Economic Advisers and, in place of the limited number of carefully planned projects recommended, urged that as many projects as possible be started as soon as possible.[50]

Thus, the perspective of the Council of Economic Advisers and the strategic interests of the president in launching a visible new program meant that the attack on poverty would not provide a means for developing a broad perspective on labor market policy. In fact, by reorienting the policy debate to focus on poverty, the new initiatives hampered thinking and institutional development around broader conceptions of labor market policy. After the declaration of the War on Poverty, existing manpower programs were reoriented to serve the poor, and with research and program funds more plentiful for those focusing on poverty, development of a broader perspective proved hard to sustain.[51]

Economic events appeared to confirm the wisdom of the poverty orientation of labor market policies. As unemployment dropped from 5.7 percent in 1963 to 5.2 percent in 1964, and then to 4.5 percent in 1965, there seemed to be less need for broader labor market policies.

Clearly, the structuralists who based their arguments on the dangers of automation had been proven wrong by the renewed vigor of the American economy.[52] The MDTA administrators found that their target group, skilled workers made obsolete by automation, were only a small fraction of the unemployed.[53] In the face of these changes, and with the excitement and energy surrounding the War on Poverty, there was little room for long-term consideration about the role labor market policies might play in upgrading the labor force, alleviating bottlenecks, managing inflation, or coping with an economic downturn.

The decision to launch the War on Poverty had lasting consequences for the ability to reorient policy in the face of altered economic circumstances. By choosing to develop some kinds of institutions and capacities rather than others, encouraging some ways of looking at problems rather than others, and by shaping interests around policies, the poverty paradigm would continue to influence the politics of employment policy long after the particular economic conditions in which it was conceived had disappeared.

The Anti-institutionalism of the War on Poverty

One of the most striking features of the manpower and poverty policies of the 1960s was their extreme fragmentation. As the new programs were put into place, they set off bitter jurisdictional struggles, and resulted in multiplication of programs rather than reform of existing institutions. The result was that one of the most fertile periods of policy experimentation in American history left little in the way of an institutional legacy for devising and implementing labor market policies.

Two questions emerge from this experience. First, why were separate administrative mechanisms set up to launch the poverty program? Second, why did efforts to reform existing institutions meet with such limited success? The first question requires explaining why the CEA and the president supported the community action approach that became the hallmark of the War on Poverty. The second question directs attention to the way interests attached to existing institutions were able to resist efforts at reform.

Ideas and Institutional Innovation

The decision to create new administrative structures for implementing the War on Poverty was made by the Council of Economic Advisers and the Budget Bureau after the broad focus of the new policy had been worked out. Their decision to frame the poverty program around local "community action agencies" was a striking departure. How they settled on community action as the mechanism to carry out the War on Poverty can be understood in part by looking at the organization of the federal executive, and in particular at the way its diverse and relatively unhierarchical structure allows alternative perspectives and innovative ideas to create niches within the executive branch.

The President's Committee on Juvenile Delinquency (PCJD) took advantage of these arrangements. A small committee operating under the protective wing of Attorney General Robert Kennedy, the PCJD had been experimenting with innovative patterns of social intervention under the Youth Delinquency and Youth Offenses Control Act passed in 1961. Guided by the "opportunity theory" of delinquency developed by Columbia University social work professors Lloyd Ohlin and Richard Cloward, the PCJD was overseeing several experimental projects that sought to expand the opportunities open to ghetto youth by community organization and mobilization.[54] Like the social Keynesians in the 1930s, the advocates of community action had built a network of allies within the federal executive. Although their success was limited, they were, much like the New Deal spending advocates, well positioned to promote their ideas during an impasse in policymaking.[55]

The poverty planners from the CEA and the Budget Bureau found community action an attractive alternative to the proposals for carrying out the attack on poverty that were submitted by the regular departments of the executive branch. They saw community action as a coordinating device that could overcome the disorganization and overlapping of responsibilities that characterized federal delivery of services at the local level. The emphasis that the PCJD put on planning and studying the results of intervention attracted budget officials, as did the promise of administrative simplicity and low cost.[56] These officials were not aiming to challenge or replace existing institutions by creating community action agencies but were seeking to make them operate more effectively by introducing a new mechanism for coordination.

The proponents of community action within the PCJD had a rather different notion of its goals. Disillusioned with the operation of urban bureaucracies and pessimistic about the possibilities for reforming existing institutions from within, they sought to secure change through anti-institutional means. The PCJD viewed community action as a mechanism that would allow the poor to challenge existing institutions.[57] In mobilizing the poor to solve their own problems, community action combined an older tradition of self-help and voluntarism with the notion of federal responsibility that had grown out of the New Deal. However, the new participatory framework enjoyed a problematic relationship to established institutions because its capacity to challenge existing arrangements was more certain than its ability to reconstitute them along new lines.

Part of the attraction of community action, then, were the diverse interpretations that its supporters attached to it. This lack of clarity about what community action actually entailed also helps to explain President Johnson's enthusiastic embrace of the idea and his insistence that the attack on poverty be immediately expanded beyond the cautious plan proposed by the poverty task force. By most accounts, the president had little sense of how community action programs (CAPs) would function; his shock when the CAPs later challenged some of his key allies among urban mayors underscores how little he understood about community action when he so eagerly endorsed it.[58]

Thus, the institutional framework of the War on Poverty can be understood as a product of the haste in which it was launched. The president's desire for a visible new initiative early in his administration lay behind his impatience to get started and the insufficient attention to organizational form that resulted. But misunderstanding and time pressures are only part of the explanation for Johnson's embrace of community action.

The problematic relationship between the modern presidency and the bureaucracy must also be considered central to the attraction of the new program, for Johnson did understand and approve of the decision to bypass existing bureaucracies and to house the new effort within the Executive Office of the President. By taking direct charge of the program, the president could claim political credit and could monitor the new policy far more effectively than if it were delegated to one of the existing departments. For Johnson, institution building meant enhancing the powers and reach of the presidency; the effects on existing administrative agencies and on administrative coherence were secondary considerations.

The creation of separate institutions to run the poverty program made sense in terms of the president's institutional and political interests, and it made sense in the schema of the other executive actors who supported it. However, dropped into the framework of existing politics and policy in the United States, the CAPs were very limited vehicles.

The CAPs had little direct power to prod existing bureaucracies into better serving the poor. One way that they might have influenced other agencies was by providing an alternative model for how to operate; as new agencies with little bureaucratic history, the CAPs were freer than established bureaucracies to experiment with diverse forms of service delivery and program operation. Yet, only limited reforms could be achieved in this way. The CAPs could not force established agencies to embrace the reforms they had pioneered; moreover, the conflict and confusion into which many of the CAPs plunged made them less than ideal vehicles for designing reform. And the struggles to control the CAPs tended to divert attention away from how to reform other institutions. As Roger Friedland has noted, "Community groups were absorbed with strategies for controlling new bureaucracies rather than transforming more important existing ones."[59]

The result was that CAPs devolved into separate institutions for the poor, and particularly the black poor, inadequately equipped to carry out many of the tasks they took on. They were particularly ill suited to implementing employment policy, as the experience of the Concentrated Employment Program demonstrated. The Concentrated Employment Program was begun in 1967 as a way to bring the various manpower services under one roof in target areas of unemployment and involve private employers in training. Local community action agencies were charged with setting up and designing the new program, targeted at the hardest to employ. Since the Concentrated Employment Program did not involve additional expenditures, it essentially left local CAPs to struggle on their own with limited resources to build the ties and organizational forms that would define the policy. It quickly became apparent that the CAPs did not have the confidence or cooperation of the business community; large corporations in particular were reluctant to provide jobs.[60] As hopes for the new program faded, it was eventually abandoned without leaving any enduring institutional framework for employment policy.

The Failure of Institutional Reform

The very existence of CAPs as competing agencies did, however, prompt some internal reform efforts, as existing institutions sought to get a share of the new resources made available by the War on Poverty. In the area of employment policy, the most important impulse for institutional reform came from the Department of Labor, which was trying to establish itself as the premier institution for administering labor market policy. The Economic Opportunity Act gave Labor charge of the youth training programs of the Neighborhood Youth Corps, but as the War on Poverty was implemented, the department sought to wrest control of other training programs from the community action agencies.[61] The department's efforts to administer these programs, and to lay claim to labor market policies more generally, prompted top department officials to challenge institutional competitors and to confront the department's own organizational weaknesses. In this way, the department's ambitions provided pressure for institutional reform.

These challenges produced only limited results. The first problem was the strong resistance posed by established interest groups protective of existing arrangements; the second was insufficient support from higher levels of the administration, particularly from the president, for such reform efforts. Thus, despite some institutional reform, attempts to mold a pastiche of disconnected institutions into a coordinated network capable of administering a national labor market policy failed. The experience of two functions central to labor market policy—vocational education and the job screening and placement activities of the Employment Service—help reveal why reform efforts often exacerbated organizational chaos instead of resolving it.

Vocational education was a particularly difficult area to reform. Advocates of an American labor market policy were aware of the importance of education, especially vocational education, to their endeavors. In the early congressional hearings about manpower policy, Princeton economist Frederick Harbison had testified that "both manpower and educational policy are so inseparable that they must be the concern of a single board."[62] But it would prove difficult to integrate vocational education into a coordinated national network of job placement and training. A state-based system of vocational education had been in place since 1917, when federal matching funds were made available to encourage the states to make vocational education part of the public school curriculum. By the late 1950s, vocational education, which continued to divide its programs into industrial arts, homemaking, and agriculture, was viewed by advocates of manpower policy as hopelessly out of touch with the labor market. But the ability of reformers to introduce change into vocational education was limited: the state-based organization and control of the system circumscribed the reach of national efforts, and the strong organization of state vocational educators in the American Vocational Association (AVA) vigilantly guarded the interests of its members in Congress.[63]

In devising and administering labor market policy, advocates of a coordinated, systematic approach to policy continually confronted the problem of vocational educators. The Budget Bureau and the Department of Labor initially sought to cut them out of the MDTA by

increasing the emphasis on on-the-job training (rather than institutional training). They also tried to assert more federal control by re-
placing automatic allocations with project-by-project negotiations
and full federal financing.[64] The AVA's successful resistance to these
measures in Congress ensured that the MDTA ultimately included a
major role for vocational educators. After the War on Poverty was
launched and training programs multiplied, vocational educators
gradually lost influence, as on-the-job training increased.[65] However, they continued to marshall sufficient strength to guard against
perceived encroachments on their terrain and managed to maintain
control over institutional training despite challenges.[66]

Some reforms were introduced in vocational education during the
1960s as the state-level vocational education establishment responded to incentives provided by new federal funds. But efforts to
make vocational education more responsive to the labor market
were not markedly successful. Investments in existing plant and per-
sonnel created a strong inertial effect that made it difficult to reorient vocational education. The vocational educators' fears of outside control and their ability to resist national reform efforts made it
nearly impossible to link vocational education effectively with the
other pieces of manpower policy. Thus, the state-level organization
of vocational education and the power of the interest association
that supported it meant that manpower policy had to work around
vocational education, hoping to decrease its role, rather than seeking to reform its operations.

A second aspect of labor market policy that reformers sought to
overhaul was the U.S. Employment Service (USES), a federal-state
organization that provided job placement for the unemployed. Because it was the only major arm of the Department of Labor operating at the local level, reformers saw it as the backbone of any labor
market policy.[67] The new manpower programs operated by the Department of Labor charged the Employment Service with screening
applicants for training and later assisting in placement. However,
the local agencies had long-established practices that undercut their
ability to administer effectively the new programs; they also had
considerable capacity to block efforts to alter their operations.

Initially established in 1933 to help combat unemployment, the
Employment Service was assigned responsibility for administering
the state-run unemployment insurance programs established after
the passage of the Social Security Act in 1935.[68] During World War II,
the Employment Service was federalized and played a critical role in
facilitating efficient use of labor for the war effort. Despite the recommendations of labor market economists that the Employment

Service remain federalized and pressure from organized labor, Congress returned it to state control after the war.[69] Employment Service administrators were strongly opposed to continued federal control and the Truman administration's emphasis on macropolicy gave it little incentive to do battle on this issue.[70]

Thus, in the early 1960s, the local Employment Service offices were poorly prepared to fulfill the new labor market policy functions that reformers hoped they would. Because they were strongly dominated by officials responsible for administering unemployment insurance, the employment services devoted little attention to job placement.[71] They functioned much more as passive labor exchanges than as the aggressive screening and placement agencies that the advocates of labor market policy envisioned. Moreover, to the extent that the employment services did connect workers with jobs, they did so in a highly prejudicial manner. They were particularly remiss in serving the "disadvantaged" and minority clients who were less attractive to employers.[72]

Efforts to make the employment services function as a key part of a more comprehensive labor market policy and to serve minorities more effectively were not successful. The autonomy of the Employment Service was a critical factor blocking reform. Although it was nominally under the authority of the Department of Labor, the Employment Service was effectively quite independent, since it was funded from employer contributions to the Unemployment Trust Fund account. The Department of Labor therefore had no significant funding leverage with which to promote reform. Moreover, the Employment Service, like the vocational educators, had a powerful state-based interest association, the Interstate Conference of Employment Security Agencies (ICESA), which was able to call on congressional allies to resist outside pressure. The ICESA derived much of its strength from its ties to state-level industrial development interests, whose primary concern was to keep the unemployment insurance tax rate low.[73]

These barriers to reform blocked several Department of Labor efforts to upgrade the operation of the Employment Service and to improve its treatment of racial minorities. Although it commanded some support among reformers and in organized labor, outright federalization was politically impossible (and not proposed) because of the strong opposition of the ICESA.[74] Instead, the Department of Labor sought to increase its authority over the Employment Service in a variety of ways that stopped short of federalization.

One attempt sought to increase the power of the Department of Labor over the Employment Service by legislation. Based on the recommendations of an outside task force headed by the dean of the University of Chicago Business School, George Shultz, the Manpower Services Act was introduced in Congress in 1966. It failed when the Johnson administration declined to support it in the face of opposition from the ICESA. A second effort the following year also failed when the ICESA teamed up with private employment agencies fearful of public competition to oppose it.[75]

With the legislative route foreclosed, the Department of Labor sought instead to increase its control over the Employment Service by administrative measures, and in particular by boosting the local monitoring capabilities of the Manpower Administration, which had been created in 1963 as the core of authority for manpower programs within the Department of Labor.[76] The first effort in 1965 to strengthen the Manpower Administration's authority over local implementation efforts ended in failure and the resignation of the manpower administrator, John Donovan.

A second attempt taking a less direct approach two years later was more successful. It reorganized responsibilities for new programs so as to centralize authority, and it strengthened the field structure of the Manpower Administration by establishing manpower regional administrators.[77] The following year, the Department of Labor secured the approval of the White House for a final effort to enhance the field authority of the Manpower Administration and to improve the coherence of Employment Service activities by administratively splitting the Manpower Administration's unemployment compensation functions from its labor market screening and placement duties. However, barraged by protests from the National Governor's Association, which had itself been prodded by the state Employment Service administrators, the White House withdrew its support for the reform effort at the last minute. A tense standoff between the Department of Labor and the president ended only when Secretary of Labor Wirtz backed down.[78]

There were real political costs involved in supporting the Department of Labor over the ICESA and its allies among the governors, but there is no indication that they would have been prohibitive had the president favored Labor's proposed reorganization.[79] The president's failure to lend consistent support to the Department of Labor's efforts to enhance its authority over the Employment Service is characteristic of Johnson's more general ambivalence about bolstering the power of some existing cabinet departments. Because their accountability to the president was less than certain, Johnson was wary of departments whose agendas might not always coincide with his.

This reluctance to enhance the power of the Department of Labor helps to explain why the president supported some very bold organizational innovations and resisted other, less controversial measures, such as reorganizing the Employment Service. In fact, in 1967 the president had endorsed a far more drastic move, when he proposed to merge the departments of Commerce and Labor into a single cabinet department, which would combine the functions of human and economic development. Announced in his State of the Union address in January of 1967, the proposal fizzled out several months later, when tentative expressions of support by key interest groups, especially organized labor, collapsed.[80] Nonetheless, in this and in other organizational initiatives, the president showed that he was not afraid to challenge established interest groups when his political objectives or his policy goals conflicted with theirs. Reorganizing the Employment Service in ways that enhanced the power of the Department of Labor was simply not a priority for the president.

These failures at reform, either via external prodding by the CAPs or by internal efforts of existing departments, gave manpower policy the distinction of being one of the most fragmented and incoherent areas of federal policy. Reoriented around the bottom of the labor market and mired in institutional conflict, the federal government's foray into labor market policy looked increasingly irrelevant to any national employment policy. As one supporter of a broader, more encompassing labor market policy remarked ruefully, the officials responsible for economic policy saw close collaboration with manpower specialists "as about equivalent to close collaboration with the Salvation Army."[81]

The Politics of Race

The political fate of the War on Poverty was deeply affected by its identification with the upheaval in racial politics during the 1960s. The initial design of the poverty program—stressing enhancement of individual capacities, and separate, new administrative mechanisms—collided with the movement for African-American political empowerment in ways that hindered further development of labor market policy. The identification of the War on Poverty with African-Americans served to reinforce the political isolation of poor African-Americans, and it strengthened political efforts to cast their problems in social rather than economic terms. Earlier debates about insufficient opportunity now vied with arguments that stressed behavioral and cultural problems as causes for poverty. Policy began to reflect these concerns by tying welfare payments to work requirements.

How did the War on Poverty become a "black program," and why were the possibilities for modifying or extending policies diminished once the program had acquired a racial meaning? To answer these questions, I examine how the political meaning of the War on Poverty changed as it was implemented in the context of the new political assertiveness of African-Americans. I then show how the place of race in party competition combined with the organization and assumptions of the War on Poverty to limit possibilities for change and to shift the onus of poverty onto the poor themselves.

The Political Meaning of the Poverty Program

The War on Poverty was not initially conceived as a "black" program by most of those involved in shaping it.[82] For President Kennedy, "the poor" conjured up the image of rural white poverty, particularly Appalachia. The economists in the CEA and Budget Bureau officials who designed the framework of the new initiative envisioned the poor in more generalized and color-blind terms. They defined poor people by income level. In their view, the political rationale for the War on Poverty was the responsibility that nonpoor Americans had to their less-well-off compatriots. Historian Carl Brauer quotes one of the poverty planners as arguing, "The program ought to be presented quite frankly in terms of the obligations which a prosperous majority owes to a submerged and desperately poor minority."[83]

It quickly became apparent, however, that the War on Poverty did not simply serve an income category. It was in practice directed at groups with distinctive social characteristics and political ties, and it very soon came to focus particularly on the black urban poor. Soon after its inauguration, the War on Poverty became identified as a "black" program.[84] Major urban areas with large African-American populations became the recipients of a disproportionately large share of the community action program funds; by 1966 over half the individuals involved in poverty programs were members of racial minorities.[85] Likewise, with the reorientation of the manpower programs that accompanied the War on Poverty, blacks came to comprise 45 percent of the total enrollment in these programs (see Tables 3.1, 3.2, and 3.3).[86] This tilt was reinforced in the popular perception by the struggles for power that erupted across the country between minority-controlled community action agencies and city governments.[87]

How did the War on Poverty become targeted at African-Americans? One explanation, offered by David Zarefsky, is simple demog-

Table 3.1
Racial Characteristics of Persons Enrolled in
Manpower Training and Development Act
Programs, 1963–1970

| | % of Total Enrollment | | | |
| | Institutional Training | | On-the-Job Training | |
Year	White	Black	White	Black
1963	76.5	21.4	83.0	13.1
1964	69.9	28.3	76.2	22.9
1965	67.7	30.1	77.1	20.9
1966	62.5	35.2	76.2	22.1
1967	59.1	38.0	73.1	24.5
1968	50.8	45.4	64.2	33.1
1969	55.9	39.7	61.1	35.4
1970	59.2	36.0	66.8	30.3

Source: Manpower Report of the President (Washington, D.C.: Government Printing Office, 1971), 303, 305.

Note: Percentages in this and subsequent tables do not total 100 because other nonwhite categories have been omitted.

Table 3.2
Racial Characteristics of Youth Enrolled in
Neighborhood Youth Corps Projects, 1965–1970

| | % of Total Enrollment | | | |
| | Youths in School | | Youths Out of School | |
Year[a]	White	Black	White	Black
1965–1966	55.8	39.0	48.2	45.2
1966–1967	52.4	43.3	47.0	49.4
1967–1968	47.3	48.0	50.2	45.6
1968–1969	46.3	47.4	48.2	47.5
1969–1970	53.7	42.5	50.3	44.2

Source: Manpower Report of the President (Washington, D.C.: Government Printing Office, 1971), 308.

[a] Years are measured from September through August.

Table 3.3
Racial Characteristics of Persons Enrolled in
Employment Programs Initiated as Part of
War on Poverty, 1966–1970

| | % of Total Enrollment | | | |
| | Concentrated Employment Program[a] | | Job Corps | |
Year	White	Black	White	Black
1966[b]			36	54
1967			—	—
1968	15.0	81.0	32	59
1969	28.0	65.0	—	—
1970	26.1	67.4	26.2	60.8

Source: Manpower Report of the President (Washington,
D.C.: Government Printing Office) 1968 Report, 317; 1971
Report, 310–11; Statistics on Manpower: A Supplement to
the Manpower Report of the President (Washington, D.C.:
Government Printing Office, 1969), 101.

[a] Program began operating in 1968; data are for fiscal
year.

[b] Data are based on a survey conducted in October 1966.

raphy. Although African-Americans comprised only 30 percent of
the poor in 1964, poverty rates for nonwhites far exceeded those for
whites. It was estimated that 47.9 percent of nonwhite Americans
were poor in 1964, compared to 14.2 percent of whites. Black rates of
unemployment were routinely double those of whites (see Figure
3.1), and those blacks who were employed were concentrated in the
lower reaches of the labor market, where their earnings were insufficient to pull them out of poverty.[88] Moreover, the most concentrated
and visible poverty, urban poverty, was disproportionately black.
Thus, targeting black poverty offered a way to achieve highly visible
results with relatively few resources.[89]

But poverty statistics and demography are not sufficient to explain the racial cast that the War on Poverty assumed: political pressures from below, inspired by the civil rights movement, were critical in refocusing poverty programs. As Paul E. Peterson and J. David
Greenstone have shown, in many cities the community action programs initially had little African-American representation; only after
black community leaders demanded representation were they ad-
mitted to the boards of many local agencies.[90] This kind of pressure,
repeated in city after city, increased the flow of resources into black
communities and enhanced black control over the local implementation of the poverty program. The focus on African-Americans was

Figure 3.1
Annual Unemployment Rate by Race, 1950–1980. *Source:* U.S. Department of Labor, *Handbook of Labor Statistics* (Washington, D.C.: Government Printing Office, 1985), 64. *Note:* Until 1972, the category "black" includes "black and other."

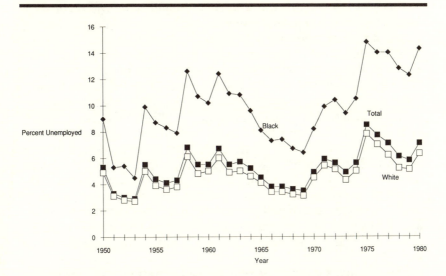

further reinforced by the response to the urban riots of the 1960s. Stunned by the violence and anger unleashed during the riots, local and federal officials alike turned to War on Poverty funds to create programs that they hoped would address the grievances expressed in the riots and redirect the energies of poor African-American communities. James Button has shown that increased funding of poverty programs was the characteristic response to the riots of the mid-1960s.[91]

The public association of the War on Poverty with African-Americans did not immediately rule out possibilities for securing broad public support for its aims. In fact, it provided an opportunity for constructing a new political rationale for poverty programs, which appealed more effectively to American values than did the notion that a prosperous majority had obligations to the poor. The belated recognition by the federal government that southern African-Americans had been denied basic civil and political rights since Emancipation meant that poverty policies could be justified on the basis of these past wrongs. Guarantees of civil and political liberties were more firmly rooted in American political discourse than notions about obligations to the poor. President Johnson seems to have counted on this source of support in 1965, when in an address at

Howard University, he promised to launch a major new initiative to help blacks "move beyond opportunity to achievement." A White House "Conference to Fulfill These Rights" to be held the following year would bring together "scholars and experts and outstanding Negro leaders," who would come up with policies to achieve this aim.[92]

This effort to redefine the political rationale of the War on Poverty failed. The White House conference was indeed held the following year, but no major new initiatives were forthcoming; in fact, support for the much more modest measures embodied in the War on Poverty was beginning to wane. Their chief political problem was their identification with African-Americans. By the late 1960s, black political incorporation no longer evoked images of passive resistance to southern racists; instead, it called up troubling memories of urban riots, which had given vent to an alienation and rage that shocked most whites. As the civil rights movement moved North, conflicts over housing and school desegregation brought race squarely into the lives of northern working-class whites, for whom southern desegregation had been a distant rumble. Moreover, in many cities, established patterns of political interaction were disrupted as blacks used CAPs to challenge local power structures. Police action and repression began to replace increased resources as a response to riots.[93]

These convulsions in American race relations took their toll on the War on Poverty. Soundings of public opinion reflected opposition to the War on Poverty. In 1967, White House Fellow J. Timothy McGinley informed Secretary of Labor Wirtz that the president was concerned about a special study he had commissioned that showed that 60 to 70 percent of the public thought "the president had gone too far in the civil rights area." The report noted that "the phrase War on Poverty is linked in the public's mind to the civil rights movement" and recommended that the phrases "the Great Society" and "the War on Poverty" both be dropped.[94] A public opinion poll confirmed that the War on Poverty had a poor reputation among whites, only 17 percent of whom thought it was doing a good job in 1968 (see Table 3.4).[95]

Similar sentiments were voiced in Congress, amplified by the losses that liberal Democrats suffered in the 1966 mid-term elections. During the House debate over the future of the Equal Opportunity Act in 1967, the fate of the poverty program appeared to be in jeopardy as Republicans and Democrats alike tried to link the poverty programs with urban riots, black militancy, and subversive political activity.[96] These challenges were warded off, but widespread misgivings about the War on Poverty suggested that, in its present form, its days were numbered.

Table 3.4
Public Attitudes toward the Antipoverty Program, 1968

Question: "In general, do you think the antipoverty program is doing a good job, a fair job, or a poor job?"		
	% of All White Respondents	% of All Black Respondents
A good job	17	38
A fair job	38	37
A poor job	24	9
Don't know	11	7
Haven't heard of antipoverty program	10	9

Source: Based on a fifteen-city survey conducted by the Institute for Social Research, University of Michigan, reported in Angus Campbell, *White Attitudes toward Black People* (Ann Arbor, Mich.: Institute for Social Research, 1971), 87.

The economic prosperity of the 1960s made it an ideal time to launch a "war on poverty." Support from the more prosperous majority would be much easier to secure in the context of a growing economy. However, even under such conditions, CEA member James Tobin later noted, willingness to divert tax dollars to the poor depended on a widespread sense of government fairness.[97] Deep-seated racial antagonisms and public perceptions that the War on Poverty provided special benefits for African-Americans made the poverty program look increasingly "unfair." Once these sentiments became politicized in party competition, the race-based rationale for the War on Poverty was easily overwhelmed.

Racial Politics and the Limits to Reorienting Policy

The individual-level/poverty cycle approach first adopted by the War on Poverty and the subsequent racial identification of poverty programs created political dynamics that would make it very difficult to shift poverty policy toward an employment approach. The problems involved in redirecting the poverty program were evident in the late 1960s when congressional liberals sought to create public service employment for ghetto residents and when the president attempted to enlist the private sector in providing work for the poor. In each case, the remedial and racial focus of the War on Poverty handicapped the effort to reorient policy.

By the mid-1960s, many government officials and politicians concerned about the poverty program began to confront the fact that

Figure 3.2
The Components of Subemployment among Residents of Poverty Areas,
1966. Reprinted from *Manpower Report of the President* (Washington, D.C.:
Government Printing Office, 1967), 76.

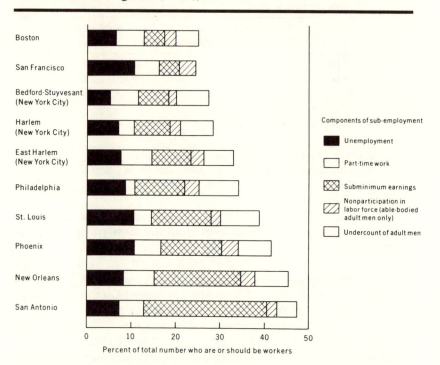

"full employment" did not solve all employment problems. The Department of Labor, with an institutional stake and an enduring interest in labor market policy, conducted several studies that spot-
lighted the relationship between poverty and employment. These
studies found that despite the falling rate of unemployment nationally, joblessness in black urban ghettos remained high. A special survey taken in November 1966 revealed that unemployment rates in
the slums of the thirteen largest cities were nearly 10 percent, a figure triple the national average.[98] As one summary of the study noted,
"For Negroes in poverty areas, unemployment rates were higher
than the worst national rates for the entire labor force recorded since
the depression of the 1930s."[99]

The department also sought to expand the definition of the employment problem with efforts to develop measures for subemployment. Concern about those working full time but earning wages
below the poverty line and those who could find only part-time work

Table 3.5
Subemployment Rates in Ten Predominantly Minority Areas, 1966

Area	Subemployment Rate (%)[a]
Boston—Roxbury area	24
New Orleans—several contiguous areas	45
New York	
Harlem	29
East Harlem	33
Bedford-Stuyvesant	28
Philadelphia—North Philadelphia	34
Phoenix—Salt River Bed area	42
St. Louis—North Side	39
San Antonio—East Side and West Side	47
San Francisco—Mission-Fillmore area	25

Source: Manpower Report of the President (Washington, D.C.: Government Printing Office, 1967), 75.

[a] The Department of Labor defined this index in the following way:

"1. People classed as unemployed since they were jobless and looking for work during the survey week;

"2. Those working only part time though they wanted full time work;

"3. Heads of households under 65 years of age who earn less than $60 a week though working full time; also individuals under 65, not heads of households, who earn less than $56 a week on a full-time job (the equivalent of $1.40 an hour for a 40-hour week);

"4. Half the number of 'nonparticipants' among men aged 20 to 64 (on the assumption that the other half are not potential workers, chiefly because of physical or mental disabilities or severe personal problems); and

"5. An estimate of the male 'undercount' group (based on the assumption that the number of men in the area should bear some relation to the number of women that exists in the population generally; also that half of the unfound men are in the four groups of subemployed people just listed—the others being either employed or not potential workers)."

led to the creation of a subemployment index, defined as including the unemployed, the underemployed, those earning wages below the poverty line, and estimates of "discouraged" and other uncounted workers. A 1966 study utilizing this index to measure subemployment in ten predominantly black urban slum areas (see Figure 3.2 and Table 3.5) clearly showed the links between ghetto distress and unemployment, underemployment, and low wages.[100] The existence of subemployment in the ghettos of American cities, Secretary of Labor Wirtz maintained, made national measures of unemployment "utterly irrelevant."[101] He saw the problem in both "personal" terms and in terms of the "job market circumstances" that ghetto residents faced. His policy solutions, however, remained within the framework set up by the War on Poverty, concentrating on intensive job readiness programs in the nation's ghettos.[102]

Also part of these efforts to rethink policy was the Department of Labor report *The Negro Family: The Case for National Action*, later known simply as the "Moynihan Report," after its principal author, Assistant Secretary of Labor Daniel Patrick Moynihan.[103] Issued in 1965, the report argued that instability in black family life, and specifically a high percentage of female-headed families, was the central problem that government policy would have to tackle if it seriously wanted to bring African-Americans up to the living standards of white Americans. The report traced African-American family dynamics to the legacy of slavery, but it also placed the employment problems of African-Americans at the center of its analysis of family life. Limiting its aim to that of "defining a problem," the report did not present policy recommendations, but one direction in which it surely pointed was that of reducing black unemployment and subemployment.

These studies and others documenting the persistence of employment problems in an economy with low aggregate rates of unemployment fueled growing doubts about the service orientation of the War on Poverty. Policymakers, members of Congress, and representatives of the poor began to call for more emphasis on employment, especially public employment. As a report by an investigative task force of the House Subcommittee on the Poverty War Program put it, "A successful employment program would in itself help to solve many of the problems of social disorganization which all too many community action agencies have sought to solve through 'organization,' 'research' and 'planning.'"[104] Public employment was a central recommendation of the Kerner Commission, appointed to probe the causes of the urban riots in 1967. Jobs were also a key demand of the Poor People's Campaign, a lobbying effort launched by the Southern Christian Leadership Conference, which brought several thousand supporters to camp in Washington, D.C., for over a month in 1968.[105] Bills supporting public employment for ghetto residents were introduced in Congress in 1967 and 1968.

None of these initiatives was adopted. Part of the reason, as those who highlight the importance of the Vietnam War correctly point out, was the strain on national finances created by the war. Even as proposals for public employment multiplied, the president was promising key members of Congress that he would hold down expenditures in exchange for a surtax aimed at slowing down the overheated economy.[106] In this context, major new expenditures on public employment would be hard to justify. But limits on spending are only part of the explanation for why public employment was rejected. The racial focus of policy was also critical. President Johnson, who had opposed public employment from the start, maintained that endorsing public employment programs in the late 1960s would be viewed as "rewarding riots."[107] In Congress, both Republicans and Democrats echoed these sentiments, leaving liberal supporters of public employment with insufficient backing to pass their proposals.

The president proposed instead to draw the private sector into providing employment for the poor. Since 1965, the Department of Labor had been experimenting with on-the-job training funds to subsidize training of workers in the private sector. The apparent success of programs in creating new jobs convinced the president that this was the way to reorient the War on Poverty.[108] In a special message to Congress on January 23, 1968, Johnson introduced the new program, Job Opportunities in the Business Sector (JOBS), as a "new partnership between Government and private industry."[109] To secure industry cooperation, the president established a new organization, the National Alliance of Businessmen (NAB), headed by Henry Ford II. The initial response of industry was unexpectedly enthusiastic: by July 1, 1969, 338,000 jobs had been pledged, and more than two-thirds of these employers had not even applied for the federal reimbursement of training costs to which they were entitled.[110] These positive signs soon evaporated. Several months later, only a fraction of the business pledges had materialized into jobs. By 1970, JOBS funds went unallocated and had to be reprogrammed for other activities.[111]

The failure of the JOBS program pointed to the problems inherent in a labor market policy targeted at the low end of the labor market. Neither business nor organized labor had a stake in the manpower policies that had been set up. Although the AFL-CIO leadership was a strong supporter of the poverty programs and some individual unions operated training programs with federal funds, the training offered by these programs held little attraction for unions as institutions or for their members as individuals. As Jack Barbash has noted, "The closer the union interest is to the workplace, the more restrictive is the outlook on training."[112] Business likewise had little interest in the training programs operated by the War on Poverty. Business participation in the JOBS program was closer to a form of charity, affordable in the tight labor markets of the late 1960s. Such public-spiritedness was short lived. As the economy grew sluggish, business cooperation evaporated. By the mid-1970s, the subsidized job-training programs had acquired such stigma that their participants were actually less likely to be hired than similarly qualified candidates who were not part of a federal program.[113]

The difficulties in sustaining business and labor support for training indicated that policymakers needed to consider more closely the relationship between training and the operation of the private sector to create a lasting role for training. But this task would have required rethinking the underpinnings of the poverty program and its relationship to the private economy. While some of the research supported by Department of Labor funds pointed in these directions, department officials had meager resources and opportunities to launch such a campaign for policy change.[114] Mired in the bureaucratic wrangling and the day-to-day press of program management, government agencies administering the poverty program sought to make incremental changes in policy, not to challenge its fundamental premises.

With these routes to reorganizing policy blocked, poor African-Americans were left with a modest set of social service and training programs, whose disconnection from the labor market made them "de facto income maintenance programs."[115] As Piven and Cloward have argued, the most significant enduring social policy benefits that poor blacks won during the 1960s were increases in welfare spending. The greatest economic gains that government action produced for blacks in the 1960s came from the growth in public sector employment, as increasing numbers of blacks were hired to staff the burgeoning social welfare bureaucracies.[116]

In the face of growing backlash and the political failure of employment alternatives, African-American organizations increasingly focused on securing what they had. This meant defending the autonomy of the Office of Economic Opportunity, winning funds for existing poverty programs, and supporting liberalization of welfare measures. These aims left black people increasingly isolated in defense of unpopular programs.[117] The most promising avenues for addressing black social and economic problems were in securing public sector jobs and in using government agencies insulated from politics—courts and administrative agencies—to pursue anti-discrimination and affirmative action strategies. Most of the burden of addressing the employment problems of African-Americans thus came to fall on public sector employment and regulatory measures to ensure equal access to employment.

Although most of those planning the War on Poverty put little stock in theories about the "culture of poverty," their arguments about the causes of poverty created fertile ground for political debates that highlighted individual irresponsibility, not insufficient opportunity, as a cause of poverty. Political proclivities to focus attention on individual conduct were enhanced by framing the problem so heavily in terms of individual attributes rather than in terms of the operation of economic institutions. This way of seeing poverty was further strengthened by the racial focus of the program, especially once the civil rights movement had lost its moral edge during the urban riots of the late 1960s. In this context, the descriptions of black culture in the Moynihan report were so politically charged that civil rights groups mobilized against it, despite substantial agreement with the report's emphasis on employment.[118]

The shifts in political arguments about poverty had policy implications that soon became apparent. Support for policies that enforced standards of individual behavior, not efforts to modify labor markets, was the logical result of this way of understanding poverty. The first major step to reorient policy along these lines occurred in 1967, when Congress imposed work requirements on welfare recipients with the Work Incentive Program (WIN).[119] With meager funds for training, and little attention to job upgrading, the WIN program at best would simply replicate all the problems of the War on Poverty job–training programs; at worst, it would serve as a means for selective punishment of welfare recipients.

Party Competition and the Failure of Cross-Racial Alliances

The racial identification of the War on Poverty and the limits of policy reform sparked interest in creating more broadly based policies and coalitions to support them. Prominent black leaders, aware of the dangers entailed in the low-resource racial policy that the War on Poverty had become, urged a reorientation of policy to emphasize the common economic interests of white and black workers. However, the organization of American party politics and the dynamics of party competition around race in the 1960s blocked the emergence of alternative coalitions more likely to support stronger, more encompassing social and economic policies that would benefit blacks and whites alike.

Black labor leader A. Philip Randolph had always supported this approach, and toward the end of his life, the Reverend Martin Luther King, Jr., also began to stress the need for such a cross-racial alliance united around common economic concerns.[120] Bayard Rustin of the A. Philip Randolph Institute sought to embody this perspective in the Freedom Budget that he drafted for Randolph and delivered at the White House Conference to Fulfill These Rights and later presented to Congress.[121] The budget called for massive increases in public spending for public works projects to create jobs and build housing and public institutions. The proposal did not receive serious attention in Congress: by the late 1960s, even congressional liberals evinced little political will to reroute policy along lines that called for massive government spending.[122]

However, supporters of the Freedom Budget had political aims that did not depend on immediate acceptance of the proposal. According to Rustin, the budget could serve as a political tool to reorient politics toward national economic goals supported by cross-racial coalitions. It was especially needed at the local level where "groups have become enmeshed in intra-community fights, ... squabbling about the election of local boards and fighting each other for the limited funds available."[123] His hope was that the Freedom Budget could serve to connect local demands to national economic issues.

The institutional organization of politics and parties in the United States made this a difficult task. American political parties had never been national organizations; party politics primarily negotiated among local power bases, rarely organizing national agendas. Rustin wanted to reverse the relationship so that national issues would determine the contours of local politics. Without nationally organized parties or government resources, there was no mechanism for bending local activities toward the national goals and broader alliances that Rustin envisioned. And in the late 1960s, reorganizing political alliances to promote cross-racial common interests would be particularly difficult.

Local Democratic party politics across the nation were in a state of upheaval as blacks, armed with new federal antidiscrimination laws, mobilized to challenge the political practices and entrenched elites that had excluded them from equal participation in state and local politics. The intellectual assumptions and operational framework of the War on Poverty were far better suited to serve as an adjunct in this struggle than they were for backing a movement to promote common interests around expansions of social and economic rights. The community action agencies evolved into a useful tool in the struggle for African-American political enfranchisement at the local level, but the strategies and tactics that enhanced black power in local politics could not also be used to promote cross-race coalitions and reorientation of the social and economic policy on the national level.[124]

The identification of social policy with racial policy created a sharp dilemma for Democratic party leaders. The political intertwining of racial policy and social policy during the 1960s meant that the traditional economic and social policy issues that had united the Democratic coalition would be overwhelmed by racial fissures.[125]

National leaders had supported measures to promote black political inclusion, but the party lacked a strategy for reconciling the interest conflicts that would accompany this opening of the political system.

Republican politicians were well positioned to benefit from the increasing salience of race in organizing political beliefs and party competition. In the 1964 presidential elections, differences in the parties' positions on racial issues had sent much of the once "solid South" into the Republican camp. Four years later, when racial rifts had intensified and spread beyond the South, the Republican party could reap the benefits of its new position of racial conservatism.[126] In the wake of three summers of black urban rioting, the issue of "law and order" provided Republican presidential candidate Richard Nixon with an appeal to white voters that highlighted racial fears.[127]

The new set of issues that dominated the campaign pulled the agenda away from the common economic concerns that had historically united the Democratic coalition. The 1968 election evidenced a curvilinear pattern, in which whites from upper socioeconomic sectors joined with blacks against a broad range of middle-income whites.[128] The racial issue proved compelling enough to defeat the Democratic contender, Hubert Humphrey, who received only 35 percent of the white vote. Although organized labor had stood as a bulwark against this emerging pattern, the movement of many non-southern blue-collar workers into the Republican ranks in 1968 indicated the appeal of the political agenda that the Republicans had fashioned.[129]

Conclusion

The War on Poverty was an extraordinary episode in American politics and policy. It provided a hothouse environment for experimenting with innovative policies and new institutional mechanisms for implementing policy. In encouraging local beneficiaries of policy to participate in the operation of government programs, the War on Poverty presaged the movement toward more responsive bureaucracies that would sweep European welfare states in the 1980s. In forging a partnership between the local and federal governments, the poverty programs pioneered a form of activity especially suited to the United States, where no strong national bureaucratic capacities existed for implementing such policy.

But prominent features of the poverty program as it developed had troubling consequences: the focus on the individual problems of the poor served to direct attention away from the broader economic sources of poverty; suspicion of established agencies, however well founded, undermined possibilities for reforming existing institutions; and the racial focus of the War on Poverty limited political possibilities for enhancing existing programs or even shifting their focus.

This chapter has argued that these features of the War on Poverty were not intentional outcomes created by a single set of actors. Rather, they were the product of different actors who were pressing against the perceived bounds of politics and established frameworks of policy understanding. The directions in which they pushed, however, were limited by their starting points. Thus, the CEA's approach to employment policy and poverty rested on its assumptions about macroeconomic policymaking; the president's enthusiasm for the poverty program stemmed from his efforts to overcome the institutional constraints on presidential policymaking. Once in place, the political meaning and policy possibilities embodied in the War on Poverty were transformed by unexpected intersections with other events. I have argued that the collision of the War on Poverty with the movement for black political empowerment was central to its political fate, although escalation of the Vietnam War also limited funding and presidential attention.

The sequencing of policy innovation and the interaction of policy with unpredicted events deeply affected the politics of employment policy. After the War on Poverty, efforts to link poverty to employment problems faced new barriers. Policy had been carved up into two realms, a politics of economic policy and a politics of poverty; no broader politics of employment united them. Poverty policy was an isolated and politically fragile invention; social obligation and economic growth were both essential for its success.[130] Social obligation offered a thin reed for planting policy in any case; when tied to policies that came to emphasize the deepest fault line in American society—racial differences—such obligation proved impossible to sustain. Political leaders increasingly laid the onus of poverty on the poor themselves, and with the collapse of the economic conditions on which poverty policies had been predicated, they abandoned the War on Poverty as an expensive and wasteful mistake. New roles would be carved out for employment policies in the coming decade, but the poor, and particularly the African-American poor, would not be among the main beneficiaries.

Four

Public Employment and the Politics of "Corruption"

DURING the 1970s, as the world economic order came unglued, policymakers across industrial nations began to question established formulas for governing domestic economies. In the United States, the Keynesian ideas that had only recently won acceptance increasingly appeared unable to remedy unemployment without creating unacceptable levels of inflation. Unfamiliar economic terrain provoked public debates about the need to establish a broader mission for employment policy and to strengthen the institutions responsible for implementing it. Most proposals envisioned a revitalized labor market policy as central to any new employment strategy. Widespread concern about unemployment suggested that it might be possible to win public support for substantially reorganizing labor market policy.

Such possibilities remained unfulfilled: most proposals to extend the reach of labor market policies died, and efforts to expand institutional capacities collapsed. Instead, a decentralized form of public service employment, focusing on cyclical unemployment, emerged as the dominant labor market policy of the 1970s. Devolving power to local officials, the new policy bore the earmarks of pork barrel politics. Even this foray into a federally supported program of public employment—the first since the New Deal—was short lived. Instead of building new support for employment policy, the implementation of public employment in the 1970s provoked widespread opposition. Less than five years after it wrote public service employment into legislation, Congress sharply scaled back funds and refocused programs to serve the bottom of the labor market. These moves served as a prelude to the total abandonment of public service employment in the 1980s.

This chapter examines the politics of labor market policies in the 1970s, asking why, of the options considered, public service employment became the central policy and why, once put into place, it was so politically fragile. I argue that party-based struggles between Congress and the president during the two Nixon administrations limited possibilities for developing new labor market capacities as each sought to control the links between politics and administration in employment policy. In the course of these partisan conflicts, the range of problems that employment policy would address narrowed, and efforts to construct new institutions for implementing labor market policy failed.

But the impetus to enact labor market policies did not die. Seeking to make unemployment the pivotal issue of party competition, congressional Democrats seized upon public service employment as their response to rising joblessness in the mid-1970s. In this way, the logic of pork barrel politics, characteristic of congressional bargaining, came to define the direction of policy. Slapped into place with little institutional preparation, and implemented by local officials drawn to its political uses, public service employment quickly provoked charges of abuse, fraud, and corruption. As its political liabilities escalated, public service employment rapidly lost support and was quickly scaled back.

New Ideas for Employment Policy

The experience of employment policies in the 1960s, together with the puzzling performance of the economy in the early 1970s, prompted a widespread reexamination of American employment policy. Professional economists in universities and analysts in the growing number of think tanks questioned the theoretical foundations of past policy and floated new ideas about the role labor market policy could play in this changed economic environment. How did these ideas envision the relationship between government and employment, and what influence did they have on the Nixon administration as it sought to craft economic policy in an uncharted environment? This section takes up these questions, beginning with a discussion of the economic puzzles that had undermined confidence in Keynesian remedies.

The Breakdown of Keynesian Employment Policy

As Nixon took office, the apparently stunning successes of Keynesian fiscal policy during the mid-1960s had been tarnished by the inability of policymakers to control the economy. Particularly worrisome were rising rates of inflation.

The economy's performance was both puzzling and alarming, for it seemed to suggest that the dominant understandings of the econ-

Figure 4.1
Unemployment and Inflation Rates, 1968–1980. *Source: Economic Report of the President* (Washington, D.C.: Government Printing Office, 1983), 225; U.S. Department of Labor, *Handbook of Labor Statistics* (Washington, D.C.: Government Printing Office, 1985), 64. *Note:* Inflation is measured by percentage of change in the consumer price index.

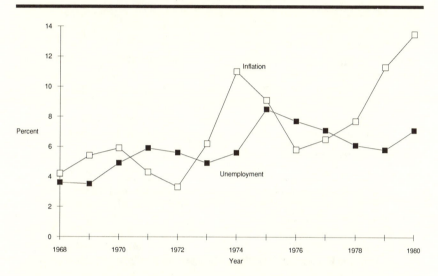

omy were no longer valid. American Keynesians had premised their policies on the notion of a stable trade-off between unemployment and inflation, graphically represented by the Phillips curve. Constructed from empirical observation, the Phillips curve presumably allowed policymakers to choose a point along the curve for the politically desired mix of unemployment and inflation. Deviations from the desired position could be corrected by discretionary action of the federal government, including tightening or loosening fiscal and monetary policy.[1]

After 1969, however, growing evidence indicated that the Phillips curve no longer offered an accurate characterization of the American economy (see Figure 4.1). The Nixon administration came into office following a strategy of moderate fiscal restraint, eschewing an activist discretionary posture toward fiscal policy in favor of a more passive "gradualism."[2] However, the recession that it intentionally induced had very little impact on inflation, even as it caused unemployment to mount. For unknown reasons, the medicine that had worked so effectively in the 1960s appeared incapable of guiding the economy in the 1970s.

Table 4.1

Shifts in Labor Force Composition, Selected Years, 1951–1969

Sex and Age Group	% of Labor Force				
	1951	1955	1960	1965	1969
Male					
16–19	3.8	3.7	4.0	4.6	4.8
20–24	6.4	4.9	5.9	6.6	6.5
25–64	55.2	55.9	53.4	50.7	48.2
65 and over	3.9	3.9	3.2	2.8	2.7
Female					
16–19	2.8	2.6	3.0	3.4	3.8
20–24	4.4	3.8	3.7	4.6	5.7
25–64	22.6	24.0	25.4	26.0	27.0
65 and over	0.9	1.3	1.4	1.4	1.3
Total male	69.2	68.3	66.5	64.7	62.2
Total female	30.8	31.7	33.5	35.3	37.8

Source: George L. Perry, "Changing Labor Markets and Inflation," *Brookings Papers on Economic Activity*, no. 3 (1970): 414. Reprinted with permission.

Table 4.2

Relative Unemployment Rates by Age and Sex, Selected Years, 1951–1969

Sex and Age Group	Ratio of Group Unemployment Rate to Prime-Age Male Unemployment Rate[a]				
	1951	1955	1960	1965	1969
Male					
16–19	3.9	3.7	3.7	5.6	6.8
20–24	1.7	2.4	2.1	2.4	3.1
25–64	1.0	1.0	1.0	1.0	1.0
65 and over	1.8	1.4	1.1	1.5	1.3
Female					
16–19	3.0	2.7	3.0	5.7	8.0
20–24	2.4	2.1	2.1	3.1	3.8
25–64	2.2	1.5	1.3	1.8	1.9
65 and over	1.2	0.6	0.5	0.8	1.3
Total male	1.3	1.3	1.3	1.5	1.7
Total female	2.3	1.7	1.5	2.3	2.8

Source: George L. Perry, "Changing Labor Markets and Inflation," *Brookings Papers on Economic Activity*, no. 3 (1970): 414. Reprinted with permission.

[a] Prime-age group consists of males 25–64 years of age.

These puzzles were accompanied by new data about unemployment and the labor force that raised further questions about policy. One central issue was the changing composition of the labor force (see Table 4.1) and the different experiences of subgroups of the work force with unemployment (see Table 4.2). The proclivity of minorities, women, and teenagers to lose jobs more frequently than did prime-aged white males appeared to account for their greater rates of unemployment.[3] This new characterization of unemployment, together with the apparent collapse of the Phillips curve, raised serious questions about the continuing utility of the employment policies fashioned in the 1960s.

Two Directions for Labor Market Policy

As the prosperity of the 1960s gave way to stagflation, decision-makers began to rethink economic policies, and the foundations of the theories that had justified employment initiatives in the previous decade came into question. Although there were many twists of argument, perspectives fell into two major camps: one sought to expand the role of active labor market policies in order to improve the functioning of the macroeconomy; the other argued that reduction of government regulation of the labor market held the key to a healthy labor market and a prosperous economy. The diversity of recommendations for labor market policies emerging in the 1970s indicated that not only had shared assumptions about the operation of the macroeconomy broken down; understandings of how labor markets function had begun to collapse as well.[4]

Proponents of active labor market policy had different views about how significantly such policy could contribute to employment objectives. A minority of labor market economists argued that labor market policies should play the central role in reducing unemployment. Led by Charles Holt and his colleagues at the liberal Urban Institute, proponents of this view based their arguments on the search-turnover theory, which maintained that high unemployment was a function of greater turnover in jobs and the long search time required to find a new job.[5] Segmentation of the labor force along age, race, and sex lines exacerbated the unemployment-inflation trade-off because these groups experienced greater turnover in their jobs and required longer search time to locate new ones.[6]

The proper role for policy, then, was to improve the functioning of the labor market to reduce turnover and make the search procedure more efficient. This approach would require substantial upgrading of the Employment Service so that it could greatly increase its capacities for matching jobs and workers. Holt and his colleagues recommended tripling the capacity of the Employment Service.[7] They also called for improving vocational counseling, instituting worker mobility programs to facilitate interregional migration, and training to fill areas of critical skill shortages. They defended the utility of manpower policy against its critics, arguing that the scale of American programs in the 1960s had been too small to assess accurately the potential contribution of such policies.[8]

The dominant viewpoint among economists who had worked on employment issues in the 1960s was to support labor market policies as a useful adjunct to macropolicy but not to expect too much of them.[9] Within the government, this perspective was represented by the National Manpower Advisory Committee (NMAC), an advisory group established under the Manpower Development and Training Act (MDTA) in 1962. The NMAC pressed the Nixon administration with its views that increasing human capital and improving the operation of the labor market could help to reduce unemployment without exacerbating inflation.[10] The NMAC argued for a broad conceptualization of manpower policy in which welfare policies and public employment would be linked to an overall comprehensive manpower policy. It called for widening the scope of manpower policy to initiate programs of job upgrading and to increase attention to underemployment. The group also voiced increasing support for public service employment, although it warned against rapidly initiating large-scale programs.[11] A long-time proponent of strengthening the Employment Service, the NMAC urged that it be federalized.

Support for public service employment also came from some advocates of the dual labor market theory, which offered a distinctive interpretation of the American labor market. The pioneers of the dual labor market theory, economists Michael Piore and Peter Doeringer, concluded from their investigations of manpower policies in the late 1960s that job training was unlikely to succeed because the only kind of jobs available to the disadvantaged, at whom they were directed, were unattractive, low-wage, dead-end jobs that encouraged employment instability.[12] They argued that the economy was divided into a primary sector characterized by relatively high-paying and secure employment and a secondary sector with low-wage, insecure employment; movement between these two sectors, they maintained, was very difficult.

In the face of this dual labor market, they argued, employment policies should facilitate the entry of disadvantaged workers into primary sector jobs, using such measures as job development services that focused on the quality of the placements rather than the quantity and strict enforcement of antidiscrimination legislation. They also stressed the importance of tight labor markets to facilitate movement into primary sector jobs.[13] Although Doeringer and Piore doubted the utility of public employment, other economists building on the insights of the dual labor market perspective strongly supported public employment programs as a means of increasing the supply of good jobs.[14]

Reconsideration of labor market policies in the 1960s and the growing unemployment of the 1970s thus created much stronger support from experts for reforming and expanding activist labor market policy. They increasingly emphasized the importance of instituting training at various levels of the labor market, not just at the bottom. Such training, they argued, could improve productivity and reduce bottlenecks, not simply increase the employability of the poor. Likewise, they envisioned a larger economic role for public employment. Public service employment could reduce the rate of unemployment without exacerbating inflation the way macroeconomic stimulation would.

Located at prestigious universities or in liberal think tanks in Washington, D.C., these advocates of new directions for manpower policy had a variety of channels for making their views heard by the new administration. Many of the labor market economists continued to have ties with the Department of Labor, which the new administration had not disrupted. The Democratic Congress provided another important point of entry for these ideas.

A very different perspective, far less favorable to government action, also took shape in the early 1970s and presented a formidable challenge to supporters of government action. The inspiration for this viewpoint was economist Milton Friedman, whose opposition to Keynesianism had made him a lonely figure until the late 1960s. In his 1967 landmark presidential address to the American Economic Association, Friedman had challenged the prevailing views about unemployment and proposed an alternative theory and policy modifications to accompany it.[15] Rather than any stable trade-off between unemployment and inflation, Friedman argued, there was a "natural rate of unemployment," which was in equilibrium with the structure of real wage rates. Lowering unemployment beyond this natural rate would only result in upward pressure on wages, that is, inflation. Moreover, because employment would tend back to its natural rate once the economy had adjusted to the new prices, it would take an accelerated rate of inflation to keep unemployment below its natural rate.

These views were an argument against using fiscal policy to reduce unemployment, since such measures would only disrupt the stability of the private economy. But Friedman did find a role for labor market policy. Arguing that the natural rate of unemployment was not "immutable," but was, in fact, shaped by many "man-made and policy-made" factors, including labor unions, the legal minimum wage, and the Healy and Davis-Bacon acts (which guaranteed union wages on government construction projects), Friedman advocated federal action to remove these obstacles to lowering unemployment. He also noted that the federal government could help reduce unemployment by improving the operation of employment exchanges and increasing the availability of information about labor supply and job vacancies.[16]

Many of these ideas were elaborated by Harvard economist Martin Feldstein, who in 1972 produced a study commissioned by the Joint Economic Committee on the feasibility of reducing the unemployment rate to 2 percent.[17] Following Friedman, Feldstein recommended that the minimum wage be dropped for youth, maintaining that this action would give employers an incentive to offer young people jobs that provided training and advancement. For adults, Feldstein argued that unemployment insurance both prolonged joblessness and increased the instability of employment. To eliminate these disincentives, he recommended taxing unemployment insurance or shifting the cost of unemployment onto the individual by setting up an "individual experience plan" that would establish individual unemployment reserves for each worker.

Feldstein also recommended some measures designed to improve the search process, similar to those advocated by Holt. Feldstein's were typically less sweeping: instead of a major expansion of the Employment Service, he called for a special Youth Employment Service, to be administered by the states.[18] Underpinning Feldstein's recommendations was an analysis that presumed that jobs were available and that existing unemployment was essentially voluntary. What had to be done was to change the terms of choice the unemployed faced so that they would prefer work to unemployment.

The views of Friedman and Feldstein had become increasingly popular among academic economists with the breakdown of the near-consensus on Keynesian ideas that had characterized the economics discipline in the United States for almost two decades. As Keynesianism faltered, Friedman and like-minded economists were well prepared to mount a challenge. Friedman's ideas quickly found their way into the Nixon administration. Nixon's appointees to the two agencies most responsible for pushing employment objectives within the administration, the Council of Economic Advisers (CEA) and the Department of Labor, were influenced by Friedman's ideas and the policy directions to which they pointed.

A Republican Labor Market Policy?

The intellectual disarray and economic uncertainty that confronted Richard Nixon in some ways paralleled the situation that Franklin D. Roosevelt had faced in the early 1930s, and like Roosevelt, Nixon allowed the members of his administration to experiment with a variety of policies. The Department of Labor borrowed ideas from the advocates of stronger active labor market policy as well as from those wanting less government action. Early initiatives from the department suggested that the administration would strengthen some federal institutions related to labor market policy and at the same time would seek to decentralize the administration of policy. This blend of centralization and decentralization would allow the president to address unemployment with an implementation strategy that would reap political advantages for the Republican party and would reduce reliance on fiscal tools that might exacerbate inflation.

Behind this activity stood the new secretary of labor, George Shultz, former dean of the business school at the University of Chicago and director of the 1965 study of the Employment Service. Shultz had long been interested in increasing the effectiveness of labor market tools, and like the labor market economists with whom he was associated on the National Manpower Policy Task Force, Shultz advocated greater coordination of manpower policies with fiscal and monetary measures.[19]

Among the measures that the new Department of Labor officials advocated for increasing the anti-inflationary functions of manpower policy was the computerization of job information. Computer job banks, still in the experimental stage, were to be expanded to seventy-six cities.[20] Accompanying the job banks was the Employment Service Reporting System, designed to track an individual's progress through the various manpower services. In addition, the department initiated studies of other proposals for reducing unemployment without increasing inflation, including lowering the minimum wage for young workers.[21] The department also favored tying manpower policy more closely to macroeconomic policy, supporting the concept of the trigger, featured in the proposed Manpower

Training Act of 1970. The trigger would automatically increase training funds by 10 percent when the national unemployment rate rose above 4.5 percent.[22]

The desire to increase information about labor markets also prompted a major new effort to collect job vacancy statistics. For several decades, economists and policymakers had pressed for better measures of the demand for labor; a major government study of employment statistics in 1962 had recommended the collection of job vacancy statistics, arguing that they were essential to better implementation of both microeconomic and macroeconomic policy. The Department of Labor had conducted a pilot study, beginning in 1964, which was widely judged to be a success. In April of 1969, the Shultz Department of Labor continued this effort by launching the first full-scale collection of job vacancy data with the Job Opening–Labor Turnover program, known as JOLT.[23]

Important antidiscriminatory measures were also put into place. The most striking product of administration antidiscriminatory action was the Philadelphia Plan.[24] Named for the city in which it was first implemented, the Philadelphia Plan sought to break down discriminatory barriers toward minorities in the construction trades by setting guidelines for the number of minority employees to be hired on construction projects financed by federal funds. First devised by Secretary Wirtz, the plan had received little backing from President Johnson and had been rescinded before Nixon took office. Within the first months of his stewardship of the Department of Labor, Secretary Shultz decided to revive the plan. Announced in June 1969 and put into effect in September of the same year, the plan was to be extended to other cities if they did not come up with "hometown" solutions that voluntarily established agreements for hiring minorities on federal construction projects.

These innovations were accompanied by efforts to increase the efficiency of manpower policy administration and, at the same time, to decentralize it. One of Shultz's first moves as secretary of labor was to institute the administrative reform of the Manpower Administration that had eluded Secretary Wirtz for so many years. In 1969 the Bureau of Employment Security (BES), the Department of Labor agency responsible for the Employment Service, was dissolved, and the Employment Service was folded into a new U.S. Training and Employment Service.[25] The dissolution of BES presumably would increase the ability of the Manpower Administration to coordinate Employment Service activities with other manpower programs. At the same time, the power of regional administrators was enhanced;

operating and planning authority devolved on them from above, and power was centralized in their hands from below.[26] The aim was to achieve a degree of administrative flexibility not possible with greater centralization and at the same time to simplify the lines of federal authority.

Not incidentally, the plan also severed lines of influence that old-line Democratic politicians had nurtured. The ease with which the reform was implemented indicated that the power of the Employment Service and its lobbying arm, the Interstate Conference, had been substantially injured in the prolonged battle of the 1960s. The Employment Service's poor performance throughout the decade had lost it some of the congressional support that had previously sustained it. More important, as the service's old allies left Congress, their replacements found the policy area altered by the ever-growing presence of the Manpower Administration. The Employment Service could not cultivate the same strong ties with these new congressional members as it could in the days before the Manpower Administration. Moreover, unlike Wirtz, Shultz and Manpower Administrator Arnold Weber enjoyed executive support for their reorganization plan: the Republican president saw reorganization of these relationships as politically advantageous.[27]

During Shultz's tenure, the Department of Labor also expanded its capacity to initiate policy. Soon after he took office, Shultz established the Office of the Assistant Secretary of Labor for Policy, Evaluation, and Research (ASPER), which sought to play the role of entrepreneur for the Nixon administration in the realm of employment policy.[28] Rather than engage in head-on combat with existing agencies within the Department of Labor, ASPER sought to propose policies that fell outside the scope of existing agency responsibilities.[29] By skirting conflicts with entrenched interests and going directly to the president, ASPER hoped to contribute to policy innovation without becoming enmeshed in the interdepartmental politics that had bedeviled Secretary Wirtz.[30]

Although the Department of Labor sought to carve out an ongoing role for the federal government in labor market policy, it also sought to transfer administrative control to local authorities. Toward that end, the administration supported legislation to decentralize and decategorize existing manpower policies under a single comprehensive authority. This was the central thrust of the Manpower Training Act presented to Congress in 1969.[31] The bill decategorized existing programs, consolidating the numerous programs (with the exception of the Job Corps) currently funded by the MDTA and the Office of Economic Opportunity (OEO) into one block grant. There were also provisions for so-called pass-throughs that would guarantee cities a certain amount of funding. Decentralization was to be achieved by providing that 75 percent of manpower funds go directly to governors who were designated as prime sponsors. The remaining 25 percent of the funds were to be used by the Department of Labor for research and technical assistance. Thus, decentralization would be accompanied by efforts to strengthen federal capabilities.

The comprehensive manpower bill that emerged from the Democratic Congress in late 1970 bore some of the decentralizing features of the administration's bill, but it retained some categorical programs. However, most offensive to the administration were provisions for spending $200 million on forty thousand public service jobs.[32] Nixon's decision to veto the bill marked the beginning of his withdrawal from innovation in labor market policy.[33]

The policies initiated during Shultz's tenure as secretary of labor can thus be interpreted as an effort by the Department of Labor to craft a Republican microeconomic employment policy that would reduce federal administrative responsibility while providing an ongoing role for the Department of Labor. There was nothing inherently objectionable to Republicans about using federal policy to make labor markets work more efficiently. The administration showed itself ready to experiment with ideas borrowed from each of the major streams of thought about employment policy in an approach that was at once pragmatic and politically conscious.

Party Competition and the Limits of
Labor Market Policy

Economic uncertainty and the search for partisan advantage spurred policy experimentation in the first years of the Nixon administration, but institutional changes and policies enacted since the 1930s would make it difficult for a Republican president to connect labor market policy with political objectives. The need to compromise with a Democratic Congress on legislation would make it still harder. Weighing the opportunities and risks associated with such policy activism, the administration first sought to assert control over policy but ultimately pulled back from the innovations it had initially supported.

What determined administration strategy, first in deciding to foster innovation and later in scaling back efforts to create a Republican labor market policy? How did the administration's shifting strategies create new boundaries for employment policy? This section examines these questions, paying particular attention to the pressures of party competition and the struggle for executive control over policy.

Presidential Strategy and Labor Market Policy

The dominant prod to action on labor market policy was the president's concern about the effects of unemployment on his prospects for reelection. President Nixon was particularly attuned to the political dangers of joblessness, as he blamed his loss to John F. Kennedy in 1960 on high rates of unemployment in the late 1950s.[34] Nonetheless, inflationary pressures in the late 1960s led the president to accept recommendations for tighter fiscal policy. Initiatives in labor market policy would indicate the administration's commitment to addressing unemployment and might eventually serve as a substitute for fiscal policy.

Policy activism on labor market policy could also be a way to realize Republican political objectives. As we have seen, the policy initiatives of Nixon's first term were not simple extensions of the policy routes mapped out during the Johnson administration; instead, they were redesigned to bend policy to Republican political aims, rather than those of Democrats. By shifting control to the states, the administration hoped to concentrate authority at the level of government at which Republicans exercised the most influence.[35] These proposals had the added advantage of responding to criticisms about the way labor market policies were administered in the 1960s. Many long-time supporters of labor market policy, such as the NMAC, saw such decentralization as a solution to the duplication and tangled lines of authority in manpower policy.

Finally, Republican activism sought to tilt labor market policy toward constituencies that the party hoped to capture. This meant turning policy away from "the disadvantaged"—poor African-Americans—toward blue-collar workers and the black middle class.[36] In 1969, Secretary Shultz had noted that the continued focus of federal programs on the problems of the disadvantaged, together with rising inflation and unemployment, could exacerbate the alienation of blue-collar workers from the federal government.[37] Although the department never launched the major initiatives targeted toward blue-collar workers that it had considered, support for decentralization and local control decreased the emphasis on the disadvantaged. At the same time, programs meant to foster "black capitalism" aimed to appeal to the black middle class.[38]

Despite the potential political rewards of a revitalized and redirected labor market policy, this kind of activism presented dangers. If the president could not control new policy initiatives or implementation, policies could continue to nourish Democratic political networks and advantage Democratic constituents. President Nixon had good reason to doubt his ability to oversee effectively new policy measures. Richard Nathan has forcefully argued that Nixon's mistrust of the bureaucracy stemmed from well-founded fears that it would not ably serve a Republican administration with new political goals.[39] Nixon had not inherited the sparsely developed federal executive that Roosevelt had. Instead, the institutional arrangements for devising and implementing policy that he confronted had been constructed by Democrats and organized to serve their political purposes. A Democratic Congress, with well-established ties to the bureaucracy, meant that policy innovation could be a highly politicized process, which the new Republican president could not control to his satisfaction. Moreover, even carefully designed strategies could be subverted by government employees whose loyalties the administration had reason to suspect. Nixon was particularly wary of initiatives emerging from the cabinet departments: major staffing increases during the 1960s made the loyalty of many officials suspect, and the considerable independence enjoyed by cabinet departments made it possible for them to undercut the president in a variety of ways.[40]

Compounding the dangers of partisan competition over policy was the dispersal of authority for policymaking within the federal executive, which made it difficult for the president to link policy to a coherent political strategy. The broad array of domestic policy initiatives proposed in the first years of the Nixon presidency did not add up to such a strategy. For example, the administration decided to go ahead with the Philadelphia Plan even though it antagonized organized labor, a constituency that Nixon had assiduously sought to cultivate. In doing so, the administration jeopardized longer-term political objectives for the tactical advantages of setting organized labor and civil rights leaders at each others' throats over the plan.[41] Such conflicts in policy would do little to contribute to the political coherence and electoral prospects of Republicans.

In order to gain firmer control over the initiatives emerging from his administration, Nixon instituted a series of organizational changes in 1970 that Nathan has called the creation of a counter-bureaucracy.[42] The president tightened his circle of policy advice and centered authority in the White House Domestic Council. As Domestic Council working groups assumed responsibility for initiating policy, the Department of Labor's input diminished. The department's influence on policy declined further when Secretary Shultz was named to head the new Office of Management and Budget (OMB). After Shultz's departure from the Department of Labor, the goal of decentralization became the only focus of administration efforts in the realm of manpower policy.

The White House used a variety of tactics to undercut the possibility of independent action by the Department of Labor. A key area of contention was the department's control over labor statistics. In 1971 administration officials moved to manage debates over employment by curbing the independence of the Bureau of Labor Statistics (BLS). Early that year, the administration disagreed with the interpretation of newly released economic statistics that the BLS had presented at its customary news conference. To prevent civil servants from presenting independent interpretations of economic data, press conferences with professional career appointees were suspended; questions were henceforth to be directed to the Secretary of Labor, a political appointee.[43]

The consolidation of power around the president and the White House had internal repercussions in the Department of Labor that diminished its ability to serve as a center of policy innovation. In 1970, after Shultz's departure, the department shifted from concern with policy development to an emphasis on program analysis.[44] The scope of research was narrowed and focused increasingly on budgetary questions and cost-benefit considerations. As this mode of analysis took over, the department conducted considerably less policy research on how to link manpower policy to broader economic policy than there had been in the preceding Democratic administration or during Shultz's tenure as secretary.[45]

The desire to break the Department of Labor's capacities was also evident in legislation promoting decentralization of manpower programs. The form of decentralization that the administration now favored, manpower revenue sharing, aimed to reduce the role of the federal government considerably more than the Manpower Training Act had. Only 15 percent of funds would be set aside for the federal government; the rest would go directly to local and state governments.[46] Although Nixon maintained that there would be an ongoing role for the Department of Labor and its components, including the Employment Service, the legislation would have dramatically undercut the Employment Service by leaving it up to local discretion whether or not to use it.[47] Manpower revenue sharing would also reduce the role of the Department of Labor by automatically allocating money to localities without prior approval.[48] When resistance from the heavily Democratic Congress blocked approval of this form of revenue sharing, the administration redoubled its efforts to use administrative means to make manpower programs a strictly local function.[49]

The president's efforts to gain control over policy by reducing the independence of the cabinet departments thus had substantive policy repercussions. The experiments in labor market policy that the Department of Labor had begun halted, and the possibilities that the department would play a role in future innovation diminished.

Party Competition and Employment Policy

Centering policy in the White House did not put an end to efforts to address growing unemployment; by 1971, however, macroeconomic policy, not labor market policy, had taken center stage. Macropolicy promised quicker results, and the pressure of the coming election made the president more willing to risk boosting inflation. The administration's shifting positions on macroeconomic policy are directly tied to the way it perceived the threat of party competition.

In 1971, the administration sought to stem the recessionary tide by loosening up the national budget and by proposing a budget that provided enough expansionary force to bring the economy back to full employment. When unemployment continued to mount and inflation showed no signs of ebbing, Nixon grew fearful of the political ramifications of his economic policy. He responded on August 15, 1971, with a "New Economic Policy." Prompted primarily by the crisis in the international monetary system, the new economic package ended international gold convertibility of the American dollar and imposed a ninety-day wage-price freeze. The president also proposed a series of tax revisions designed to stimulate business activity and recommended a package of spending cuts totaling $4.7 billion.[50]

Despite the turn to macroeconomic stimulation (and Nixon's often-cited remark that he was now a Keynesian), the new policy was severely criticized by Democratic politicians, who hoped to make the economy the key issue in the coming presidential campaign.[51] Organized labor joined with Democratic members of Congress and their allies in the economics profession in denouncing the tax breaks for business, which were the main stimulatory device of the New

Economic Policy. They argued instead that tax breaks should be weighted more heavily toward individual consumers.[52] Organized labor's bitter denunciations of "Nixon's failure" in managing the economy and ongoing cooperation with congressional Democrats promised to help Democrats in the coming election.[53]

Nixon's 1972 landslide punctured Democratic hopes of regaining power. The strains of the Vietnam War and racial strife had rent Democrats in 1968; reforms since that time had opened the party but rendered it incapable of acting as a coherent entity.[54] George McGovern's campaign and subsequent defeat displayed the bitter fruits of the party's inability to restructure and redistribute power. Not only were Democrats unable to take advantage of Nixon's difficulties in managing the economy; they pursued issues that exacerbated the divisions in the Democratic electorate. Although McGovern's economic program identified full employment as the first priority, much of the campaign focused on the candidate's proposed Minimum Income Grant Program, which would provide a $1,000 federal grant for each American. Poorly thought out and ill defended, the "Demogrant" directed political attention to the issues most likely to divide the Democrats' main constituents.[55]

Divisions that had begun to appear in 1968 deepened as Democrats lost more of their traditional base of support. The AFL-CIO refused to endorse a presidential candidate, depriving McGovern of the considerable aid of the federation's Committee on Political Education (COPE). Election results confirmed what had been apparent enough during the campaign. Nixon had torn into formerly Democratic strongholds, capturing 66 percent of the blue-collar vote and, for the first time ever, winning a majority of the union vote.[56]

The 1972 election changed Nixon's perception of the political costs of unemployment and, with it, the policy activism that had surrounded the issue during his first term. This transformation in the electoral pressure altered Nixon's strategy toward employment as a policy issue. Not only did the president continue his efforts to incapacitate the Department of Labor; he also abandoned his pre-election conversion to Keynesianism.

The appointment of building trades union leader Peter Brennan as secretary of labor in 1973 initiated a period in which the department was wholly excluded from national policymaking.[57] Allowing little input from the department, the OMB cut Department of Labor programs for the following year by 26 percent.[58] During Nixon's second term, the Department of Labor ceased to function as a center of policy development. Its research capacities were refocused on activities that would justify department programs to the OMB. As a growing center of power within the administration, the OMB based its judgments on both political and more narrow cost-benefit considerations.[59] Neither left much room for experimentation with an expanded federal role in labor market policy. In fact, under the new political and organizational conditions, ASPER was seen "as too often trying to tear the department and its programs down."[60]

Macroeconomic policy, too, shifted away from a concern with unemployment after the election. The administration evinced little concern about provoking recession and unemployment to wring inflation out of the economy. Pitting spending against inflation and higher taxes, the president vowed to hold down spending in his message on the proposed 1974 budget, and he promised to impound funds if Congress sought to revive any programs slated for termination.[61] This "return to the old-time religion"[62] eventually took its toll in unemployment: from an annual rate of 4.9 percent in 1973, it rose to 5.6 percent the following year and shot up to 8.5 percent in 1975 (see Figure 4.1).

The administration's decision to deemphasize the employment goal in national economic policymaking was accompanied by upward revisions in the definition of what constituted full employment.[63] By 1973, Nixon's CEA had moved away from using a single number to define full employment, saying that changes in the composition of the labor force had made it impossible to estimate a single figure.[64] The council did, however, believe that the rate had moved upward from the 4 percent goal that had been the yardstick during the 1960s. Administration officials also argued that the changing composition of the labor force had altered the meaning of unemployment figures. Treasury Secretary John Connally made such a case before the Joint Economic Committee in 1972, suggesting that policymakers should not "be carried away by an unemployment figure of say, 6 percent" when the rate for male heads of households was only 3 percent.[65]

Nixon's activism on employment ended once the president's perception of unemployment as a political issue changed. When Democrats proved unable to mount a credible political challenge, the president felt free to pursue other policy options, most centrally the fight against inflation. The administration not only abandoned innovation in labor market policy; it also went back to its original, "Friedmanesque" views on macropolicy. The Democratic Congress would provide the only remaining source for initiating activist policy on employment measures.

The Democratic Congress and Public Service Employment

For Democratic congressional leaders, unemployment was the most promising issue on which to quarrel with a Republican president. Throughout Nixon's presidency, congressional Democrats challenged his macroeconomic policies, but their most effective action came in support of public service employment. First initiated as an emergency policy in 1971, public service employment was established on a more permanent basis by the Comprehensive Employment and Training Act of 1973 (CETA), and it rapidly became the main activity conducted under the new legislation.

During the Nixon administration, the Joint Economic Committee (JEC) in Congress was a major vehicle for Democrats challenging the administration's employment policies. Senator William Proxmire (D. Wisc.), vice chairman (and later chairman) of the JEC, repeatedly pressed administration spokesmen on their plans for coping with unemployment.[66] The JEC's well-publicized hearings provided a platform for economists associated with the Kennedy and Johnson administrations, most of whom urged the president to adopt more expansionary monetary and fiscal policy.[67] The JEC also challenged the administration's redefinition of full employment, vigorously disputing the idea that the changing composition of the labor force made older understandings less significant.[68]

During the 1960s, many congressional Democrats had come to support public jobs, but President Johnson's opposition had prevented this growing consensus from reaching legislation. Once freed from loyalty to the president and confronted with rising joblessness, however, Democrats in Congress seized upon public employment as a remedy for unemployment. In contrast to the 1960s, when public jobs were advocated to attack hard-core unemployment in black urban ghettos, in the early 1970s, as unemployment became more widespread and city finances grew increasingly strained, the potential increased for public employment to serve a broader segment of the population.

In 1971, after House leaders had decided to make unemployment a major Democratic issue, Democratic leaders in both houses of Congress defied the administration by presenting public service employment legislation.[69] By mid-1971 they had passed an Emergency Employment Act (EEA). Pressured by the coming election and an even less acceptable public works bill, Nixon unenthusiastically signed the measure. The act allocated $2.25 billion for a two-year transitional program of public service employment. It gave special consideration to regions with particularly high unemployment by setting aside special continuing funds for areas with unemployment rates above 6 percent.

The passage of the Emergency Employment Act was facilitated by the numerous interpretations attached to it. The administration viewed the measure as a temporary program; the president's original opposition to public employment had been somewhat mitigated by language stressing the transitional nature of the jobs. Many Democratic supporters, however, saw the EEA as the first installment in a permanent program of public jobs. Among Democrats, the loose eligibility standards of the Public Employment Program (PEP) established by the EEA was its most attractive feature. The program would provide employment to the growing number of unemployed technical and professional workers and to veterans returning from Vietnam as well as to the hard-core unemployed. Moreover, the EEA allocated funds directly to states and localities, granting them considerable leeway in how the funds were spent. With few federal strings attached, emergency jobs for the unemployed had broad appeal.

After passage of the EEA, liberal Democrats began to push more forcefully for an ongoing commitment to public service employment. The continuing deterioration of the economy had convinced many leading Democratic mayors and congressional representatives that a permanent program of public jobs was essential.[70] These Democratic supporters of public employment introduced legislation in late 1971 and early 1972 to create five hundred thousand public jobs. No action was taken that year, and the following year, in the face of a declining unemployment rate and the end of the election season, Nixon terminated the Emergency Employment Act. Nonetheless, Democrats had made public employment a viable issue for the first time since the New Deal. PEP's favorable impact gave public employment a positive public image and helped to consolidate a coalition of support among the nation's local officials.[71] The breadth of support for public jobs ensured that such programs would remain a major feature of the Democratic employment policy agenda.

In 1973, a legislative compromise over manpower policy gave the president the decentralization he had long sought, while Congress secured provisions for public service employment.[72] CETA replaced the MDTA and OEO, decategorizing over a dozen programs that had functioned under their authority. Operating responsibility was granted to local governmental units with a population of over one hundred thousand, which were designated as prime sponsors. But

Table 4.3
Distribution of CETA Appropriations by Type of Program, 1975–1980

Category	% of Total CETA Funding					
	1975	1976	1977	1978	1979	1980
Comprehensive training programs[a]	48	36	31	28	23	36
Public service employment	34	53	46	58	58	38
Special youth programs[b]	5	3	16	5	12	18
Summer youth programs[c]	13	8	7	9	7	7

Source: Calculated from data in Donald C. Baumer and Carl E. Van Horn, *The Politics of Unemployment* (Washington, D.C: Congressional Quarterly Press, 1985), 19. Used with permission.

[a] Includes programs for native Americans, migrants and seasonal workers, and veterans; the private sector initiative program; and research and demonstration programs.

[b] Includes Jobs Corps programs, Youth Employment and Training programs, Youth Community Conservation and Improvement projects, and Young Adult Conservation Corps programs.

[c] Temporary, part-time jobs for low-income young people during the summer months only.

congressional Democrats had preserved something of a federal role as well. The Department of Labor was charged with establishing guidelines on eligibility and program activity and was also responsible for approving project plans and monitoring ongoing programs. The major victory for the Democrats, however, was a title authorizing public service employment for areas with 6.5 percent unemployment rates for three months or more.

Although public service employment was initially only a small part of CETA, after the passage of the Emergency Jobs and Unemployment Assistance Act of 1974, it took precedence over all other aspects of CETA (see Table 4.3). Enacted as a response to surging unemployment in late 1974, this measure added a new title to CETA authorizing $2.5 billion for temporary public service jobs.[73] In the words of one Department of Labor official, "Public service employment became synonymous with CETA and we forgot about [training] which is really the guts of the program."[74]

The Politics of "Corruption"

The public service employment instituted in the 1970s marked a sharp shift away from the version of labor market policy fashioned under the War on Poverty or the experiments of the early Nixon administration. No longer would the federal government play a strong role in monitoring and implementing policy. Legislative decentralization, together with the destruction of Department of Labor capacities under the Nixon administration, meant that localities had wide discretion over how they administered public service employment. These circumstances created considerable room for abuse, and sometimes outright fraud, especially after the CETA program was dramatically expanded in the first year of the Carter administration. The slipshod manner in which public service employment was implemented evoked time-honored arguments equating public spending with corruption.

This section examines why labor market policy took the form of a poorly organized program of public jobs in the 1970s, stressing the limits inherent in designing and implementing policy without effective participation and guidance from the executive. The political fate of public service employment also highlights the difficulties of reforming policy in a context of poorly developed institutional capacities.

Congress and Pork Barrel Politics

The Democratic Congress had been a staunch defender of a federal role in employment policy. But, Congress was a limited vehicle for producing labor market initiatives. Without the Department of Labor (or some equivalent executive agency) involved in policy development, the range of congressional initiatives would be truncated. Moreover, without presidential leadership, congressional proclivities to fragment policy in ways that widely dispersed benefits increased; in the 1970s the declining strength of political parties made this tendency more pronounced.[75] In this context, labor market policy became a decentralized program of public jobs in which localities could use the funds with few strings attached.

The absence of executive branch assistance in policymaking narrowed the range of policy innovation by limiting the information and perspectives available to congressional members formulating policy. Without active support from the Department of Labor, congressional representatives found it difficult to secure some kinds of data that would have been helpful in defining issues and strengthening the case for innovation. The subemployment index, constructed at the insistence of Secretary Wirtz, provides an example. By drawing attention to an issue that conventional unemployment statistics had masked, the new measure strengthened arguments that employment policy was central to solving the problems of the ghetto.[76] Under Nixon, the administration not only attempted to control the interpretation of economic statistics but also sought to limit the statistics that were produced. In 1972, leading manpower policy advocate Senator Gaylord Nelson requested assistance from the Bureau of Labor Statistics in creating a subemployment index that would be part of the regularly reported employment statistics. The Department of Labor refused on the grounds that there was no accepted definition of subemployment and that such an index would cost too much in any case.[77]

The Department of Labor had also formerly been an important source of innovation and support for diverse initiatives. In the 1960s, the policy development arm of the Department of Labor had served as a forum for new ideas in employment policy.[78] Because policies emerging from the Department of Labor tended to take a long-range view and sought to enhance the role of the department, they encompassed ideas less likely to emerge from Congress. Through experiments with such programs as mobility grants, the department hoped to expand the range of policies considered feasible by Congress. The Department of Labor, driven by its institutional interests, was also more likely than Congress to initiate legislation that challenged the stranglehold of some interest groups over institutions or policy, such as that of the local employment agency administrators.

By contrast, in Congress there were strong pressures to support decentralization and local discretion in allocating resources. Foremost among those pressing for decentralization were local officials, who the Nixon administration assiduously courted in support of its revenue-sharing proposals. Aware that hard-pressed localities would welcome federal aid to cope with severe budget crises, the administration built up widespread bipartisan support for revenue sharing among local politicians.[79]

Mayoral enthusiasm for special revenue sharing in turn put pressure on Democrats to support public service employment with substantial discretionary authority for local officials.[80] With the national leadership of the Democratic party in crisis, mayors had assumed an increasingly important role in the Democratic coalition, making their desire to choose the beneficiaries of manpower programs difficult to ignore. Although the congressional liberals, who had most strongly backed manpower policies, were reluctant to grant such latitude to localities, they lacked the support needed to enact policy on their own terms. In the end, both the EEA and CETA gave the localities considerable discretion about who would participate in the new programs and what kinds of jobs they would perform. In the eyes of Congress, the place of public service employment within a broader employment policy became less important than the need to provide financially strapped localities with additional resources.

Enacting labor market policy in this form had important ramifications for the ability of policy to address black unemployment and underemployment. The decentralized administrative framework set up for public service employment had no provisions to ensure that "the disadvantaged"—workers less attractive to employers for a variety of reasons, including race—would be served by the new program. An Urban Coalition report on the EEA revealed that the poor were underrepresented among the beneficiaries of the program, and it charged that participants from high unemployment areas received lower wages than other participants. The report also criticized the lack of effort to alter civil service systems to allow program participants to make the transition into permanent employment.[81]

With public employment inadequately addressing the persistent joblessness in the black ghetto, and other programs abandoned, the Work Incentive Program (WIN) became, by default, the major employment policy directed at poor African-Americans.[82] But the program, initiated more to ferret out the undeserving than to provide training or jobs, had a poor record of moving its participants into good jobs.[83] Congressional Democrats made some efforts to address the problems with WIN, but on the whole they preferred to stay away from the difficult and divisive problem of black unemployment. In the early 1970s, the ratio of black to white unemployment rose above its historical average of two to one as the recession took its toll on the black community (see Table 4.2).[84]

The form and context in which public employment programs were enacted also had ramifications for the successful administration of these programs. Implemented by a Department of Labor whose resources had been slashed and by local governments with little experience with such programs, the administration of CETA was, not surprisingly, fraught with difficulties. Although the act had called for an important federal role, the administration used CETA's passage as an occasion to cut the federal portion of the budget. Just as the Department of Labor was gearing up for its new responsibilities, it was deprived of the resources to staff the new programs. Many of the old staffers of the Manpower Administration were ill suited for their new responsibility to provide technical assistance. Under the MDTA and OEO, they had functioned primarily as contractors and had little experience with actual program administration.[85] Considerable confusion in CETA's early days can be traced to the incompetence of the Department of Labor and the inexperience of many local authorities in operating manpower programs.[86]

As unemployment climbed to post-Depression highs, the federal government responded with the first public employment programs since the New Deal. Public service employment was actively supported by a broad coalition of local and national officials and fortified by strong public approval.[87] But the single-minded emphasis on public employment and the fragility of the framework on which it was erected cast doubts on the durability of the new policy.

Expansion without Institution Building

The election of Jimmy Carter as president in 1976 gave a boost to public service employment. The new administration adopted public employment as a central component in its unemployment strategy and in so doing infused CETA with an economic rationale it had been lacking. Public service employment would stimulate the economy, but by targeting stimulus at the unemployed, it would minimize the dangers of inflation. In this way, public service employment would become an important adjunct of macroeconomic policy.

As unemployment spiraled in the first half of the 1970s, calls for expanding labor market policy mounted. CETA legislation had mandated the creation of a body of policy analysts and interest group representatives to study and make recommendations about employment policy. The group, the National Commission for Manpower Policy, sought to avoid the old debate about whether unemployment was structural or cyclical and to recommend policies that would address each type of unemployment. Beginning in 1974, the commission held numerous conferences that brought policy analysts together with representatives of business, labor, and minorities to consider the shape labor market policy should take and the role it could play.

One theme that ran throughout the many studies that the commission sponsored was the idea that employment and training programs needed to be seen as an integral part of national economic policy, and that preventive programs should be developed to replace the current remedial and reactive manpower policies. The need to forge links between macroeconomic policies and employment and training programs was another recommendation that appeared repeatedly in the commission's publications.[88]

These ideas were strongly represented in Carter's Department of Labor. The new secretary of labor, Ray Marshall, was a Texas economist who had long supported various forms of "selective intervention" to complement macroeconomic policy. Marshall advocated improving the operation of labor markets through such measures as better labor market information, increased emphasis on job training, and antidiscriminatory measures.[89] As secretary of labor, he also pushed hard for public service employment, maintaining that it was the cheapest and least inflationary way to reduce unemployment.[90] In order to maximize the anti-inflationary impact of public service employment, he sought to increase federal control over the allocation of CETA funds.

The new CEA chairman, Charles Schultze, former Budget Bureau director under President Johnson, represented a more traditionally Keynesian viewpoint, which stressed aggregate stimulation by means of tax cuts as the best way to cope with unemployment. Schultze tended to regard federal spending, including spending on public employment, as an inefficient and slow means of stimulating the economy. In some respects the differences between Marshall and Schultze recapitulated the debate between the Department of Labor and the CEA in the early 1960s. Yet by 1977, thinking on both sides of the issue had moderated; Schultze's Keynesian views were not pitted so starkly against the structuralist view represented by Marshall as in the early 1960s. The new CEA head preferred to emphasize general measures, such as tax rebates and temporary tax cuts, but was not averse to some spending on public employment.[91] Likewise, Marshall strongly supported macropolicy.

The initial stimulus program that the president proposed soon after he took office reflected the influence of both Marshall and Schultze. It also bore the imprint of the Democratic Congress, which was pushing for major public works jobs programs, and of state and local governments advocating countercyclical aid to localities.[92] The overall package provided $31.6 billion of stimulation, to be pumped into the economy over a two-year period in the combined form of tax cuts and direct job creation. Schultze was primarily responsible for the proposed $50 tax rebate to each taxpayer as well as the proposed investment tax credits for business. Congressional pressure produced an additional $4 billion for the public works jobs program Congress had passed the previous year. Public works were to be accompanied by a sharp increase in CETA funds for public service employment and a new youth employment act that would add another $1 billion of expenditures for employment and training. Finally, an extension of countercyclical revenue sharing was included.

The package went beyond the president's proposals, providing nearly double Carter's requests for local assistance and public jobs.[93]

Carter's decision to embark on such economic stimulus indicates the importance of networks of expertise in shaping policy agendas. The president had been wary of major stimulatory efforts, preferring instead to concentrate on various programs for structural change, such as tax reform. Yet his main economic policy advisers persuaded him to support a stimulus package. Coming from outside Washington, with an entourage of Georgians to run the White House, the new president had drawn most of his key economic policy advisers from the respected mainstream of Democratically aligned economists who had effectively functioned as a network since the 1960s.[94] Keynesian perspectives, now somewhat more supportive of labor market measures, continued to dominate that network.[95] In the face of the consensus for fiscal stimulus among members of this network, the president accepted the main features of the approach they outlined, modified by an emphasis on the public service employment and job-training activities of the Department of Labor.[96]

However, the decentralized institutional framework inherited from the Nixon administration was poorly equipped to administer a rapidly expanded program, and the pressure for quick action left little time for the "slow laborious" task of devising an effective labor market policy and building the institutions to implement it.[97] Neither the Department of Labor nor localities were organized to handle the public service employment program. Although CETA had been operating for several years before the expansion, the Department of Labor was ill equipped to offer technical assistance to local operations. The department was also understaffed; the number of CETA public service jobs doubled from May to November of 1977, but the number of federal officials assigned to preside over the program remained the same as in 1975.[98]

At the local level, elected officials retained fundamental operating authority for CETA; not surprisingly, they used the new jobs for their own political purposes. Charges that local governments were substituting CETA workers for employees they would have hired anyway cast doubt on CETA's ability to have any effect on unemployment. Hasty approval of some projects left little time for reflection about the quality of the jobs being created, providing targets for ridicule in the national press.[99]

Secretary Marshall was obliged to preside over a major program expansion and an overhaul of the apparatus that administered it at the same time. The result was that the Department of Labor added to local confusion by issuing ill-thought-out and often contradictory

administrative orders about public service employment.[100] It also
meant that there was little chance to develop the relationships and
create the institutions needed to administer labor market policies
other than public service employment.

"Corruption" and the Collapse of Support

Congressional and presidential enthusiasm for public service employment evaporated quickly. Faced with mounting charges of corruption, waste, and mismanagement, politicians scurried to dissoci-
ate themselves from the program and pressed for extensive revisions
in CETA legislation meant to guard against abuse. By 1978, the inability to sustain public service employment as an economic policy
ultimately cast it back into the realm of a remedial social policy, with
all the attendant political problems.

The confusion and disarray that surrounded the expansion of
CETA led to some misuse and, on occasion, outright fraud in the
administration of public service employment funds. These abuses,
along with colorfully unorthodox uses of CETA money, provided
ammunition for a barrage of media stories portraying CETA as an
expensive and wasteful boondoggle.[101] In Congress, these worries
intensified already existing doubts about whether the effects of fiscal
substitution were so great that CETA was doing little more than pick-
ing up the tab for services local governments would have provided
anyway.[102]

Aware of the damage that such negative perceptions could do, the
Department of Labor launched a public relations effort to improve
CETA's image, but the political problems of CETA were not so easily
repaired. In 1978, the Carter administration began to distance itself
from public service employment, declining to use presidential pres-
tige to build up support for the program.[103] As CETA began to be
perceived as a political liability, the Department of Labor's star
began to wane as well. In late 1977, when the Economic Policy
Group, Carter's main economic policymaking body, was reorganized, Marshall was excluded from the steering committee.[104] Cast
into an administrative framework that could not efficiently support
a major expansion, public service employment did not emerge as a
central pillar of employment policy, as its advocates had hoped.

The reauthorization of CETA in 1978 revealed that the charges of
corruption and waste had diminished support for public service employment in Congress. Although many of the changes proposed in
the reauthorization package were responses to the severe problems
that had accompanied the rapid expansion of public service employ-

ment in 1977, the tenor of the congressional debate, especially in the House, revealed substantial hostility to the very notion of public service employment. The many reports of fraud and abuse of CETA funds created an atmosphere in which many supporters of CETA felt compelled to endorse cuts. As one liberal remarked, "[T]he way to show you're against abuse is to be against the program."[105] Congressional action on CETA showed more desire to retaliate for mismanagement with cuts than to strengthen the administrative structure that had proven incapable of supporting the massive program expansion Congress had authorized in 1977.[106]

The administration's proposed revisions to CETA aimed to increase the emphasis on the poor. Income eligibility limits sought to ensure that CETA slots would be reserved for those who were poor as well as unemployed. Lower caps on CETA salaries and duration of employment were proposed to end the fiscal substitution problem. The administration also sought to emphasize training and encourage private sector participation. Despite these many alterations, the administration did not propose any substantial reductions in CETA slots. During the initial consideration of the bill, the House almost rejected it altogether, so strong was the sentiment against CETA. Proposals cutting substantial sums from the president's request likewise narrowly missed approval. Only after a break in the consideration of the bill, during which state and local governments lobbied heavily for it, did Congress pass CETA. The reauthorization retained most of Carter's recommendations but tightened numerous restrictions and reinforced Department of Labor monitoring to prevent abuse.[107]

CETA's new constituency led political support to wane still further after 1978. By focusing on the structurally unemployed and the poor, the program lost much of the backing that had sustained it through the most severe bouts of criticism. Especially damaging was the dampened enthusiasm of state and local officials, who could no longer rely on the program for an extra source of workers or patronage.

The legislative changes of 1978 also created new problems that hindered CETA from functioning as a major part of employment policy. Most federal energy went into monitoring abuse rather than into providing technical assistance to improve local programs. As Baumer and Van Horn note, "The relentless effort to eliminate fraud, waste, and abuse represented a triumph of bureaucratic process over program substance."[108] The local flexibility that CETA was supposed to promote was sacrificed for fear of abuse.

CETA's extreme vulnerability to charges of corruption is striking. Evaluations conducted during the administration of CETA have shown that although abuse existed, it occurred infrequently and that fiscal substitution was significantly reduced by changes in the regulations guiding CETA.[109] Nonetheless, suspicions about corruption nearly incapacitated CETA in the late 1970s and created the negative image of the program that led to its abandonment in 1982. Why were charges of corruption so politically potent if actual instances of abuse were so few?

One answer lies in the long-standing power that the theme of corruption carries in American political discourse. The identification of government spending with corruption stretches back to the nineteenth century, and has been revived at regular intervals.[110] Because they tap so effectively into cultural antipathies to government power, charges of corruption and fraud are staples of policy debate in the United States. Those who oppose a policy for a variety of reasons find abuse and mismanagement to be effective themes for rallying opposition. These cultural proclivities are fed and reinforced by very real problems that the federal government has confronted in administering programs in a federal system with a weak national bureaucracy. Accordingly, programs that rely on complex administrative mechanisms are particularly prone to public charges of fraud or corruption. The major New Deal jobs programs, the Civil Works Administration (CWA) of 1933–1934 and the Works Progress Administration (WPA) begun in 1935 were both denounced as corrupt at various points, and each endured public investigations into charges of fraud.[111]

If charges of corruption are commonplace, they are not always successful in undermining social policy. Programs that are bureaucratically insulated or protected by legal guarantees are more able to weather a storm of public criticism than are those without such protections. CETA was vulnerable on both counts: it was poorly institutionalized, housed in a weak department, and it was unable to claim legal safeguards. Moreover, as unemployment began to drop and inflation rise precipitously in the late 1970s, public attention and political concern shifted away from the problem of jobs. In this context, supporters of CETA had few resources for waiting out charges of corruption.

Conclusion

The experience with public service employment in the 1970s helped to reshape public thinking about what was possible in the realm of employment policy. Tainted by the old bugaboo of government waste and corruption, labor market policy began to look much less desirable than it had at the beginning of the decade. Arguments that the American government was simply not capable of undertaking such programs resonated with the widely publicized failings of CETA. Skepticism about the prospects for labor market policy abounded.

By provoking doubts about labor market policy, the experience with public service employment also created new conceptions about the trade-off between different policies. Having failed to function as a complement to economic policy by reducing unemployment without increasing inflation, labor market policy lost its status as a potential solution to the economic problems of the 1970s. Instead, new arguments blaming government spending for inflation suggested that public employment was part of what was wrong with the American economy. These views would prepare the ground for a major shift in public thinking about what government could and should do in the domain of employment.

Five

The Political Collapse of Full Employment

FOR THE THIRTY years that followed World War II, American presidents had, in words, if not always in their actions, supported the goal of full employment. For Democrats, the objective was especially salient, but Republican politicians, wary of electoral repercussions, also highlighted employment concerns. During the late 1970s, in an economic context of sharply rising inflation, full employment receded as a political issue. And as full employment lost its place as a pivot of partisan competition, arguments that government could play only a limited role in affecting employment began to set new boundaries for government action. By appointing a staunch inflation fighter to head the Federal Reserve and deliberately provoking a recession before the election of 1980, President Jimmy Carter apparently abandoned the struggle against unemployment that had guided federal action and formed a central tenet of Democratic party policy since the New Deal.

What accounts for these changes in the position of employment as a political issue, and how did ideas about limiting the government's role become influential? Two major explanations, each linked to broader arguments about American exceptionalism, have been offered to account for shifts in economic policy in the late 1970s. One traces the shift to business influence, pointing to the striking political mobilization of American business and financial interests during the 1970s.[1] A second explanation highlights the role of public opinion: strong and widespread opposition to inflation joined with antipathy to federal power to overwhelm negative sentiments about unemployment.[2]

Although evidence exists to back up each claim, I argue that to understand properly the role of business and public opinion, debates about employment policy in the late 1970s must be seen as the final stage of a policy sequence that began in the 1940s. Explanations that highlight the role of public opinion make sense when we understand how policy alternatives became limited to approaches that pitted inflation and unemployment directly against each other. Similarly, business leaders were more easily able to dominate policy when coalitions supporting alternatives could not come together. Thus, to understand why full employment lost its force as a political issue, we need to analyze the political collapse of alternative policies and the failure of a coalition opposing business views to emerge.

This chapter explores these questions by examining efforts to create alternative policies in the Congress and in the executive branch during the late 1970s. In Congress, support for new planning mechanisms and guarantees of full employment were embodied in the Full Employment and Balanced Growth Act, known as the Humphrey-Hawkins Act, after its congressional sponsors. At the same time, the executive branch sought to develop new capacities that would allow the federal government to target its intervention more precisely in order to attack inflation without increasing unemployment. Neither initiative was sustained. Although the Humphrey-Hawkins Act passed in 1978, the legislation was a shell of the original bill, neither enhancing planning capabilities nor guaranteeing full employment. Similarly, the administration's efforts to control wages and prices and to initiate sectoral policies quickly unraveled.

I explain the failure of these alternatives by showing how the development of employment policies during the preceding decades handicapped proposals for extending government power in the late 1970s. Existing policy packages provided little groundwork upon which to build such new policies: the institutional framework and the organization of interests would have had to be substantially reoriented to support policies that expanded the government role. Neither congressional policymaking nor policy initiation from within the federal executive provided pathways that could sustain efforts to reorganize policy. And in each case, President Carter's ambivalence about the role of government undermined these initiatives. The failure to define a new set of public measures addressing employment problems quickly eroded existing public support for government action. Instead, politicians found it increasingly attractive to argue that government was the problem and not the solution, paving the way for a historic shift in the government's commitment to address employment problems.

Legislating Full Employment?

In the mid-1970s, unemployment rates not seen since the Great Depression galvanized a heavily Democratic Congress into action. The apparent failure of Keynesian strategies to alleviate joblessness rekindled interest in planning and, for a brief moment, thrust ideas once rejected back into the national spotlight. The legislative vehicle for planning, the Humphrey-Hawkins bill, briefly provided a rallying

point for congressional Democrats concerned about unemployment. Its popularity, however, quickly waned. Instead, the principal
congressional action on unemployment during the 1970s—apart
from the Comprehensive Employment and Training Act—was to extend a variety of passive policies that provided temporary income
assistance to the jobless.

How did planning ideas rise to prominence, only to quickly disappear, and why did more passive policies succeed? This section answers these questions by highlighting the disjunction between planning and the institutions, interests, and intellectual developments of
the preceding decades. Working with the legacy of past employment
policy, supporters of planning in Congress found that they had few
resources for making planning a credible policy alternative.

Planning for Full Employment: The
Humphrey-Hawkins Act

The Humphrey-Hawkins bill brought together two distinct responses to the economic uncertainty of the 1970s. The first sought to
institute planning mechanisms that would allow more predictable
and flexible economic policy; the second would guarantee full employment. Support for planning emerged from within a network of
liberal elites, which included sections of organized labor and a few
business leaders; guarantees for full employment were initially proposed by black representatives in Congress, whose constituents had
been hardest hit by rising unemployment. By merging these overlapping but distinct concerns, the Humphrey-Hawkins bill would
have redrawn the politics of employment policy. In contrast to
the Keynesian strategies followed since the war, the Humphrey-
Hawkins bill proposed new institutions that would encourage the
federal government to intervene in the economy in more selective
and directive ways. And by guaranteeing jobs as a central part of
employment policy, the bill provided a way of rejoining a key African-American policy interest to the mainstream of economic policy.

The reemergence of planning in national policy discussions came
from outside the mainstream of the institutions and networks that
had set the terms of economic policy for most of the postwar period.
Instead, a few prominent dissenters from the Keynesian consensus,
joined by a handful of liberal elites, used the media to put planning
on the national agenda. Ties with liberal members of Congress provided the channel into policy debate.

Foremost among the intellectual proponents of planning was
Harvard economist Wassily Leontief, whose work on input-output

analysis had won him the Nobel prize in economics in 1973. In early 1974, Leontief launched a crusade for planning on the editorial pages of the *New York Times* with a call for a national economic planning board. Arguing that a "well-staffed, well-informed and intelligently guided planning board" could have prevented the economic problems of the mid-1970s, Leontief called for a revival of Roosevelt's National Resources Planning Board. Unlike "the powerless and understaffed Council of Economic Advisers," the new body would be able to collect information on all sectors of the economy and would then use this comprehensive information to outline policy options.[3]

Although the planning board would not gather much new information, it would bring together economic data previously scattered throughout the federal bureaucracy and the private sector.[4] Thus the board would give economic policymakers a holistic vision of the national economy in detailed sectoral terms. Leontief was highly critical of the tendency among economic policymakers to describe the economy in terms of a single aggregate measure, such as the rate of inflation, unemployment, or GNP.[5] He cited as an example the Council of Economic Advisers (CEA), which he argued, could only manipulate "about three or four variables ... the government budget in the aggregate, certain aspects of taxation, certain aspects of monetary policy...." The result was that the council's recommendations were "limited to the classical Keynesian variety."[6]

Although Leontief's ideas did not arouse much interest among his fellow economists, they did attract support from organized labor and even some liberal business leaders. Eleven prominent supporters of some version of planning came together in early 1975 to form the Initiative Committee for National Economic Planning. Headed jointly by Leontief and United Auto Workers president Leonard Woodcock, the group's proposal was signed by nearly seventy supporters, including business and labor leaders, as well as academics.[7] New York University economist Abraham Gitlow remarked, "[T]he roster of names associated with the [planning proposal] does not look like the membership list of some small and peripheral clandestine group. They are people of experience and sophistication."[8]

The committee saw its proposals for economic planning as a way to correct the uncoordinated and short-sighted perspective of current economic policymaking. It projected a vision of planning that would not take the place of the decentralized market but would influence private economic decisions to meet democratically determined economic objectives.[9] The particulars of the planning process were left open, but the committee envisioned expert teams of scientists and engineers (rather than economists), who would be responsible for laying out sector-specific options for the national economy. These options would then be evaluated in public hearings, and a final report would be issued by the White House. The plan would not set mandatory goals but would be used to evaluate the effects and desirability of legislation, including measures that would spur production in the direction laid out by the plan.

At its first press conference, the committee had announced its intention to propose legislation to create a new national Office of Economic Planning in the White House and a Joint Planning Committee in Congress.[10] Former presidential candidate, now Senator, Hubert Humphrey (D. Minn.), along with Republican liberal Jacob Javits (R. N.Y.), took the lead in putting the Initiative Committee's proposals into legislation. In 1975, Humphrey introduced the Balanced National Growth and Economic Planning bill, originally drafted by the Initiative Committee.

The bill called for an Economic Planning Board in the Office of the President, which would draw on a comprehensive store of information about the economy to devise a proposed Balanced Economic Growth Plan and would suggest policies for reaching the goals of the plan. A process of democratic planning would follow, in which local governments and private interest groups would participate in developing and revising the plan. The final step before adoption would be congressional review. Humphrey argued that the bill provided a vital corrective to current economic policymaking. In contrast to existing policymaking, in which all key actors, including the CEA, focused only on the coming year and in which the annual budget constituted the major planning document of the federal government, the procedures set up in the new act would promote more long-term planning.[11]

The apparent failure of Keynesian policies in the mid-1970s thus gave planning broader support than it had enjoyed in decades, but its political appeal remained limited. The legislation created new institutions and procedures for policymaking, but it did not set specific employment targets or guarantee particular results. With unemployment soaring to its highest point since the Great Depression, legislation effecting change over the long term did not promise much political payoff.

Congressional sponsors of planning solved this problem in 1975 by tying their bill to a broad full employment measure written by the Congressional Black Caucus. The Equal Opportunity and Full Employment Act of 1976 was first proposed in June 1974 by Representative Augustus Hawkins (D. Calif.), an active member of the Congressional Black Caucus. In its earliest and most sweeping form, the Hawkins bill had attracted support primarily from African-Americans, their close allies in Congress, and the labor movement.[12] This first bill, intended as a rallying effort around the employment issue, guaranteed jobs for all who wanted to work. If national economic policies failed to generate sufficient employment, the shortfall would be made up by federally financed jobs on projects designed by local planning councils. Workers on such federal jobs would be paid the prevailing wage rate. Most controversial, the bill made the right to employment legally enforceable, allowing individuals to sue if they were denied a job.

As unemployment began to climb rapidly upward in 1975, Hawkins's bill attracted growing support. It was reintroduced in somewhat revised form in 1975, this time also sponsored in the Senate by Humphrey. Still providing a legally enforceable right to employment, the bill established 3 percent unemployment as an interim goal to be achieved in eighteen months. It required the president to present a "Full Employment and National Purposes Budget," much as the original Full Employment bill of 1945 had. It also explicitly called on the Federal Reserve to bring its policies into line with a national effort for full employment and required the board to prepare an annual statement outlining how its policies in the coming year would be consistent with the goal of full employment.

Unlike the planning bill introduced the same year, Hawkins's bill did not create a new economic planning board but relied on a strengthened Council of Economic Advisers to coordinate the activities of government agencies and to see that they conformed to the National Purposes Budget. But the fortified council that Hawkins envisioned would differ from the current CEA, as it would be responsible for housing a National Advisory Council on Full Employment composed of representatives of labor, industry, public interest groups, and state and local governments.

In March of 1976, the planning proposals of the Initiative Committee and the concern for full employment animating the various Hawkins bills came together in the Full Employment and Balanced Growth Act of 1976. Proposed as an amendment to the 1946 Employment Act, the new bill aimed to fulfill the promise of the original Full Employment bill of 1945. In Humphrey's words, the bill, "put full employment back in the Employment Act."[13] The new bill kept the 3 percent unemployment goal, to be reached as soon as possible, but with a deadline of four years. The president, the Congress, and the Federal Reserve were all directed to participate with state and local governments in devising a plan to allow "full use of the resources and ingenuity of the private sector of the economy." It made the federal government the "employer of last resort" by establishing

public jobs paying the prevailing wage whenever they were necessary but eliminated the legally enforceable job guarantee.[14]

In 1976, the congressional Democratic leadership, seeking to
make unemployment a major issue for the upcoming campaign season, threw its support behind the Humphrey-Hawkins bill. For a
brief moment, it appeared certain that the bill would pass, forcing
President Ford into a politically damaging veto.[15] Instead, congressional leaders refrained from bringing the bill to the floor that year.
Its fate remained in doubt for two years, until it finally passed in a
form that made it no more than a symbolic gesture.

The Politics of Symbolism and the Demise of
  Humphrey-Hawkins

The burst of congressional support for Humphrey-Hawkins in 1976
was deceptive. The bill made a good weapon in the political competition of an election year, but it quickly became evident that the
ideas it embodied had no political or institutional ground in which
to germinate. Interest group support was weak; even among those
who favored the bill, support was shallow. Moreover, Humphrey-
Hawkins had virtually no backing from the network of experts who
had staffed the institutions of economic policymaking for the past
three decades. It had served well as a political document, but once
questions about mechanisms and trade-offs were posed, congressional support began to evaporate. In the end, President Carter endorsed a symbolic Humphrey-Hawkins Act as a gesture toward African-Americans, who had strongly supported his campaign.

Organized labor testified in favor of the Humphrey-Hawkins bill
in 1976, but the level of commitment varied widely across the labor
movement. Unions traditionally more amenable to government action, such as the United Auto Workers and the International Union
of Electrical Workers and Machinists, had been early and staunch
supporters. But the AFL-CIO was considerably less enthusiastic.
AFL-CIO president George Meany initially opposed the measure as
unrealistic, but as unemployment rose and the election approached,
he was persuaded to back the revised version of the bill, stripped of
its legal guarantee of a job.[16]

Business organizations vigorously denounced Humphrey-Hawkins. Leading business groups, including the Chamber of Commerce,
the National Association of Manufacturers, and the Business
Rountable testified against the bill during the 1976 hearings.[17] Business leaders who had earlier taken an interest in planning were less

enthusiastic about guarantees of full employment. For them, planning held some attraction as a way to achieve more predictability in government intervention, including regulation, taxation, and credit policy.[18] But beyond that, the majority of American businesses were skeptical about measures that would enhance government involvement in the marketplace. Among the few business leaders who had supported broader notions of planning, the meanings they attached to it varied widely. Most simply wanted more long-term thinking about economic issues and better coordination of government action; only a tiny fraction supported more thoroughgoing versions of planning that envisioned corporatist forms of economic policy-making.[19]

Expert support for Humphrey-Hawkins was also very weak and isolated. The call for planning in the mid-1970s had come from voices that were outside the mainstream of the economics profession. But, unlike the prospending Keynesians of the 1930s and 1940s, those supporting planning during the 1970s did not constitute an emerging "school" inside an academic profession. Far from being at the center of an emerging network, many of the most important intellectual forces behind the Humphrey-Hawkins bill were the same individuals who had drafted the Full Employment bill of 1945. Much of the actual legislation was crafted by Leon Keyserling, head of the CEA under Truman. By training a lawyer, Keyserling had long advocated planning and spending measures opposed by mainstream liberal economists. He also had a scorn for economists working within the mainstream, which was widely returned in kind.[20]

The isolation of the experts backing Humphrey-Hawkins was intensified by the fact that academic economics had moved in directions uncongenial to the notion of planning. Planning of any sort required knowledge of and interest in institutions, and the discipline of economics had steadily moved away from concern with institutions. Instead, the increasing status of mathematical economics within the discipline highlighted individual-actor models that eschewed attention to institutions. In the area of employment policy, the dominance of the neoclassical model meant that non-Keynesian economists were far more likely to sympathize with the Friedman/Feldstein view, which called for selected microeconomic measures, not planning.[21]

In contrast to spending advocates of the 1930s, the intellectual supporters of planning in the 1970s did not have a growing network within the executive branch, nor were there any likely footholds on which to build one. The Council of Economic Advisers had been dominated for decades by mainstream economists with little inter-

est in planning. Other major agencies involved in economic policymaking were, if anything, even less amenable to ideas about planning. Without ties to administrative agencies, proposals for planning
appeared hollow; arguments about administrative feasibility were
less convincing and the sources of support more narrow. Congressional supporters of planning could find few sources of economic
expertise to draft the bill and few to defend it convincingly in congressional testimony.[22]

Particular features of the Humphrey-Hawkins bill made it an easy
target for opponents. It had won support as a political vehicle advocating full employment, and as a political weapon to wield against
Republicans who favored recessionary policies. It was, however,
short on specifics. The bill offered little guidance about the particular mechanisms that would bring the nation to full employment,
and, most important, it addressed the problem of how to achieve
full employment without inflation only cursorily.[23]

These omissions provided the basis for damaging objections from
inside the heart of the Democratic economic policy network. The
strongest and most effective criticism came from Charles Schultze,
former budget director under President Johnson and future CEA
chairman under Carter, then at the Brookings Institution. In his congressional testimony on the bill, Schultze declared his sympathy
with the general goals of the measure, but argued strongly against
passage because of its inflationary consequences.[24] Schultze was
particularly opposed to the provision that made the federal government the employer of last resort, and he stressed the problems that
the prevailing-wages clause could cause. He declared his approval of
using public service employment for countercyclical purposes but
warned against making public employment a permanent policy of
the federal government, as the bill aimed to do.

The hearings abruptly halted the momentum that the Humphrey-
Hawkins bill had gained in Congress. Although the Democratic leadership still hoped to use the measure as a political vehicle, their
freshman colleagues feared that in the wake of such damaging testimony, support for the bill would hurt them in the upcoming election. These members of Congress persuaded the House leadership
to refrain from bringing the bill to the floor in 1976.[25] This marked a
turning point in the political fortunes of Humphrey-Hawkins; after
1976, the bill was progressively weakened until it was an essentially
toothless measure.

The swift demise of planning for full employment highlights the
limits of Congress as the sole arena for promoting planning. Various
features of the bill that helped win it support in Congress under-

mined its credibility and provided targets for opponents. The statement of a specific target rate of unemployment and the date for reaching it, for example, made a dramatic symbol, useful in political debate, but was difficult to defend in policy discussions, particularly when the mechanisms for attaining these goals were only vaguely defined.

Moreover, the congressional forum made it difficult to specify mechanisms that would lead to the economic goals the bill identified. One central problem was that Congress could not endorse wage-price controls as an anti-inflationary mechanism and retain the support of organized labor.[26] Organized labor had just emerged from the experience of broad controls imposed by the Nixon administration in 1971 as part of its New Economic Policy and eventually lifted in 1974.[27] Implemented by an administration that was deeply opposed to controls but felt the need for a dramatic political gesture, the experiment had left bitter feelings on all sides. Organized labor had been particularly disillusioned by the far more strict control applied to wages. Labor leaders were ill disposed to endorse controls two years later, especially if they came with no guarantees about how the program would be administered.

By themselves, congressional leaders were in no position to make credible promises about administration of a system of controls; support from the executive branch, which would actually implement controls, would have been necessary. But the Humphrey-Hawkins bill was a partisan measure, supported by the Democratic leadership to pressure the Republican executive and to provide a galvanizing issue in the upcoming presidential campaign. It could not at the same time serve as a vehicle for finding common ground and building bridges between the administration and Congress.

Thus, the political function that congressional leaders staked out for the Humphrey-Hawkins bill led to a bill strong on symbolism but hard to defend as a blueprint for policy. In a more stable political and institutional environment, Democratic congressional leaders might have been able to push it through even under these conditions. But the Democratic freshman representatives, elected on the wave of post-Watergate hostility toward the Republican party, were extremely cautious about anything that might affect their reelection prospects.[28] Public charges by Democratic economists that the Humphrey-Hawkins bill was inflationary were sufficient to tip the balance away from the legislation for a large number of the freshman Democrats in Congress.

After the election of Jimmy Carter as president in 1976, Humphrey-Hawkins was refashioned as a symbolic measure. During the campaign, Carter had announced his support for the bill, but hedged with the proviso "given my current understanding of the bill."[29] However, this guarded support came after the candidate had repeatedly resisted pressure from the Congressional Black Caucus to support the bill. Carter's turnabout came only in the aftermath of ill-fated remarks about "ethnic purity" that threatened to cost him substantial black support. Once in the White House, Carter's ambivalence about Humphrey-Hawkins returned, and he retreated to supporting the general goals of the bill without endorsing the legislation itself.[30]

The administration decided to support the bill only in late 1977, as a symbolic gesture to the black community, which had strongly supported his campaign.[31] The administration's bill set a target of reducing unemployment to 4 percent by 1983 but did not make the federal government the employer of last resort or specify any other means by which the goal was to be reached. Finally, the new version of the bill acknowledged the danger of inflation, elevating price stability to a goal equal in importance to that of full employment.[32]

If Humphrey-Hawkins, as supported by the administration, was primarily symbolic, after congressional debate, even the nature of the symbolism was in doubt. In Congress, where Humphrey-Hawkins was now identified as a "black" measure, promoted primarily by the Congressional Black Caucus, the desire to underscore the importance of the anti-inflation goal was even greater than that of the administration. Republican conservatives used debate over the bill as a forum to argue for strengthening the federal commitment to reducing inflation and to balancing the budget. Under the leadership of Senator Orrin Hatch (R. Utah), the bill sent to Carter included specific numerical goals for reducing inflation, targeting 1988 for a zero inflation rate. It also called for the reduction of federal spending to the lowest level consistent with national needs.[33] Numerous other goals, including measures to increase productivity and to move to parity for farm prices, were tacked onto the bill, indicating that it had become an ineffectual wish list for a broad range of groups, most of which had little commitment to planning or to full employment.

The experience of the Humphrey-Hawkins bill highlighted the difficulty of instituting planning mechanisms with Congress as the central vehicle. Unorthodox ideas became highly vulnerable in the course of public hearings, and political pressures made the bill stronger on symbolism than on mechanisms for achieving the goals it set out. By the time the last version of the bill was considered, the public debate made it clear that inflation was the central economic problem and budget cutting was the way to solve it.

The Political Success of Passive Policies

The political failure of full employment, as embodied in the early versions of the Humphrey-Hawkins bill, did not mean that Congress had turned away from viewing unemployment as a government responsibility. Although congressional members could not agree on the commitments embodied in Humphrey-Hawkins, they continued to support extensions of passive policies that would tide the unemployed over bouts of joblessness. Throughout the 1970s, extensions of unemployment insurance and expansion of Trade Adjustment Assistance (TAA) indicated that when Congress could hand out divisible benefits through established channels, it was willing to do so. In debates about expanding these programs to cope with rising unemployment, congressional members rarely raised questions about whether it was the federal government's responsibility to assist the unemployed.

During the 1970s, in the context of rising unemployment, Congress approved changes in unemployment insurance that extended benefits substantially beyond the twenty-six weeks initially provided by the program. Among other changes that expanded coverage, the Employment Security Amendments of 1970 set up a permanent program that extended benefits for up to thirty-nine weeks. The program would be automatically triggered when unemployment reached specific national or state levels. Once unemployment began to climb in the 1970s, Congress put into place a variety of emergency measures providing supplemental benefits that increased the period for receiving benefits to as high as sixty-five weeks.[34] With these changes, the program lost many of its insurance features and effectively began to function as an income support program for those who had lost their jobs.

The changes that Congress approved during the 1970s revealed a willingness to take some responsibility for alleviating the distress caused by unemployment but a reluctance to consider structural changes, even if they linked the unemployment insurance system more closely to the broad objectives of economic policy. From the Kennedy administration on, presidents had sought to establish such links by proposing changes that would allow unemployment insurance to function as a countercyclical spending device.[35] One of the central objectives of these reform efforts—higher benefit levels and increased coverage—was to ease the drop-off in workers' purchasing power during periods of rising unemployment and thus help brake a recessionary spiral. But such modifications interfered with the states' prerogatives established by the 1935 Social Security Act, which were strongly defended by business. In most cases, Congress rejected changes that increased the federal role in setting standards for unemployment insurance.

The federal-state structure of unemployment insurance, which granted the states substantial control over the program, was thus a continuing obstacle to making unemployment insurance a counter-cyclical tool. Although some congressional leaders lamented the "piecemeal remedies" that Congress had enacted during the 1970s, they were unable to agree on structural reforms that would tie un-employment insurance to broader economic objectives or ensure the adequacy of benefits.[36] But numerous emergency provisions for extending the duration of benefits in the 1970s made unemployment insurance increasingly resemble a more generous and nonmeans-tested "welfare" program.

Another existing program, the Trade Adjustment Assistance pro-gram, which provided funds to workers unemployed as a result of foreign competition, was also greatly expanded during the 1970s. First authorized in 1962 as part of the Trade Expansion Act, the pro-gram was designed to ensure labor support for trade liberalization. The act provided that workers who had become unemployed be-cause of an import concession granted in trade negotiations would be compensated. A complex administrative process for determining eligibility placed the initial determination in the hands of the Tariff Commission, which approved no applications during the 1960s.[37]

With the upsurge in unemployment during the 1970s, however, Congress substantially liberalized Trade Adjustment Assistance in order to ward off organized labor's growing support for protection-ism. The Trade Act of 1974 loosened eligibility requirements and gave the Department of Labor responsibility for approving applica-tions. As a result, the number of beneficiaries and the cost of the program soared. In 1976, TAA served 48,824 beneficiaries at a cost of $69.9 million; two years later, these numbers had soared to 156,599 beneficiaries at a cost of $258.3 million.[38]

Congress took the initiative in expanding TAA in 1974. Organized labor, stung by the previous administration of the program and wor-ried about rising competition from international trade, offered little support.[39] Business was more enthusiastic, hoping to neutralize labor's rising protectionism. Because TAA was administered through the unemployment insurance program, it did not require the crea-tion of new institutional structures. But the very factors that had made it easy to achieve a consensus on expanding TAA ensured that it would do little more than offer limited income support to dislocated workers. Although the 1974 law contained provisions for worker retraining and readjustment, nothing was done to create the programs and institutional links needed to reach these objectives, nor was the program implemented in ways that emphasized adjustment goals.[40] As a consequence, only 3 percent of TAA funds went for retraining purposes; the rest provided direct cash aid for workers.[41]

The expansion of these passive programs during the 1970s revealed congressional willingness to address unemployment, but it also underscored the limits of congressional action. Extending these policies increased the bifurcation of American social policy along racial lines. Because the recipients of unemployment insurance and Trade Adjustment Assistance were individuals who had enjoyed a stable attachment to the labor force, the programs did little for those who had not able to establish such ties. Racial minorities were more likely to be served by the less generous Aid to Families with Dependent Children (AFDC) program and by poorly funded, short-term remedial training programs.[42]

The limits of congressional action were also revealed by Congress's inability to tie these programs to a broader employment policy. The structural changes needed to create such links were rejected because they entailed expansions of federal power. This reluctance to increase federal authority inherently advantaged business, which found it easier to influence these policies at the state level. But congressional action on passive policies did not simply respond to business interests: where Congress could increase benefits without structural change, it was willing to do so whether business agreed or not. Thus, increases in the duration of unemployment insurance were approved throughout the decade despite business opposition.[43] What remained unclear, however, was how long political support could be sustained for major expenditures on income assistance that did little to promote reentry into the labor market.

Executive Institutions and the Scope of Economic Policy

The problems encountered by the broad congressional proposals for planning suggest that less sweeping measures, pursued from within the executive branch, might have been more successful in creating alternative capacities to control inflation without increasing unemployment. Yet, such endeavors, which included Department of Labor initiatives to create tripartite cooperation and executive efforts to hold down wages and prices, fizzled out in the late 1970s. No enduring institutional relationships useful in controlling inflation emerged from the various attempts to create new forums for anti-inflationary action. Central to the failure of these efforts was the lack of stable support from business or labor.

To understand why executive branch efforts to create new forums for managing inflation in the late 1970s failed, it is necessary to look beyond the immediate circumstances of business and labor opposition in order to place these attempts within the broader context of federal economic policy. The version of Keynesianism that established the framework for economic policy in the United States had never regarded these relatively interventionist tools as desirable features of economic policy. This antipathy to intervention had several consequences for anti-inflation policy. First, it meant that executive actors responsible for economic policymaking rarely placed much emphasis on institutionalizing the relationships between labor and management essential to such anti-inflation strategies. As a consequence, these mechanisms were resorted to only in periods of extreme political pressure, and they were put into place without the underlying relationships necessary for their success.

Second, even when they were tried, these anti-inflationary initiatives did not become the organizing principles of economic policy; instead, they constituted only one of several policy thrusts. Because of this, the attitudes of business and labor toward government were often determined by other policies, which appeared more enduring but did not necessarily promote cooperation. In this context, labor and business had only weak incentives to comply with government anti-inflationary measures, and considerable motivation to seek their own advantage in alternative policies. Without such cooperation, tripartite forums and inflationary controls were doomed to failure, and the scope for economic policymaking was restricted.

The Department of Labor and the Failure of
Tripartite Cooperation

Because organized labor was its central constituency, the Department of Labor had an institutional stake in creating alternatives to unemployment as a cure for inflation. In the 1970s, as inflation began to climb upward, the department began to search for ways to promote labor-management cooperation on wages and prices. In their most ambitious guise, the department's initiatives in the 1970s sought to reorganize the framework of industrial relations that had been set up during the 1930s and 1940s by creating a more consensual tripartite approach, in which business, labor, and the government would come to agreements about prices and wages.

Much of the impulse to move in this direction came from John Dunlop, Gerald Ford's secretary of labor. A labor market economist at Harvard with considerable government experience and strong ties to organized labor, Dunlop had long argued in favor of developing capacities to control inflation in different sectors. In contrast to the macroeconomists of the CEA, Dunlop stressed the importance of institutions and the need to build new forums for business-labor consultations. Like Leontief, Dunlop criticized the dominant tendency of economists to focus their research on aggregate measures. Dunlop's model, in contrast, emphasized patterns of group decision-making. Rather than studying the Phillips curve in the aggregate, he argued, policy-relevant knowledge would have to take into account wage contours—the relationship of wages to one another—on a quite specific basis. The dominant models of wage determination and the Phillips curve, he maintained, had "helped restrain private and public policies to create jobs and have simplified dangerously the complex issues of inflation. . . ."[44]

As secretary of labor and as a member of Ford's Economic Policy Board—upon which he made his acceptance of the position of labor secretary conditional—Dunlop argued for incomes policies based on an understanding of the processes, both formal and informal, of wage determination in the United States. His varied experience in government and his long friendship with organized labor had convinced Dunlop that wage restraint could be effectively achieved only by inducing labor and management to cooperate in making and administering national economic policy.[45] He envisioned a kind of corporatist national economic policymaking in which government policymakers would draw labor and business leaders "into their thinking—not only to provide information but . . . to secure a kind of consensus, a kind of acceptance of policies because they'll work better that way."[46]

One vehicle for promoting such consensus was the President's Labor-Management Committee, established in 1974 by President Ford. As coordinator of the committee, Dunlop presided over regular meetings of sixteen leading labor and business figures to consider a broad range of economic policy questions and make recommendations to the president. Among the policy areas they considered were taxation, regulation, and housing.[47]

Dunlop also pursued more pinpointed sectoral initiatives, most notably in the construction industry, the source of the most dra-

matic wage increases in the early 1970s. During the Nixon administration, Dunlop had headed the Construction Industry Stabilization Committee, a tripartite board set up in March 1971 to approve
wage rates in the construction industry.[48] When the operating authority for that committee lapsed in 1974, Dunlop pressed for the
creation of a new forum for labor-management negotiations in the
industry. These efforts culminated in the Construction Industry Collective Bargaining Act of 1975, which established a new labor and
management national bargaining committee in the industry.[49]

Instead of providing a stepping-stone for creating new labor-
management forums in other sectors, the act was followed by a political controversy that led to Dunlop's resignation and signaled the
kind of difficulties that advocates of tripartite cooperation would
have in the future.[50] Organized labor had agreed to support the bill
if it also included a provision legalizing common situs picketing,
which had been outlawed by the Supreme Court in 1951. Legaliza-
tion of common situs picketing was an important issue for the building trades since it would allow them to picket an entire construction
site even if only one contractor was the target. They viewed it as a fair
exchange for the restrictions on collective bargaining contained in
the rest of the bill. Dunlop had worked out a compromise between
employers and labor on the issue and had secured the president's
support. Employers, however, reneged on the agreement, and, in the
face of unprecedented business mobilization, Ford vetoed the measure.[51] Dunlop resigned soon after, effectively marking an end to
efforts within the Ford administration to build labor-management
cooperation that would help control inflation.[52]

Carter's secretary of labor, Ray Marshall, did not initially emphasize such labor-management forums as a way to combat inflation.
Instead, his earliest efforts focused on public service employment,
which he viewed as a selective measure serving much the same purposes, but providing more direct benefits to the unemployed. With
the political backlash against the Comprehensive Employment and
Training Act (CETA) and increasing concern over inflation, however,
Marshall began to advocate what he called a sectoral approach to
inflation. The approach borrowed from Dunlop the idea of establishing a cooperative relationship between labor and business under
the auspices of government.

As Marshall elaborated the idea, cabinet members would be
charged with establishing task forces of labor and management representatives, who together would explore the inflationary pressures
in their sectors, including supply factors other than wages, and
would collaborate in devising solutions to the problems. The es-

sence of the approach was to establish a framework within which long-term patterns of corporatist-style cooperation could emerge. Marshall viewed such cooperation as far preferable to altering behavior through sanctions, as wage or price controls would. The sectoral policy would, moreover, be more flexible than a program of general sanctions or explicit numerical standards for wages and prices because it would more easily accommodate adjustments in particular sectors.[53]

These ideas had little impact on policy within the Carter administration. The department did not turn its attention to developing these policy options until 1978, after it had lost much of its influence within the administration. Moreover, these ideas promised few economic or political payoffs in the short term. Institutionalizing such new relationships was a long-range project, unlikely to produce substantial results in the near future. Nor did this approach offer much that would allow the president to make a dramatic public gesture against inflation.

In neither the Ford nor the Carter administration, did the president exhibit much support for the long-term efforts to build labor-management cooperation. In each case, the press of more immediate political pressures made executive attention to such institution-building efforts sporadic and rendered presidential support fickle. Moreover, the Department of Labor was not a good site for developing these new institutional forums; the department's long-standing ties to organized labor left it open to charges of constituency bias. Without consistent presidential support or strong institutional sponsorship, tripartite cooperation was not likely to win labor or business backing, especially when it entailed sacrificing other political aims with a better chance of success.

Executive Initiative: The Council on Wage-Price Stability

Presidential efforts to master inflation by implementing wage-price controls or strong guidelines fared little better than did Department of Labor attempts to create forums for tripartite cooperation. The political difficulties these programs experienced reflected their ad hoc status within economic policy. Wage-price controls have rarely been favored by the network of economists supplying policy advice to American politicians. Instead, presidents, faced with public pressure to "do something" about inflation, have been drawn to controls as a means of making a strong public statement about their intention to fight inflation.

President Carter's decision in 1978 to implement a program of strong guidelines, to be administered by the Council on Wage and Price Stability (COWPS), reflected the political problems inherent in using guidelines as a last resort. New institutional mechanisms had to be constructed with little previous groundwork, and, by 1978 this task was complicated by the suspicions that Nixon's earlier implementation of controls had engendered. Moreover, COWPS did not set the terms of economic policy during the last two years of the Carter administration. Its anti-inflation strategies were only one of several policy directions that the administration pursued. Not surprisingly, COWPS not only failed to have much impact on the economy; it also helped to heighten antagonism among government, business, and labor, and it further reduced confidence in government solutions to inflation.

The Nixon administration's program of mandatory controls, first announced in 1971, did little to ease the path for COWPS. Nixon's decision to freeze wages and prices and then impose mandatory controls marked an about-face in policy that reflected executive desire to project an image of mastery over a drifting economy. The dramatic endorsement of controls did not signal a conversion on the part of Nixon's economic advisers; instead, it was a highly political move that showed how easily political concerns can overrule expert apprehensions.

Since the 1960s, the CEA, appointed by Democratic presidents, had sought to keep wages and prices within acceptable bounds by issuing guideposts and relying on exhortation to secure compliance.[54] The weakness of this approach became apparent in the late 1960s and early 1970s, when inflation began to appear impervious to such measures. In 1970, the Nixon administration began to issue periodic "inflation alerts," designed to pressure industry and labor by drawing attention to wage and price rises, but the president remained adamant about his opposition to controls. In the middle of 1971, however, Nixon took the world by surprise with his New Economic Policy, whose main domestic component included a ninety-day wage-price freeze, to be followed by a system of progressively less restrictive controls which remained in effect for three years.[55] Against the counsel of most of his economic advisers, the president had responded to growing calls for some sort of wage-price action (although not necessarily controls) from politicians, business leaders, and labor leaders, including the Committee for Economic Development, Federal Reserve Chairman Arthur F. Burns, and AFL-CIO president George Meany.[56]

Economically and politically, the experiment was less than successful. As soon as the controls were lifted, a burst of inflation ensued, as industry and labor sought to catch up for lost gains.[57] Neither business nor labor was pleased with its experience under controls. Labor leaders had been unhappy from the start, charging that the freeze was inequitable. The administration of the program, which they claimed ignored union perspectives, only enhanced their discontent.[58] Business leaders likewise judged the controls a failure, arguing that market distortions and government intrusions simply promoted inefficiency. Economists of both the Keynesian and monetarist schools found that the experience confirmed their worst expectations about the ineffectiveness of controls.[59]

In light of this experience, President Carter initially rejected wage-price controls as an economic tool. Instead, the new president simply sought an extension of the Council on Wage and Price Stability, a small agency established in 1974 after the Nixon controls were abolished, charged with monitoring several potential sources of inflation, including government regulations, collective bargaining, and anticompetitive private behavior.[60] The administration's first response to rising inflation in 1978 was a mild effort that included cuts in wage increases for federal workers and a rather vague "deceleration" program that aimed to bring prices and wages down without establishing specific goals or sanctions for noncompliance. The program had few results. As CEA chairman Charles Schultze later remarked, "We preached and promoted and jumped up and down, but with little effect."[61]

In late 1978, pressed by rising inflation, the president unveiled a program of voluntary guidelines to be administered by COWPS. Several provisions of the plan sought to allay labor's fears that wages would be held down more effectively than prices would: one proposal would allow the federal government to refuse to do business with firms that violated the guidelines; another provided for "real wage insurance," a version of a tax-based incomes policy that would compensate labor for rises in inflation exceeding a contractually established rate.[62]

Despite the voluntary nature of the program and the assurances to labor, there was little enthusiasm for the plan from any quarter. Miffed at having been excluded from consideration of the package and still concerned that the provisions for price control were not nearly as strong as those for wages, organized labor denounced the proposal in strong language. AFL-CIO head George Meany was particularly incensed by the plan and announced his support for mandatory wage-price controls instead.[63] Concerned about labor's implacable hostility and complaints that COWPS decisions were arbitrary, in late 1979, the administration set up a tripartite Pay Advisory Committee and a Price Committee to recommend changes in the pay standard and to review the council's decisions.[64] But less than a year later, it was clear that the guidelines were having little impact on inflation, that neither labor nor business had been won over, and that the administration had not increased public confidence in its ability to manage inflation.[65]

The failure can be traced in part to the administration's vague approach to the problem of securing compliance with the guidelines. Lacking legal sanctions, the main weapon in the hands of administrators was that of adverse publicity for violators. But, as W. Kip Viscusi, former deputy director of COWPS observed, the publicity sanction was of limited utility, especially once a pattern of noncompliance had emerged.[66] The limitations of the sanction became clear very soon after the guidelines were established. The president's efforts to secure compliance by initiating biweekly meetings with industry leaders ended in failure. An alternative compliance mechanism was the tripartite model of industry, labor, and governmental consultation advocated by Dunlop as secretary of labor. As head of the Pay Advisory Committee, Dunlop sought to use that body to create tripartite cooperation around the goal of lower inflation.[67] But since there was no agreement within the administration on such an approach, the Pay Committee was instead seen as a competitor by COWPS. Haggling between the two groups further undermined the credibility of the government's anti-inflation program.[68]

The difficulties that surrounded compliance revealed a more general problem: the guidelines were not the centerpiece of economic policy. Instead, they competed with a range of initiatives, many of which worked at cross-purposes. In part, this confusion stemmed from the difficulties of implementing such a complex package in the context of divided national institutions. Congressional opposition to using federal procurement and regulatory policy for economic goals and its lack of enthusiasm for real wage insurance meant that sanctions that the administration had once considered as part of the package were not available.[69] But the conflicts between COWPS and the Pay Advisory Committee also indicated that the administration did not have an integrated vision of economic policy. Instead, it had various sectoral policies, overlaid with the guidelines program.

In this context, the guidelines became little more than hollow symbols, announcing the administration's intention to fight inflation. Immediate political pressures undermined possibilities for creating enduring forms of cooperation between business and labor. The appearance of a policy took the place of the institutional innovation and reordering of public-private relationships needed to implement an anti-inflation program.

Business, Labor, and the Limits on Innovation

For the anti-inflation strategies advocated by the Department of Labor and by the president to work, they had, at a minimum, to convince business and labor that the burden of economic change would be distributed fairly or that the procedures outlined by the government offered the best outcome each group was likely to secure. This was not easily accomplished, in part because of the inherent difficulties of implementing incomes policies in the decentralized political and economic structure of the United States—difficulties that were compounded by presidential ambivalence about the purposes of such strategies. But other policies, particularly those in the regulatory arena, were simultaneously shaping interests and promoting mobilization along lines that made a cooperative reconciliation of interests around inflation unlikely in the 1970s.

The decentralized political and economic structures of the United States created inherent difficulties for administering incomes policies by making it harder to strike and keep bargains. The incomplete and loose organization of labor and business increased the possibility that parts of each group would seek their own advantage outside any potentially common agreements. Without overarching interest organizations, such behavior would be difficult to contain. Similarly, institutional fragmentation left federal officials poorly equipped to guarantee particular action on the part of the government; the need for congressional approval or institutional cooperation rendered government action uncertain.

Some economists have argued that these structural factors pose insuperable barriers to creating incomes policies in the United States; others, most notably John Dunlop, have maintained that by creating regularized forums for business-labor consultation, it would be possible to overcome the problems of fragmentation.[70] But, as we have seen, it was difficult to sustain presidential interest in the effort to create new forums for labor-management cooperation. Short-term political pressures often diverted the president's attention or, as in the case of President Ford, caused the withdrawal of presidential support. Moreover, much of the president's interest in these strategies was simply to provide the public with assurance that the administration had an anti-inflation program. As Herbert Stein, a member of the CEA under Nixon, put it in 1970, a "realistic discussion of incomes policy" starts "from the proposition that we are mainly concerned with a political, public-relations problem."[71] But reassuring the public could come into conflict with building new forums of cooperation, and when the two clashed, the president's interest lay in the immediate rewards that symbolism could offer.

In the 1970s, these barriers to creating business-labor cooperation on inflation were reinforced by initiatives that government was taking in other policy arenas, most notably in regulatory policy. During the late 1960s, and especially in the first half of the 1970s, America's corporations felt themselves to be under siege by a new movement of social regulation. Spurred by the public interest movement, new laws in occupational health and safety, pollution, product safety, and a host of related areas were put on the books.[72] The new regulations not only increased government monitoring and business reporting responsibilities; they also allowed individuals unhappy with corporate behavior to sue.

This burst of regulatory legislation helped to galvanize the business community into action. New organizations, such as the Business Roundtable, which included the chief executive officers of the largest American corporations, were created and older associations, such as the Chamber of Commerce and the National Association of Manufacturers, were revitalized.[73] The spurt of organizational creativity greatly increased business ability to intervene in politics, and allowed business groups to take better advantage of new techniques of exercising political influence, including grass roots organizing and political action committees (PACs).[74] Particularly important in boosting business's political influence was the unusual degree of unity among diverse business interests that new organizations sought to foster.[75]

Mobilized and unified as it had not been for decades, the business community decided to take on organized labor. Business's decision to oppose the common situs picketing bill in 1975 indicated its desire and ability to advance its own interests at the expense of creating more consensual relations with labor to cope with inflation. Prospects for building labor-management forums to control inflation further evaporated in mid-1978, when a broad spectrum of business leaders and organizations launched an all-out attack on a proposed labor law reform bill that unions had long sought.[76] The defeat of the bill further emboldened business in its new agenda, and soured labor on efforts at cooperation.

Business's success at curbing labor's power substantially diminished incentives for working out an accord under the auspices of the federal government. At the same time, it reduced labor's belief that government could protect its interests. Under these circumstances, the federal government's vacillation and uncertainty about the role of tripartite cooperation or wage-price controls doomed the development of these mechanisms.

The system of industrial relations that had emerged from the New Deal and remained in operation until the 1970s would not be reconstructed along more consensual lines without considerable initiative on the part of the federal government. Uninterested in promoting changes for most of the postwar period, the federal government could not muster sustained support for the several initiatives launched in the 1970s. As government wavered, and business enhanced its ability to win on its own terms, prospects for creating alternatives to recession to remedy unemployment diminished further.

Presidential Strategy and the Rhetoric of Limited Government

The efforts to sustain employment objectives in an inflationary economy were further undermined by the president. Rather than nurturing such initiatives, both Ford and Carter deployed presidential rhetoric in the fight against inflation in ways that weakened political support for them. A central feature of this rhetoric assigned the responsibility for inflation and other economic problems to the federal government itself. By blaming government for the nation's economic problems, both presidents helped to narrow the range of anti-inflation strategies. Such rhetoric strengthened the public appeal of free market economists and their business allies, who backed recession and unemployment as the only cure for the American economy. It also bolstered popular antipathy to the federal government, helping public opinion to crystallize in favor of recessionary strategies.

This presidential rhetoric is most puzzling in the case of Jimmy Carter. As leader of the Democratic party, a diverse coalition that had highlighted employment objectives and had thrived on a patchwork of federal programs since the 1940s, Carter had much to lose by embracing policy strategies that used the market mechanisms rather than government authority to allocate the benefits and costs of economic change. Personal beliefs are not sufficient to make sense of the president's decision to fault government for national economic woes. Although he was a fiscal conservative and had run for office as a Washington outsider, Carter initially deployed policy and rhetorical strategies that were well within the Democratic mainstream.

To understand why antigovernment rhetoric became the central theme of Carter's final two years in office, it is necessary to examine the weakness of the federal executive in the late 1970s and evaluate the presidential strategies used to govern in a political and bureaucratic environment that seemed increasingly out of control. These strategies provided a common political focus for business organizations seeking to reduce the government's control of the economy and for broad-based popular frustration with government. The political union of these forces, I show, set new, more narrow boundaries on employment policy.

Presidential Strategy: The Tensions between Governance and Policy

When Carter took office, he, like other presidents, had to confront two problems: how to formulate a substantive policy agenda that was politically appealing and how to handle his relationships with the executive bureaucracy and Congress in order to get his agenda approved and implemented. The second task, that of governing, posed a particular challenge for Carter. Not only had the president inherited a fragmented executive branch, further weakened by the Watergate scandal; he also had to grapple with the unsolved economic puzzles of the 1970s. After his initial efforts to make government more efficient and rational had failed, the president increasingly emphasized his belief in limited public power; at the same time, he sought to shift blame for the nation's problems onto a bloated federal bureaucracy and a recalcitrant Congress. Such a governance strategy was not easily reconciled with much of the president's substantive policy agenda, and in time it sharply limited the scope of that agenda.

In the realm of economic policymaking, President Carter initially followed the advice of his mainstream Keynesian economic advisers. Economic policy did not strongly attract the president, Erwin Hargrove has noted, because it "did not provide opportunities for bold, dramatic steps of presidential leadership," as did many foreign policy issues.[77] As we have seen, the Council of Economic Advisers urged the president to follow the conventional Keynesian wisdom of stimulating the economy when he took office in 1977. Although the president was wary of a major program of economic stimulus, the broad consensus among his advisers persuaded him to move in this direction. The package of spending and tax cuts that the president proposed and Congress approved early in 1977 was designed to pull the economy out of its slump.[78]

For the second task, handling the bureaucracy and the Congress, Carter drew on his own experience as governor of Georgia, where he had overhauled the state bureaucracy to make it more rational and efficient. He sought to do the same in Washington, launching a reorganization plan for the executive branch that aimed to facilitate coherent policy initiatives.[79] The same impulse was evident in his efforts to reorganize and rationalize social policies, such as welfare, and to carve out new areas of coordinated government activity, as in energy policy.[80] The president believed that better organization would allow the government simultaneously to pursue liberal policy goals and lower expenditures by ridding social programs of coordination problems that created perverse incentives and increased costs.

Both the policy and the governance strategy quickly unraveled. As the stimulus package disintegrated amid the chaos of the CETA program and mounting inflation, the president looked increasingly incapable of addressing the key issues that confronted him. He responded with a two-track anti-inflation strategy. The first track featured the guidelines administered by COWPS, later coupled with a sort of social compact with labor in hopes of achieving wage restraint. The second path, reflecting the president's deepest convictions, aimed to cut spending and reduce the deficit to curb inflation.

Carter also had to seek new strategies to address his governance problem. As efforts to achieve rationality and efficient organization through comprehensive reform faltered, the president returned to the antigovernment themes that had served him so well in his presidential campaign.[81] Engulfed by interest group claims that he could neither satisfy nor control, Carter identified the "special interests" and Congress as the nub of the problem.[82] A central aim of the new governance strategy was to reduce demands on government by making moral appeals to the nation to be less selfish. As James Caesar has noted, Carter sought "a change in the basic political culture—a kind of moral regeneration that would limit and discipline the special interests."[83] This governance strategy reverberated in economic policy with an increased emphasis on attacking the deficit. Carter had long been identified as a "fiscal conservative," but not until his midterm shift in strategy did these inclinations come to the fore in his economic policy. Increasingly, he pointed to the deficit as the source of inflation and identified spending fueled by interest group demands as the cause of the deficit.

Attacking the deficit became a way to assert presidential authority over the executive and congressional networks that he could not control. But it was a strategy that posed dangers for Democratic economic policy. There was by no means a consensus that deficits were responsible for the inflation of the 1970s. Mainstream Democratic economists laid the blame on supply shocks, in fuel and food prices in 1974 and in fuel prices again in 1979.[84] In a 1979 memo to the Economic Policy Group, Secretary of Labor Ray Marshall argued that the president should deemphasize the role of the deficit. Acknowledging that the deficit had "been a contributing factor," he went on to say that it was "*not* the primary cause of inflation. Overemphasis of the deficit impedes the political education needed to cure what is essentially a political phenomenon."[85]

The attack on the deficit offered another kind of political education, and it was one that constricted the possibilities for an active government response to economic problems. The renewed anti-statist political rhetoric was not only much more amenable to the second of Carter's substantive policy tracks, that advocating recession; it, in fact, helped to diminish the political prospects of the first track, which called for government action. Although Carter was reluctant to embrace openly the strategy of recession as a means to control inflation, his attacks on government led away from alternative policies, which would have required new government capacities to oversee the economy.

"New" Ideas and the Political Meaning of Employment Policy

Carter's antigovernment rhetoric provided a common political voice for the diverse concerns expressed by the business community and uncovered in soundings of public opinion. The president's political arguments added credibility to the promarket economic theories that business-funded policy organizations were vigorously promoting. They also tapped into and nurtured antigovernment sentiments in public opinion, already primed by the Watergate scandal and two decades of federal policies that had strengthened rather than muted such attitudes. By emphasizing the frustration with government that "the public" and business both shared, politics helped to crystallize new political meanings in which federal employment programs were part of the wasteful and intrusive polices that needed to be dismantled if the economy were to revive.

The business community's support for free market economic ideas in the 1970s marked a new form of mobilization. With the breakdown of consensus among academic economists, business leaders sought to promote economic ideas that promised the least government involvement. The ideas of the monetarists, increasingly influential within the academic community, had a powerful allure for business because they envisioned an economy with minimal government involvement, free from the unpredictability and "distortions" caused by labor unions, government regulation, and discretionary action. These ideas had an obvious appeal to such groups as the Chamber of Commerce and the National Association of Manufacturers, who had rarely supported the spending initiatives of the past two decades and who were now actively battling both unions and government regulation.

For employment policy, this approach meant reducing government activity and relying on private adjustment to economic change. Since the early 1970s, a growing number of economists associated with the business community had argued that government spending caused inflation.[86] This perspective diverted attention away from the efforts to build tripartite cooperation, and it left little room for Keynesian-style macroeconomic stimulation, especially in an inflationary economy. Such views about macroeconomic policy were complemented by emerging neoclassical explanations of unemployment, which highlighted individual incentives to work, rather than the operation of broad economic forces, as the key determinant of employment status. This approach to unemployment posed a challenge to several targeted employment programs, such as CETA, that provided public service employment, and it cast doubt on the wisdom of the various extensions of unemployment insurance.

Business organizations regarded the promotion of these ideas as an essential part of their mobilization in the 1970s. Business-funded think tanks, which developed and publicized such ideas, were an important new feature on the political landscape of American politics.[87] Often more overtly political and policy focused than their liberal counterparts, these organizations commanded resources and employed tactics that secured them a serious hearing in policy debates. But their contribution was less in pioneering new ideas than in packaging and marketing ideas.[88] Similarly, the greatest success these organizations experienced was not in securing support for specific policies but in shifting the terms of the policy debate. Their activities were complemented by business-funded academic research, which pointed research trajectories in directions that business hoped would support its policy preferences.[89]

Business, then, had poured considerable resources into formulating a comprehensive alternative to the prevailing assumptions governing economic policy. By the time President Carter began to emphasize the importance of balancing the budget in order to control inflation, these ideas had become attached to a much larger, comprehensive policy package for transforming the relationship between the government and the economy. Presidential support for part of that menu gave an already mobilized business community increasing confidence that it could press for the whole of its agenda. Compared with the resources backing market-oriented solutions to inflation and unemployment, ideas favoring new forms of government intervention were poorly equipped to compete.

Business-backed ideas about the role of government in the economy reinforced more broadly based antigovernmentalist sentiment pervading public opinion in the 1970s (see Table 5.1). As James Savage has noted, "[T]he charge that an administration's deficits were fiscally irresponsible, a sign of bureaucratic inefficiency, as well as a symbol of government operating beyond the scope of public control, remained politically potent particularly as federal social interventionism became less popular during the 1970s."[90] The symbolic appeal of the balanced budget made it increasingly difficult to defend Keynesian macroeconomic policy. The attack on deficits resonated with the increasing burden of taxation felt by middle-income Americans, as inflation pushed them into higher tax brackets. And as the balanced budget became a code for reducing government, it became tied to the growing movement to reduce taxes.[91]

The joining of antigovernmentalism and the politics of balanced budgets also made it more difficult to defend selective employment measures. The memory of the upheaval surrounding the implementation of the War on Poverty, together with the administrative problems rampant in CETA, reinforced the association of employment policies with intrusive, wasteful "big government," which was now identified as the source of the nation's economic dilemmas. "Big government" was also associated with the racial interventionism that marked government action in the 1960s and 1970s.[92]

Presidential rhetoric and business's new ideas thus helped to crystallize new political meanings for employment policy. The racial identification of the War on Poverty and the fraud and corruption associated with CETA were now undergirded by a more encompassing perspective that viewed government interventionism as wrong

Table 5.1
Public Confidence in Government, 1964–1980

Question: "Do you think that people in the government waste a lot of money we pay in taxes, waste some of it, or don't waste very much of it?"	

Year	% Replying "Wastes a Lot"
1964	47
1968	59
1970	69
1972	66
1974	74
1976	74
1978	77
1980	78

Source: Data reported in Seymour Martin Lipset and William Schneider, *The Confidence Gap: Business, Labor, and Government in the Public Mind* (New York: The Free Press, 1983), 17.

per se. Public receptivity to this message did not necessarily reflect any broad understanding or acceptance of the economic ideas that business supported.[93] Nor did it mean that public support for government action on employment issues had evaporated: public opinion polls in the late 1970s continued to show majority backing for government action on employment issues.[94] But it did signal a shift in the public debate.

Economic ideas, as popularized by business, interacted with popular frustrations with government to create new political meanings that identified government action as the source of the nation's economic problems. In the domain of employment, this meant increased public receptivity to arguments that employment goals could be attained by reducing government activity. This encompassing logic provided the basis for policy changes that looked to private action to solve employment problems.

Shifting Boundaries: The New Logic of Employment Policy

The Democratic failure to develop alternative employment policies and the resonance of business solutions with public frustrations helped to shift the boundaries of political debate on employment policy. Throughout the postwar period, the definition of the "employment problem" had been a narrow one, generally restricted to unemployment, as officially defined. Policy debates about employment issues concerned the ways that government could reduce unemployment. By the end of the Carter administration, public discussion had so shifted that the relevant question was not how government should act on the narrow problem of unemployment but whether government should act at all on this issue. The new logic, which called for minimal government initiative and prized private over public action, was evident in a range of policy proposals that broke with past assumptions. Although not all were approved, and few passed unaltered, employment policy was effectively transformed to reflect a sharply narrowed scope for government activity.

During the last two years of his administration, President Carter made a series of important policy decisions that reduced government's role in employment. CETA, as we have seen, was cut back and redirected to the most needy. The president's proposed 1980 budget reflected the belief that recession was the only way to deal with inflation; it called for substantial cuts in social programs in order to curb inflation.[95] Most significant, however, was Carter's decision to appoint Paul Volker to head the Federal Reserve in 1979. Pressed by the financial community, which was unimpressed with the administration's anti-inflation program and anxious for higher interest rates to prop up the dollar on international markets, the president responded by appointing Volker, a known and respected inflation fighter.[96]

In October 1979, under Volker's tutelage, the Federal Reserve announced a break with established practices. The board would no longer directly manipulate interest rates; instead, it would seek to control the growth of the money supply. Although economists disagree about whether this decision marked a triumph for monetarism, the implications for employment policy were indisputable.[97] Throughout the postwar era, monetary policy had functioned as the handmaiden of fiscal policy; the change in the Federal Reserve's approach signaled a new, more independent role for monetary policy, which would effectively divorce it from concerns about employment. The relatively insulated decisionmaking processes of the Federal Reserve would be further removed from employment concerns by focusing on bank reserves rather than interest rates.

By appointing Volker and embracing stringent budget cuts, Carter had put into place an economic policy that sacrificed employment to control inflation. In the fight to reduce inflation, employment was to be much more determined by market forces than Keynesians had once believed necessary.

President Carter's actions were a prelude to the more deliberate and ambitious attempts to remake policy and politics under Ronald Reagan. Although pronouncements of a "Reagan revolution" were certainly overblown, policymaking during the two Reagan administrations did manifest a clear shift in the role of government. In employment policy, the change was revealed in a new starting point for deliberations: the operating assumption was that government action would worsen the economy by interfering with individual, market-driven adjustment. The burden was now on supporters of government action to show that their proposals would work. With Keynesian remedies in disrepute, this was a difficult task. American supporters of government intervention had no successful models or established practices to which they could point. And they now had to combat the new logic of employment policy that the administration was promoting. Central to that logic was the idea that individual initiative could solve the economy's problems; government, it was asserted, blocked the necessary enterprising activity.

In the realm of macroeconomic policy, the lure of achieving economic prosperity through lower taxes and less government was a strong one. The administration's embrace of supply-side economics did not win many intellectual adherents, but the breakdown of consensus in the economics profession meant that there was little to counter the theory's obvious political attractions.[98] For selective employment policies, the logic of microeconomics, clothed in concern about individual incentives, became central to policy debates. CETA was discontinued on the grounds that, in addition to being a lightning rod for waste and fraud, it hindered movement into the private labor force by shielding workers from the market. Although a new job training program, the Job Training Partnership Act, was enacted in 1982, its modest size reflected deep skepticism about the efficacy of government action.[99]

The same logic was applied to passive policy. Congressional debates about whether to continue the extensions of unemployment insurance in the early 1980s revealed far more attention to the effects on individual incentives (thus questioning the existence of the programs) than to the issue of who should bear the tax burden for the extensions.[100] Although extensions were approved over the administration's objections in 1982, new rules reduced eligibility. These changes took a toll on coverage: availablity of unemployment benefits declined during the recessions of the early 1980s, in contrast to the increases that had occurred in previous recessions.[101]

The employment policy created during the Reagan administration, like much of American policy, was a grab bag of approaches. The new logic did not emerge in pure form, but its influence in redrawing the boundaries of policy was nonetheless unmistakable. The absence of a credible alternative had changed the status of employment as a political issue. Although politicians continued to view unemployment as a political danger, it no longer provided the spur to action it had in the 1960s and 1970s. The troubled history of employment policy in the United States provided an ample stock of effective arguments for politicians of both parties who were anxious to limit public responsibility and curb government action.

Conclusion

During the 1970s, the American economy was confronted by a range of new economic problems challenging the Keynesian framework that had guided economic policy in one form or another since the 1940s. A variety of political actors responded with proposals to increase the government's capacity to intervene in the economy in more coherent and pinpointed ways. But the development of ideas and politics over three decades had bequeathed a meager legacy for supporters of such proposals. Political and private institutional arrangements presented formidable obstacles to elaborating and winning support for augmenting planning or sectoral capacities.

Alternative, business-sponsored proposals, eschewing government action and reinterpreting unemployment as an individual choice, offered an increasingly attractive route to a middle class bearing a growing tax burden in an inflationary economy. Politicians seeking to address broad public discontent with the government and the economy helped to join these strands together into a new political configuration. As the logic of individual initiative replaced older notions of government responsibility, the boundaries of employment policy constricted, and the scope of government activity narrowed.

Six

Policy Boundaries
and Political Possibilities

POLICY decisions are, most obviously, choices among alternatives. But neither the range of alternatives nor the parameters of choice remain constant over time. Instead, notions about what is possible and desirable change as distinct definitions of problems emerge, and as conceptions about what government is able to do and what it should do shift. Arguments about American exceptionalism, which point to enduring features of politics or culture, cannot take us very far in understanding the scope or the nature of such shifts. Because they emphasize constraints, these accounts underestimate the possibilities for change. General models of policymaking, on the other hand, are too open ended; they provide few tools for understanding the recurrent features of policy and the persistent exclusion of some alternatives.

To make sense of the shifts as well as the regularities in policy, I have argued that we need a historical approach that pays attention to sequences of change and examines the way that policy "collides" with unanticipated events. By shaping the definitions of problems and creating political meanings for policies, these processes organize the terms of policy debate and effectively set boundaries for policy innovation. Such boundaries mark off a domain in which some questions are asked and others are left unspoken, some issues are defined as problems amenable to public action and others are regarded as natural or inevitable phenomena, and some lines of action are embarked upon with little controversy while others are not even broached.[1]

I have examined the emergence of boundaries in American employment policy by exploring the changing definitions of employment-related problems and by studying conflicts in which supporters of contending formulations sought to impose their visions on policy. We can now look more closely at what the case of employment policy tells us about policy change in the American political system and consider the present possibilities for employment policy.

Sequences of Change and Bounded Innovation

This account of the emergence and eventual eclipse of employment policy in the United States emphasizes the need to understand how the elements that combine to produce policy innovation are connected and in particular to see how they are linked over time. Scrutiny of these links reveals the ways in which innovation is bounded and at the same time illuminates the directions in which change is likely to proceed.

Identifying Contingencies and Boundaries

The notion that policies are the product of sequences of change that set boundaries on innovation suggests that explanation must comprehend contingency as well as boundaries, and must identify the influence of each. Contingency means that decisions about policy—defining a problem, delimiting its scope, and devising a strategy of intervention—are often the product of circumstances that cannot be readily anticipated or controlled. Because such factors as economic pressures, social movements, and effective politicians all may push outcomes one way rather than another, particular decisions may be seen as contingent. However, such decisions also exercise an enduring effect on future possibilities by limiting the kinds of choices likely to emerge for consideration. In this way, possibilities open at any one time are also bounded by earlier choices. If we look at the development of employment policy, we see both contingency and a bounding process at work.

In some instances, contingent factors reinforced the direction in which interests and institutions were moving, helping to close off alternative possibilities. One such case immediately after World War II was the failure of the widely anticipated postwar depression to materialize. The economic boom that occurred as the legislative framework for American employment policy was being debated sealed the fate of the original Full Employment bill and bolstered the decision to defederalize the U.S. Employment Service. By the time these pieces of legislation were considered, economic prosperity had strengthened the forces arrayed against them by reducing a sense of urgency about the economy and diverting public attention to other issues, including labor strife. The economic boom was particularly damaging to American Keynesians because the stagnationist analysis embodied in the Full Employment bill was predicated on an enduring tendency to depression in the American economy. If such a tendency did not exist, the Full Employment bill's effort to strengthen federal control of the economy would appear to be unnecessary.

Although it is not possible to predict precisely how employment policy would have developed had the original Full Employment bill passed and the Employment Service remained federalized, several features of both the bill and the service suggest that they would have created a broader scope for employment policy. The passage of the Full Employment bill would have made spending versions of macroeconomic stimulation more feasible by enhancing the executive's coordination capacities. Moreover, the bill's declaration of a right to employment for all Americans who sought to work could have provided symbolic support for proponents of more aggressive government action on employment. Maintaining the Employment Service as a federalized agency would have greatly enhanced the possibilities for administering a variety of labor market policies. It might also have made the creation of a separate administrative structure for the labor market policies of the War on Poverty unnecessary. As we have seen, the poor record of the state employment agencies and their unwillingness to respond to national directives was repeatedly cited as a central problem of labor market policies during the 1960s.

In other cases, contingent factors created new political meanings for employment policy. For example, the emergence of the southern civil rights movement and urban riots in the mid-1960s helped to transform the political profile of labor market policy. The poverty program initially envisioned by the Kennedy administration was not racially focused, nor did it emphasize political mobilization as the central means of alleviating poverty. Once the new programs began to be implemented, however, a new political assertiveness on the part of African-Americans, inspired by the civil rights movement, transformed the War on Poverty. Black local political leaders, with the tacit agreement of the Office of Economic Opportunity, sought to use the community action program in particular as a vehicle for black political empowerment.[2] The Johnson administration reinforced the racial focus of the poverty program and emphasized its service delivery aspects by using poverty agencies to funnel resources to black communities in the aftermath of the urban riots that spread throughout the North.

The collision of employment policy with black political mobilization had a major impact on the contours of employment policy. It strengthened the remedial focus of labor market policy, split the social and the economic more sharply, and encouraged the creation of separate, racially focused programs. It made these policies easier to abandon when support for black programs fell in the late 1960s, even though the labor market problems of African-Americans were in many ways growing more severe. By itself, black political mobilization did not make these responses inevitable, but in the context of the policy approach approved by the Council of Economic Advisers (CEA) and the institutional framework inherited from the 1940s, a conjunction of powerful forces pushed labor market policy toward a racially targeted remedial form.

The economic climate in the late 1940s and the emergence of the civil rights movement are only two instances in which unanticipated events helped to shape the development of employment policy. Other contingent factors that shaped employment policy can also be identified. President Kennedy's assassination helped break the legislative logjam that had limited the domestic initiatives of his own administration. The escalation of the Vietnam War limited possibilities for reorganizing the employment programs of the War on Poverty by decreasing the funds available for domestic purposes. The sudden jump in unemployment—sparked by OPEC price increases in oil— after CETA was enacted led the training aspects of the legislation to be ignored in favor of public service employment.

Each of these instances of contingency affected employment policy in a variety of ways. They contributed to changing the definition of the problem to be solved, expanding or narrowing the scope of the policy, shaping the institutional framework that would administer policy, or recasting the terms of political debate that surrounded policies. In and of themselves, such contingencies did not determine the direction that policy took, but in each case they made possible routes that would have been less likely in their absence.

The process of bounding works to restrict possibilities: over time, sequences of policy development narrow the range of alternative policies. Central to this narrowing process is the creation of institutions.[3] Institutions exercise an enduring effect on what is possible later, not so much by preventing change (although they occasionally do that) as by sending change off in particular directions. There are several ways in which institutions leave their imprint on future possibilities. First, the existence of institutions affects what is possible later by channeling action: institutions encourage research along specific lines and orient political mobilization in some directions rather than others. Second, existing institutions affect the operation of new institutions. Supporters of rapid change will often seek to create new institutions rather than to reform older ones. But because new institutions must compete with or operate in the interstices of already existing ones, their character, too, is stamped by the past. Finally, the failure to create policies and the absence of institutions also exerts an influence into the future. If government institutions do not exist, groups may reach private arrangements that later make public intervention harder, or they may seek to address their problems in a different arena of public action, redefining the problem in the process.

Each of these ways in which sequences of policy and institutional creation bounded later policymaking is evident in the development of employment policy. Perhaps the most important institution affecting the early development of employment policy in the United States was the Council of Economic Advisers. Once created, the CEA played a critical role in keeping macroeconomic perspectives on employment at the center of policy considerations. The CEA's conception of the problem that policy should address—unemployment due to insufficient macroeconomic stimulation and lack of job readiness among the poor—dominated thinking about poverty and unemployment throughout the 1960s, even as evidence of a broader problem of "subemployment" began to emerge.

Existing institutions also blocked some types of action, limiting possible linkages and narrowing the scope of policy. One key example was the connection between public education and labor market policy. The prior establishment of a state-level system of vocational education, poorly linked to the labor market, frustrated efforts to make vocational education part of a revitalized employment policy in the 1960s. The power of vocational administrators to safeguard their own domain and the extensive reforms needed to make vocational education part of a more coherent employment policy dissuaded manpower policy experts from putting much effort into schools after their initial attempts failed. Decisions in the early 1900s to keep public schools separate from the labor market thus affected the development of manpower policy in the 1960s and, indeed, have created problems for employment policy and for public education that continue into the present.[4]

Established arrangements affected later possibilities as well by shaping the kinds of demands that particular groups made and influencing where they directed those demands. A striking feature in the development of American labor market policy was the scant interest that organized labor expressed in enhancing the training capacities of the American government. Although organized labor supported Democratic proposals for training, it never viewed these programs as essential to its own well-being. Labor had alternative arrangements that governed promotion and pay: the seniority system secured by collective bargaining. Such training as existed was an internal function of the firm. So long as these arrangements benefited labor, unions had little incentive to look for alternatives.

But, even when these arrangements came under attack in the 1970s, labor's impulse was not to seek untested alternatives but rather to throw its energies into defending existing arrangements. Groups, such as organized labor, whose whole existence has been oriented around the operation of particular institutions do not easily shift their orientations, especially when alternatives are not already in place.

The perceived failure of institutions led groups to reevaluate their strategies and to recast the terms in which they framed problems. The limited focus of the War on Poverty and its eventual demise encouraged black leaders to rely on legal regulations—the affirmative action approach—as the centerpiece of their employment strategy. Although black organizations vigorously supported broader approaches to employment when they reached the agenda, after the War on Poverty, they focused on the legal realm, where black employment problems, cast as questions of rights, stood a better chance of being addressed.

The interplay of contingency and bounding in employment policy highlights the importance of discerning the links between formally different realms of politics and policy. Changes in policy can be driven by political forces whose focus was originally quite different; institutional arrangements in different domains can limit the development of policy by narrowing its scope and directing energy in alternative directions. The first step in changing policy lies in recognizing the often invisible linkages that block or redirect the impetus for reform.

Connecting Ideas and Politics

We can get a better picture of how the broad constraints that develop over time actually operate to affect particular decisions by examining the interplay of ideas and politics. Explanations of policy or political change have long contended over the relative influence of ideas and political power as the determinants of policy. This study suggests that this problem is most fruitfully addressed by asking how ideas and politics fit together and by discerning how and why that fit changes over time. Ideas can help transform politics and open new policy possibilities, as they did in the 1930s. But their ability to influence policy depends on political and administrative institutions that organize interests and political competition along favorable lines.[5]

There are two distinct ways in which the term "ideas" is used in accounts of policymaking. The first meaning is captured by the concept of a public philosophy.[6] The ideas that constitute a public philosophy express broad concepts that are tied to values and moral principles and that can be represented in political debate in symbols and rhetoric. A second usage of "ideas" refers to a more programmatic set of statements about cause and effect relationships and a method for influencing those relationships. The language expressing programmatic ideas is the technical or professional terminology of the expert.[7]

Although these two types of ideas shade over into each other, and on occasion interlock, it is useful to differentiate them because their influence on policy and politics is distinct. Public philosophies play a central role in organizing politics, but their capacity to direct policy is limited; without ties to programmatic ideas, their influence is difficult to sustain. Likewise, programmatic ideas are most influential when they are linked with a public philosophy; but these ideas must also forge links with administration. Programmatic ideas developed without reference to administration may be technically strong but are likely to be politically impotent. The influence of ideas on politics is strongest when programmatic ideas, tied to administrative means, are joined with a public philosophy; unhinged, the influence of each becomes difficult to sustain.

In American employment policy, much of the period from the 1940s to 1980 was characterized by a dissociation of programmatic ideas and public philosophy. The social Keynesianism championed by Alvin Hansen had joined a set of programmatic, administratively rooted ideas with a broader vision about politics, most fully articulated by Roosevelt's 1944 Economic Bill of Rights. After the failure of this vision, ideas as public philosophy became increasingly disjointed from the technical policy ideas, and the technical ideas grew more divorced from administration. The growing distance of these two types of ideas and their separation from administration impoverished both.

Because programmatic ideas increasingly developed without political or administrative moorings, it became difficult for them to influence policy in any regular way. Although the expression of these ideas grew ever more sophisticated, and American social scientists commanded data banks that made their European counterparts envious, their ability to chart new policy directions involving government action was narrowing. Research relevant to employment policy emphasized the movement of aggregate measures and micro-economic models, leaving untouched a middle ground concerned with sectors and institutions that the government was grappling to address.[8] In the absence of sufficient applicable research, purely po-litical criteria held sway. This was particularly evident in the 1970s, in the federal responses to growing unemployment and inflation, ranging from wage-price guidelines to pork barrel–style public serv-ice employment.

Not only did they fail to open new paths, but technical ideas often wound up undermining the effort to improve government action. In labor market policy, for example, the growth of evaluation research did little to improve policy. The tools of evaluation research were first applied by liberal researchers hoping to forge the best new poli-cies to attack poverty. Initially unrecognized was what Henry Aaron has called the "profoundly conservative tendency" of such analyses.[9] Limitations in the available data and the failure of models to capture the interrelations among programs meant that research and evalua-tion studies were likely to "detect the failures but [would] have no way to indicate the hypothetical potential success."[10]

The fragmented context of American policymaking exacerbated these tendencies: research and evaluation typically proceeded along narrow, program-based lines that offered little perspective on the connections among different policies.[11] The negative assessments of programs that often emerged from these studies provided ammuni-tion in the ongoing political struggles over these programs. Results of individual program evaluations did not automatically protect or destroy programs, but the prevalence of negative evaluations helped to bolster broad political arguments against government in-tervention.

The dissociation of the two kinds of ideas also impoverished pub-lic philosophy. During the 1960s and 1970s, rhetorical appeals grew in importance, but they were increasingly unanchored in program-matic content. The War on Poverty, for example, was declared with little effort to assemble support based on a rationale for the specific policies to be undertaken. As Jeffrey Tulis has put it, "[T]he president offered a metaphor, whose premise provided the answers."[12] The difficulty in matching politics and programmatic ideas lay behind the exhaustion of New Deal liberalism and the crisis in public philos-ophy that characterized the 1970s.[13] Yet, as party ties became attenu-ated, rhetoric and symbols bore more of the burden of organizing electoral politics.

Much of Ronald Reagan's early political success can be attributed to the way he fused a bold and appealing rhetoric to a set of programmatic ideas about how the economy worked. Although widely rejected by economists, supply-side economics resonated with the growing disillusion with government action among mainstream economists. Most important, however, supply-side economics appeared plausible, in part, because it was clearly "doable" within the context of American politics and institutions. But the merging of programmatic ideas and public philosophy was more apparent than real in most policy areas during the Reagan administration. As the decade progressed, the disjuncture between rhetoric and government action on the economy grew. While the rhetoric remained firmly promarket, policy was actually a disjointed blend of initiatives.[14] In this sense, the Reagan administration did not so much resolve as elide the problems of uniting philosophy with programmatic ideas about the economy.

Ideas and the Problem of Positive Government in the United States

The experience of employment policy suggests that the development, access, and plausibility of ideas calling for new kinds of government capacities are handicapped by the difficulty of uniting politics, ideas, and administration in the United States. The problems that this would cause were recognized by some supporters of a broad, more encompassing employment policy immediately after the war. The political scientist E. E. Schattschneider argued that a national employment policy would be impossible without "responsible" programmatic parties. He urged that parties establish permanent research organizations that could fuse policy and politics in what he called "political planning." Stressing the inherently political nature of devising and mobilizing policy ideas, he warned that "parties simply cannot afford to rely on non-party research and publicity to do the job."[15]

Yet that is just what presidents and parties had to do in the United States. This meant that connections among politics, administration, and policy were forged in piecemeal and sporadic ways, when cooperation among technical experts, particular interests, and government agencies could be effected or when the president threw the weight of his office behind policy innovation. In some policy areas, including Social Security, these conditions were unproblematic; in others, such as medical care, they permitted only partial success.[16]

In employment policy, by contrast, the most important private interests, business and labor, had little incentive to extend policy; the dominant experts paid little attention to administrative issues; and the relevant government agencies were either hostile or weak. Moreover, the president did not have much incentive to back employment policy innovation as long as America remained economically strong and Keynesian policy appeared sufficient to manage unemployment. In this context, the scope of employment policy remained limited, and proposals for extending it continued to be contested. Nothing in the political, intellectual, or administrative history of employment policy provided a foothold for extending or revitalizing the government's role during the 1970s, when it became clear that the older approach had broken down.

Where the difficulties of uniting politics, administration, and ideas are less severe, policies may be enacted more easily. The successes of deregulation and tax reform in the 1980s provide a telling counterexample to employment policy: in neither of these cases did ideas about reform have to contend with arguments about administrative feasibility or with opposition to building new government capacities.[17] In this context, technical ideas were able to influence policy more easily and could benefit from their attachment to an appealing rhetoric.

Supporters of proposals that create new forms of government activity face a more difficult task. Although they might also fashion an appealing rhetoric and find political support for such concepts as fairness or opportunity, their rhetorical claims remain unconvincing and their support ephemeral if government's capacity to act is widely doubted. When there is a history of administrative failure, as in the case of employment policy, the rhetoric becomes even less likely to influence policy.

Political Possibilities and Employment Policy

By the 1980s, transformations in the international economy, the organization of work, and the composition of the labor force all had helped to undercut existing approaches to employment policy in the United States.[18] The pattern of innovation and failure that characterized the postwar era ended as unemployment lost much of its force as a political issue. But these developments in the international political economy have also created possibilities for launching a new policy sequence in which employment policy embraces a broader scope, allowing it to appeal to a wider range of interests and putting it on a firm administrative footing. By examining the emerging features of the American response, we can assess the influence of past employment policies on the current approaches to economic change, and we can consider what is at stake in the way government responds to broad economic changes.

Employment Policy and American Citizenship

As they grope for responses to the pressures of international economic competition, national policymakers are not only rethinking policy strategies; they are also implicitly reevaluating the conceptions of citizenship underlying policy since World War II. This process has focused attention on two questions that have important implications for how the boundaries are drawn between public and private life. The first asks whether problems lie in the operation of the economy or in individuals. The second asks what the government's responsibility is in the domain of employment. How a nation answers these questions reveals much about its guiding conceptions of citizenship.

For most of the postwar period, the response to these questions remained ambiguous in the United States. In contrast to the full-employment welfare states in Europe, American policy avoided promises to ensure employment, and it established only a limited scope for identifying problems in the economy. But both Republican and Democratic policymakers accepted responsibility for minimizing unemployment, and politicians worried about the political consequences of joblessness. Neither party sought to extend policy to issues of underemployment, low wages, or the organization of work, but both supported different programs designed to enhance job readiness. Definitions of what was a structural economic problem and what was an individual problem tended to place the balance of responsibility on the individual; economic problems were construed as limited to cyclical fluctuations. Nonetheless, the range of training and public service employment programs enacted during the period also indicated acceptance of some measure of public responsibility to help the individual adjust to economic fluctuations. This rather equivocal formulation was politically viable as long as the favorable international position of the American economy ensured prosperity. Guarantees of "social citizenship" were not necessary in a land that could credibly claim to deliver on a promise of equal opportunity.

The decline of the United States as the preeminent world eco-

nomic power forced these fundamental issues to the surface of national policy debates during the 1970s and 1980s. Out of those
debates emerged a new, more sharply drawn formulation of the division between public and private responsibilities regarding employment. The dominant thrust of policy now assigned the central problems and responsibilities of employment to the private individual
and advocated a sharply limited role for government. Government's
task of ensuring equal opportunity was supplanted by an emphasis
on enforcing citizens' obligations to work.[19] These changes in the
assumptions underlying policy were bolstered by new explanations
for unemployment; government's limited role was a conspicuous
premise of theories about "the American underclass" and policy debates over workfare.

The resurgence of neoclassical assumptions about unemployment among economists provided a rationale and language for the
new politics of employment policy in the 1980s.[20] In these formulations, unemployment is not a problem that policy can actively address. It is either the short-term product of misinformation about
the market, a voluntary choice of individuals who prefer leisure to
work, or an extended search by individuals looking for jobs. This
perspective is reinforced by the concept of a natural rate of unemployment; government policy will only create new economic
problems, such as inflation, if it tries to tamper with the natural
rate.

These economic ideas were complemented by new ways of thinking about the problems of the black poor. Disproportionately high
rates of unemployment and subemployment among African-Americans are particularly troubling in the United States because they
raise questions about equal rights, where the government's mandate
to act is clear. During the 1980s, the concept of the underclass
helped to recast the problem of black poverty as a behavioral issue
that called for special attention to the work habits of the black poor.
Although some of the most prominent explanations for the existence
of the underclass emphasize the structural economic roots of persistent poverty found disproportionately among minorities, the pre-
dominant political use of the concept has focused on the behavioral
problems of the poor.[21]

Such perspectives on unemployment and poverty were often
voiced in policy debates during the 1980s; they were an essential
component of the workfare programs adopted in many states during
the decade.[22] These programs embodied two (often contending) definitions of the central problem: one view maintained that welfare
recipients did not work because they lacked sufficient motivation;

the other saw the problem as one of inadequate preparation and support for work. The logic of the first commanded coercion and punitive sanctions for those who did not work; the second called for a range of enrichment and supportive services to increase job readiness. State-level workfare programs represented a blend of these two approaches, although the balance varied from state to state.

These state-level experiments culminated in the Family Support Act of 1988, which offered both coercion and supportive services to bring welfare recipients into the labor force.[23] Without substantial funding, however, the act's balance shifts decisively toward the punitive and coercive. Thus, in practice, low levels of funding have ensured that views about insufficient work motivation of the poor have guided policy to a far greater extent than have the views arguing for increased supportive services.

These debates about work and welfare have largely ignored the history of employment policy in the United States. They present a highly selective reading of past policy and a narrowly drawn picture of contemporary problems. By placing the onus of responsibility on the individual, workfare ignores the policy failures of the past that left black communities with destructively high rates of unemployment, particularly during the 1970s.[24] Moreover, debates about workfare and obligation divert attention from the most important questions about work and citizenship currently facing American policymakers.

Changes in the American economy and society have altered the relationship between work and economic well-being. While the most dire predictions about a nation of low-wage service workers are overdrawn, it is clear that sharper divisions now separate different levels of the labor market. Most striking has been the decline in the wages of men in the lower reaches of the labor market, which work-welfare programs do nothing to address.[25] Compounding these labor market shifts are economic and cultural changes that have increasingly left women responsible for supporting families.[26] Work-welfare programs have addressed this problem more directly, with child support programs and increased support for child care, but these initiatives are poorly funded and affect only a tiny segment of the population. For the most part, the problems of combining work and family are a private responsibility, falling heavily on the shoulders of individual women.

Uncushioned by government action, economic adjustments may have profound social consequences. The deep recessions of the mid-1970s and early 1980s ravaged many communities, and in particular minority neighborhoods, which continued to suffer even after prosperity had returned for much of the nation.[27] For those with few resources, social disorganization ensued as the routines and resources of worklife disappeared. As a consequence, these communities have been further battered by the growth of the underground economy, accompanied by skyrocketing homicide rates and increases in crime.[28] In the absence of public action, the problems in these communities did not solve themselves; they multiplied instead.

Changes in the structure of the labor market limit or expand opportunity as they pull workers into or out of the labor force. But because workers, in addition to being factors of production, are members of communities and participants in social networks, these changes have profound effects on the nature of society. In the United States, over the past ten years, policy has largely ignored these concerns; instead, the burden of economic adjustment has been borne by private individuals, often those with the fewest resources.

Creating Possibilities

What are the possibilities that American policymakers and politicians could construct an alternative approach to employment issues as they search for ways to respond to transformations in the international economic system? I conclude by considering how new policy sequences may be launched and by sketching the features of an employment policy that combines ideas, politics, and administration in politically sustainable forms.

The start of a new policy sequence is most visible when there is a "big bang" of innovation. Yet the "big bang" analogy is somewhat misleading. It underestimates changes that have already prepared the way for such shifts in policy, and it overstates the degree to which policy is transformed afterwards. In fact, small changes transform policy, even in a political system in which policy shifts seem to occur all at once. Small changes not only prepare the ground for major shifts but may also chart the direction of those transformations by providing working examples of new policy and creating new conceptions about what is possible and desirable.

During the past decade, alterations to the economic and social environment have created the potential for making small changes in employment policy that could point the way toward a fundamental reorientation in scope and mission. Support for such revitalized employment policies could be won by linking these policies with problems that have attracted broad public attention, including concern about American competitiveness, dissatisfaction with public education, and the worries about a growing "underclass."[29]

The concern among business leaders about the quality of the American labor force and its impact on American competitiveness creates possibilities for building support for a broader, more encompassing labor market policy.[30] But to attract employer interest, employment policy would have to build much stronger ties to the private sector, attending more closely to the needs of the private economy. This does not mean, however, that policy need blindly follow the dictates of business; government could influence business goals relevant to employment policy by creating incentives to adopt some strategies rather than others. The availability of highly skilled workers, for example, may prompt movement away from a competitive strategy based on low-wage labor.

Widespread dissatisfaction with American public education provides another potential opening for expanding employment policy.[31] The problem of school dropouts, the growth of youth unemployment, and the difficulty of making the transition from school to work all suggest the need for rethinking the institutional links between school and the labor market. Apprenticeship programs, which have attracted increasing attention, are only one of the ways in which public schools could contribute to an enhanced labor market policy. As preeminent community institutions, schools could also serve as centers of information about the labor market and programs of adult education.[32]

Finally, concern about the emergence of an American underclass has drawn attention to the links between economic change and community stability. The economic dislocations of the 1980s have highlighted the importance of local institutions in cushioning the effects of economic transitions.[33] This experience suggests the need for "bottom-up" community-organizing strategies as an essential component of employment policy. Local organizations, including community development corporations, churches, and schools, can all be enlisted in increasing the effectiveness and extending the reach of labor market policies.

In the context of a set of broader employment policies, such mobilization could avoid being limited by the institutional isolation that characterized organizing during the War on Poverty. A community-organizing strategy builds on distinctive strengths and weaknesses of American federalism, which lacks a strong central bureaucracy but features a strong tradition of local activism. The growth of state-level administrative capacities during the 1980s, together with the community-based organizations created during the 1960s, may prove helpful in sustaining such local activism.[34]

These potential impulses for revitalizing employment policy suggest an approach different from the one that dominated policy in the past. They indicate the need for building stronger ties between public and private action, creating a broader scope for policy, and devoting greater attention to the institutional links that join policy areas. The resulting policy would contribute to reconciling the social and economic objectives of employment policy and would provide ways of addressing the needs of minorities without explicit targeting.

Reliance on macropolicy would be replaced by greater attention to the specific relationships and institutions that undergird the economy. Learning how and where the government might affect those relationships in order to influence the quantity and quality of employment is thus central to redesigning policy. Labor market policy would be expanded to serve different levels of the labor market, thereby losing its remedial character. The task of labor market policy would be more than simply addressing unemployment, its primary charge in the past. Problems of relieving bottlenecks, upgrading skills, and enhancing geographic mobility would all fall into the domain of labor market policy.[35]

This conception of employment policy calls on government to play a different role than it has in the past. It emphasizes the need for government to act as a catalyst for private activity rather than simply as a regulator or director of a separate public realm.[36] This approach channels market trends toward public goals, rather than compensating for the market, as in the 1960s and 1970s, or capitulating to it, as in the 1980s. Increasing this type of intervention would actually strengthen the political appeal of regulatory and public sector approaches, such as affirmative action and public employment programs; a more balanced blend of approaches would both reduce the pressure on such policies to carry the burden alone and help mitigate their status as political flashpoints. In this way, employment policy that incorporated a variety of approaches could enhance the political acceptability of policies contested during the 1960s and 1970s by changing the context within which they are evaluated.

These are some of the most promising possibilities for assembling new packages of policy. By remaking institutional links and bringing interests together in different ways, they provide the raw material for launching a new employment policy sequence. Implicit in this scenario is the notion that change is possible; institutional structures constrain, but they do not bind in the same way at all times and are themselves subject to change.

Accordingly, we have choices to make about employment policy. At root, these are decisions about the kind of society we will have, not because employment policy can remedy all social ills, but because it is the cornerstone of any public strategy to ensure economic security. Without it, there is little foundation for a national community based on individual dignity and mutual respect.

Notes

Preface

1. E. E. Schattschneider, "Party Government and Employment Policy," *American Political Science Review* 39 (December 1945): 1148.

Chapter One

1. On economic policy during the Reagan years, see Isabel Sawhill, "Reaganomics in Retrospect," in *Perspectives on the Reagan Years*, edited by John L. Palmer (Washington, D.C.: Urban Institute Press, 1986), 91–120.

2. For an overview of the work ethic in America, see Daniel T. Rodgers, *The Work Ethic in Industrial America, 1850–1920* (Chicago: The University of Chicago Press, 1974).

3. See Robert Y. Shapiro, Kelly D. Patterson, Judith Russell, and John T. Young, "The Polls-A Report: Employment and Social Welfare," *Public Opinion Quarterly* 51 (Summer 1987): 268–81; the survey data reported in James R. Kluegel and Eliot R. Smith, *Beliefs about Inequality: Americans' Views of What Is and What Ought to Be* (New York: Aldine De Gruyter, 1986), 153–55; and the discussion in Jennifer Hochschild, *What's Fair? American Beliefs about Distributive Justice* (Cambridge: Harvard University Press, 1981), 183–84.

4. They go on to note, "Given the levels of support for providing jobs—even in the abstract—it is in some ways surprising that this preference has had such little impact on public policy since 1960." See Robert Y. Shapiro and Kelly D. Patterson, "The Dynamics of Public Opinion toward Social Welfare Policy" (paper prepared for delivery at the 1986 Annual Meeting of the American Political Science Association, August 28–31, Washington, D.C.), 33–34.

5. See Karl Polanyi, *The Great Transformation* (Boston: Beacon Press, 1944), for a view of markets as social constructs.

6. For analyses of recent changes in the relationship between family and work, see Sylvia Ann Hewlett, Alice S. Ilchman, and John J. Sweeney, *Family and Work: Bridging the Gap* (Cambridge, Mass.: Ballinger, 1986); and Naomi Gerstel and Harriet Engel Gross, eds., *Families and Work* (Philadelphia: Temple University Press, 1987). For a consideration of some of these issues in a historical context see Joan Wallach Scott, "Work Identities for Men and Women," in *Gender and the Politics of History*, edited by Joan W. Scott (New York: Columbia University Press, 1988), 93–112.

7. For a survey of some of the ways that social and economic policy has affected families, see the essays in Irene Diamond, ed., *Families, Politics and Public Policies: A Feminist Dialogue on Women and the State* (New York: Longman, 1983).

8. For a discussion of the boundaries of American policy in this era, see Ira Katznelson, "Rethinking the Silences of Social and Economic Policy," *Political Science Quarterly* 101 no. 2 (1986): 307–25.

9. For a survey of measures aimed at combating unemployment in Europe, see the essays in Jeremy Richardson and Roger Henning, eds., *Unemployment: Policy Responses of Western Democracies*, Sage Modern Politics Series vol. 8 (London: Sage Publications, 1984); for a review of labor market policies in the United States and Europe, see Margaret Gordon, *Social Security Policies in Industrial Countries: A Comparative Analysis* (Cambridge: Cambridge University Press, 1988), ch. 12; on macroeconomic policy and planning in France and Britain, see Peter A. Hall, *Governing the Economy: The Politics of State Intervention in Britain and France* (New York: Oxford University Press, 1986).

10. See Herbert Stein, *The Fiscal Revolution in America* (Chicago and London: The University of Chicago Press, 1969), ch. 7. On "proto-Keynesian" ideas in the United States, see Walter Salant, "The Spread of Keynesian Doctrines and Practices in the United States," *The Political Power of Economic Ideas: Keynesianism across Nations*, edited by Peter A. Hall (Princeton, N.J.: Princeton University Press, 1989), ch. 2; and Bradford A. Lee, "The Miscarriage of Necessity and Invention: Proto-Keynesianism and Democratic States in the 1930s," ibid., ch. 6.

11. Quoted in Ester Fano, "A 'Wastage of Men': Technological Progress and Unemployment in the United States," *Technology and Culture* 32 no. 2 Pt. 1 (1991): 288.

12. See, for example, Alvin Hansen, "Social Planning for Tomorrow," in *The United States after the War*, edited by Alvin Hansen, F. F. Hill, Louis Hollander, Walter D. Fuller, Herbert W. Briggs, and George O. Stoddard (Ithaca, N.Y.: Cornell University Press, 1945), 3–34. On the defeat of the Full Employment bill and the crafting of its replacement, the Employment Act of 1946, see the classic account in Stephen Kemp Bailey, *Congress Makes a Law* (New York: Vintage, 1950); see also Robert M. Collins, *The Business Response to Keynes, 1929–1964* (New York: Columbia University Press, 1981), esp. ch. 4.

13. Collins, *The Business Response to Keynes*, ch. 7; see also Herbert Stein, *The Fiscal Revolution in America*, chs. 15–17.

14. A notable case is the 1968 surtax, which economists, following Keynesian logic, had urged be enacted as early as 1966. See Lawrence C. Pierce, *The Politics of Fiscal Policy Formation* (Pacific Palisades, Calif.: Goodyear Publishing, 1971); and Ronald F. King, "The President and Fiscal Policy in 1966: The Year Taxes Were Not Raised," *Polity* 17 (Summer 1985): 685–714.

15. Many observers have argued that the Reagan administration ultimately fell back on modified Keynesian economics after the initial splash of supply-side rhetoric. See Alan S. Blinder, *Hard Heads, Soft Hearts: Tough-Minded Economics for a Just Society* (Reading, Mass.: Addison-Wesley, 1987), 105–8; and Benjamin M. Friedman, *Day of Reckoning: The Consequences of American Economic Policy under Reagan and After* (New York: Random

House, 1988). Some have argued that Reagan invented a new style of "conservative Keynesianism." See, for example, Robert Kuttner, "Reagan Redefines Keynesianism," *Boston Globe*, January 9, 1989.

16. On the problems with the WPA and the way they affected later discussions of policy, see James T. Patterson, *America's Struggle against Poverty, 1900–1980* (Cambridge: Harvard University Press, 1981), 64–67, 186–87.

17. There is a large literature on labor market policies. Good overviews include Janet Wegner Johnston, "An Overview of U.S. Federal Employment and Training Programs," in Richardson and Henning, *Unemployment*, 57–115; Ewan Clague and Leo Kramer, *Manpower Policies and Programs: A Review, 1935–75* (Kalamazoo, Mich.: W. E. Upjohn Institute for Employment Research, 1976); Donald C. Baumer and Carl E. Van Horn, *The Politics of Unemployment* (Washington, D.C.: Congressional Quarterly Press, 1985).

18. Baumer and Van Horn, *The Politics of Unemployment*, 157–62.

19. See Dean L. May, *From New Deal to New Economics: The American Liberal Response to the Recession of 1937* (New York and London: Garland Publishing, 1981), ch. 4. The first National Recovery Administration head, Hugh Johnson, and Roosevelt brain truster Rexford Guy Tugwell were among the few who viewed the earliest public works programs as means of stimulating the economy through "pump priming," as it was called at the time. Arthur M. Schlesinger, Jr., *The Coming of the New Deal* (Boston: Houghton Mifflin, 1958), ch. 17.

20. Sweden has the most comprehensive labor market policies among Western nations; Germany also has an extensive labor market policy. For a summary, see Gordon, *Social Security Policies in Industrial Countries*, ch. 12. On Sweden, see Gosta Rehn, "Swedish Active Labor Market Policy: Retrospect and Prospect," *Industrial Relations* 24 (Winter 1985): 62–89. On developments in West German labor market policy during the 1970s and 1980s see Douglas Webber and Gabriele Nass "Employment Policy in West Germany," in Richardson and Henning, *Unemployment*, ch. 8. For an illuminating discussion of labor market policies in both countries, see Paul Osterman, *Employment Futures: Reorganization, Dislocation and Public Policy* (New York: Oxford University Press, 1988), ch. 6.

21. For a critique of American labor market policies that notes these features, see E. Wight Bakke, *The Mission of Manpower Policy* (Kalamazoo, Mich.: W. E. Upjohn Institute for Employment Research, 1969).

22. On planning in the United States prior to the 1970s, see Otis L. Graham, Jr., *Toward a Planned Society* (New York: Oxford University Press, 1976). On the Humphrey-Hawkins Act see Helen Ginsburg, *Full Employment and Public Policy: The United States and Sweden* (Lexington, Mass.: D. C. Heath, 1983), ch. 3; and James W. Singer, "Humphrey-Hawkins Hangs On," *National Journal* 9 (May 7, 1977): 724.

23. On the Chrysler bailout, see Robert B. Reich and John D. Donahue, *New Deals: The Chrysler Revival and the American System* (New York: Times Books, 1985).

24. This viewpoint had its most influential proponent in Ford's secretary

of labor, John T. Dunlop. See John T. Dunlop, "Inflation and Incomes Policies: The Political Economy of Recent U.S. Experience," *Public Policy* 23 (Spring 1975): 135–66.

25. Housing policy exhibits a similar pattern of innovation and abandonment of policy. See Bruce Headey, *Housing Policy in the Developed Economy* (New York: St. Martin's Press, 1978).

26. See Anthony King, "Ideas, Institutions and the Policies of Governments: A Comparative Analysis: Part III," *British Journal of Political Science* 3 (October 1973): 409–23; Lawrence J. R. Herson, *The Politics of Ideas: Political Theory and American Public Policy* (Homewood, Ill.: Dorsey Press, 1984).

27. On antistatism and individualism in American political culture, see Louis Hartz, *The Liberal Tradition in America* (New York: Harcourt, Brace and World, 1955); on the effects of such ideas on policy, see King, "Ideas, Institutions and the Policies of Governments," 419. On the work ethic, see Rodgers, *Work Ethic;* and David H. Freedman, "The Contemporary Work Ethic," in *Employment Outlook and Insights*, edited by David H. Freedman (Geneva: International Labour Office, 1979), 119–35. For a view that the work ethic was not widespread among workingmen in the nineteenth century and needed to be inculcated by industrialists, see Herbert Gutman, *Work, Culture and Society in Industrializing America* (New York: Vintage Books, 1966), chs. 1–2.

28. On variations in public support for various kinds of work programs over time, see Shapiro et al., "Polls-A Report," 268–81.

29. For an argument that highlights the impact of public opinion on policy but notes problems as well, see Benjamin I. Page and Robert Y. Shapiro, "Effects of Public Opinion on Policy," *American Political Science Review* 77 (March 1983): 175–90; see also Alan D. Monroe, "Consistency between Public Preferences and National Policy Decisions," *American Politics Quarterly* 7 (January 1979): 3–19. For a view more skeptical of the influence of public opinion, see Paul Burstein, "The Sociology of Democratic Politics and Government," *Annual Review of Sociology* 7 (1981): 291–319.

30. See, for example, Herbert McCloskey and John Zaller, *The American Ethos: Public Attitudes toward Capitalism and Democracy* (Cambridge: Harvard University Press, 1984), 272; King, "Ideas, Institutions and the Policies of Governments," 423.

31. McCloskey and Zaller, *The American Ethos*, 289.

32. See Robert B. Reich Introduction to *The Power of Public Ideas*, edited by Robert B. Reich (Cambridge, Mass.: Ballinger, 1988), 5.

33. Andrew Shonfield's *Modern Capitalism: The Changing Balance of Public and Private Power* (New York: Oxford University Press, 1965) is a model for this approach. Shonfield argues that cultural differences are at the heart of cross-national differences in economic policy, but he roots his analysis in institutional factors.

34. This view of culture is elaborated in Ann Swidler, "Culture in Action: Symbols and Strategies," *American Sociological Review* 51 (April 1986): 273–86.

35. Michael Kalecki, "Political Aspects of Full Employment," *Political Quarterly* 14 (October-December 1943): 322–31.

36. For a review of this approach, see Michael Shalev, "The Social Democratic Model and Beyond: Two Generations of Comparative Research on the Welfare State," *Comparative Social Research* 6 (1983): 87–148; for a pathbreaking analysis of the United States that drew on this perspective, see Andrew Martin, "The Politics of Economic Policy in the United States: A Tentative View from a Comparative Perspective," Sage Professional Paper in Comparative Politics no. 01–040 (Beverly Hills and London: Sage, 1973).

37. For an analysis discussing variation in business attitudes in the United States, see Alan Barton, "Determinants of Economic Attitudes in the American Business Elite," *American Journal of Sociology* 91 (July 1985): 54–87.

38. Peter Gourevitch, *Politics in Hard Times: Comparative Responses to International Economic Crises* (Ithaca and London: Cornell University Press, 1986); Thomas Ferguson, "From Normalcy to New Deal: Industrial Structure, Party Competition, and American Public Policy in the New Deal," *International Organization* 38 (Winter 1984): 41–93.

39. Recent works that have begun to tackle these questions include the essays in Hall, *The Political Power of Economic Ideas*, particularly the concluding chapter by Peter A. Hall; Paul Quirk, "In Defense of the Politics of Ideas," *Journal of Politics* 50 (February 1988): 31–41; Martha Derthick and Paul J. Quirk, *The Politics of Deregulation* (Washington, D.C.: Brookings Institution, 1985), especially ch. 7; and Reich, *The Power of Public Ideas*. Students of international relations have been particularly interested in the role of ideas. See John S. Odell, *U.S. International Monetary Policy: Markets, Power, and Ideas as Sources of Change* (Princeton, N.J.: Princeton University Press, 1982); and Judith Goldstein, "The Impact of Ideas on Trade Policy: The Origins of U.S. Agricultural and Manufacturing Policies," *International Organization* 43 (Winter 1989): 31–71.

40. See the discussion by Carl Kaysen, "Model Makers and Decision-Makers: Economists and the Policy Process," *Public Interest*, no. 12 (Summer 1968): 80–95. In fact, economists associated with business organizations have on important occasions differed with their membership or constituencies on matters of economic policy. See Collins, *The Business Response to Keynes*, on the role of the Committee for Economic Development; and Kim McQuaid, *Big Business and Presidential Power* (New York: Morrow, 1982), 354 n. 38, for the differences between Business Council economists and business leaders over the 1968 surtax.

41. Peter Gourevitch's analysis of support coalitions in *Politics in Hard Times* acknowledges the importance of such mediating institutions, while affirming the centrality of social interests. Contrast his analysis with that of Thomas Ferguson, "From Normalcy to New Deal." Ferguson presents a sophisticated rationale for the emergence of different sectoral interests but devotes little attention to how these interests get translated into policy.

42. Thomas Ferguson and Joel Rogers, *Right Turn: The Decline of the*

Democrats and the Future of American Politics (New York: Hill and Wang, 1986), come perilously close to presenting such a view of politics. See the more complex and institutionally sensitive analysis of America's "right turn" in Thomas Byrne Edsall, *The New Politics of Inequality* (New York: Norton, 1984).

43. John Kingdon, *Agendas, Alternatives, and Public Policies* (Boston: Little Brown, 1984). See the discussion about the streams on pp. 20 and 92–94 and the discussion about "first principles" on 200–201.

44. Christopher Leman, *The Collapse of Welfare Reform: Political Institutions, Policy, and the Poor in Canada and the United States* (Cambridge: MIT Press, 1980), 23.

45. Kingdon, *Agendas, Alternatives, and Public Policies*, ch. 4; on the garbage can model, see Michael Cohen, James March, and Johan Olsen, "A Garbage Can Model of Organizational Choice," *Administrative Science Quarterly* 17 (March 1972): 1–25.

46. On analogical reasoning in decisionmaking, see Ernest R. May, *"Lessons" of the Past: The Use and Misuse of History in American Foreign Policymaking* (New York: Oxford University Press, 1973); Richard E. Neustadt and Ernest R. May, *Thinking in Time: The Uses of History for Decision Makers* (New York: Free Press, 1986); Yuen Foong Khong, *Analogical Decision-Making and Foreign Policy: Explaining America's Vietnam Options* (Princeton, N.J.: Princeton University Press, forthcoming).

47. On the notion of sequences, see Sidney Verba, "Sequences and Development," in *Crises and Sequences in Political Development*, edited by Leonard Binder et al. (Princeton, N.J.: Princeton University Press, 1971), 283–316. For a discussion of policy sequences applied to the case of housing, see Headey, *Housing Policy in the Developed Economy*.

48. See the discussion in Stephen D. Krasner, "Approaches to the State: Alternative Conceptions and Historical Dynamics," *Comparative Politics* 16 (January 1984): 223–46; Stephen D. Krasner, "Sovereignty: An Institutionalist Perspective," in *The Elusive State: International and Comparative Perspectives*, edited by James Caporaso (Beverly Hills and London: Sage Publications, 1989), 69–96; Edward G. Carmines and James A. Stimson, *Issue Evolution: Race and the Transformation of American Politics* (Princeton N.J.: Princeton University Press, 1989). On path dependence, see Paul A. David, "Clio and the Economics of QWERTY," *American Economic Review* 75 (May 1985): 332–37; and Douglass C. North, *Institutions, Institutional Change and Economic Performance* (Cambridge: Cambridge University Press, 1990), ch. 11.

49. For a discussion of the emergence and definitions of social problems that emphasizes relationships among different arenas, see Stephen Hilgartner and Charles L. Bosk, "The Rise and Fall of Social Problems: A Public Arenas Model," *American Journal of Sociology* 94 (July 1988): 53–78.

50. These collisions are similar to the sharp changes that are envisoned by the theory of punctuated equilibrium. Developed by biologists Stephen J. Gould and Nils Eldredge, the theory has attracted the interest of political scientists concerned with explaining change over time and those seeking to

develop a nonutilitarian perspective on institutions. See Carmines and Stimson, *Issue Evolution*; and Krasner, "Sovereignty: An Institutionalist Perspective."

51. See the essays in G. Calvin Mackenzie, ed., *The In and Outers: Presidential Appointees and Transient Government in Washington* (Baltimore: Johns Hopkins Press, 1987); and Hugh Heclo, *A Government of Strangers: Executive Politics in Washington* (Washington, D.C.: Brookings Institution, 1977).

52. Peter A. Hall, "Policy Innovation and the Structure of the State: The Politics-Administration Nexus in France and Britain," *Annals*, no. 466 (March 1983): 43–59; on the relationship between the president and the bureaucracy, see Richard Nathan, *The Administrative Presidency* (New York: John Wiley and Sons, 1983); for an argument in favor of "multiple advocacy" as a system of presidential advising, see Roger B. Porter, *Presidential Decision-Making: The Economic Policy Board* (Cambridge: Cambridge University Press, 1980).

53. The capture theory is elaborated in Marver H. Bernstein, *Regulating Business by Independent Commission* (Princeton, N.J.: Princeton University Press, 1955); a classic exposition of the logic of "capture" is presented in George Stigler, "The Theory of Economic Regulation," *Bell Journal of Economic and Management Science* 2 (Spring 1971): 3–21. On the particularly political character of the American bureaucracy, see Joel D. Aberbach, Robert D. Putnam, and Bert A. Rockman, *Bureaucrats and Politicians in Western Democracies* (Cambridge: Harvard University Press, 1981), 94–100.

54. These issues have been discussed as problems of political learning. See Hugh Heclo, *Modern Social Politics in Sweden and Great Britain* (New Haven: Yale University Press, 1974); Odell, *U.S. International Monetary Policy*, 367–76; and Peter A. Hall "Policy Paradigms, Social Learning and the State: The Case of Economic Policy-making in Britain," *Comparative Politics* (forthcoming). See also the discussion about the way policy specialists limit the approaches to defining problems in Charles E. Lindblom and David K. Cohen, *Usable Knowledge: Social Science and Social Problem Solving* (New Haven: Yale University Press, 1979), 56.

55. On economists in government, see A. W. Coats, "Economic Ideas and Economists in Government: Accomplishments and Frustrations," in *The Spread of Economic Ideas*, edited by David C. Colander and A. W. Coats (Cambridge: Cambridge University Press, 1989), 109–18; William J. Barber, "Economists in a Pluralistic Polity," *History of Political Economy* 13 (Fall 1981): 513–47; William R. Allen, "Economics, Economists and Economic Policy: Modern American Experience," *History of Political Economy* 9 (Spring 1977): 48–88. One influential formulation of the relationship between experts and the government in policymaking is Hugh Heclo's concept of issue networks in "Issue Networks and the Executive Establishment," in *The New American Political System*, edited by Anthony King (Washington, D.C.: American Enterprise Institute, 1978), 87–124.

56. See the discussion of site of idea production in Derthick and Quirk, *The Politics of Deregulation*, ch. 7; on government as a site for producing

ideas, see William J. Barber, "The Spread of Economic Ideas between Academia and Government: A Two-Way Street," in Colander and Coats, *The Spread of Economic Ideas,* 119–26.

57. Derthick and Quirk, *The Politics of Deregulation,* 247; for a perspective that acknowledges the influence—as well as the limits—of think tanks, see James A. Smith, "Think Tanks and the Politics of Ideas," in Colander and Coats, *The Spread of Economic Ideas,* 175–94.

58. See Peter A. Hall's discussion of the need to link ideas, politics, and administration in "Conclusion: The Politics of Keynesian Ideas," in Hall, *The Political Power of Economic Ideas.*

59. See Theodore Lowi, "Party, Policy and Constitution in America," in *The American Party Systems: Stages of Political Development,* edited by William Nisbet Chambers and Walter Dean Burnham (New York: Oxford University Press, 1975), 238–76; David Mayhew, *Placing Parties in American Politics* (Princeton, N.J.: Princeton University Press, 1986), 244–56, 327–31.

60. Nelson Polsby has emphasized the importance of understanding the incentives of politicians as a spur to innovation. See Nelson Polsby, *Political Innovation in America* (New Haven and London: Yale University Press, 1984), 159–67.

61. One of the earliest applications of these ideas to politics is in James Buchanan and Gordon Tullock, *The Calculus of Consent* (Ann Arbor: University of Michigan Press, 1962). A reflection on some costs of parsimony is found in Albert O. Hirschman, "Against Parsimony: Three Easy Ways of Complicating Some Categories of Economic Discourse," *Economics and Philosophy* 1 (1985): 1–21.

62. See Kenneth Shepsle, "Institutional Equilibrium and Equilibrium Institutions," in *Political Science: The Science of Politics,* edited by Herbert F. Weisberg (New York: Agathon Press, 1986); see also Terry Moe, "Interests, Institutions, and Positive Theory: The Politics of the NLRB," *Studies in American Political Development* 2 (1987): 236–99.

63. Such beliefs may in fact frame their evaluations about how to achieve electoral success. See Erwin Hargrove's discussion of Jimmy Carter in *Jimmy Carter as President: Leadership and the Politics of the Public Good* (Baton Rouge and London: Louisiana State University Press, 1988), ch. 2.

64. Fred I. Greenstein, "Change and Continuity in the Modern Presidency," in *The New American Political System* edited by Anthony King (Washington, D.C.: American Enterprise Institute, 1978) 65. On the use of rhetoric, see Jeffrey K. Tulis, *The Rhetorical Presidency* (Princeton, N.J.: Princeton University Press, 1987).

65. On the pressure for the president to move quickly (or "to move it or lose it"), see Paul Light, *The President's Agenda: Domestic Policy Choice from Kennedy to Carter with Notes on Ronald Reagan* (Baltimore and London: Johns Hopkins University Press, 1982).

66. On the need to investigate the sources of preferences see Aaron Wildavsky, "Choosing Preferences by Constructing Institutions: A Cultural Theory of Preference Formation," *American Political Science Review* 81 (March 1987): 3–21; James G. March and Johan P. Olsen, "The New Institu-

tionalism: Organizational Factors in Political Life," *The American Political Science Review* 78 (September 1984): 734–49.

67. For an argument stressing the role of culture in interest construction, see Wildavsky, "Choosing Preference by Constructing Institutions." For a study that examines political institutions as the source of interest definition, see Sven Steinmo, "Political Institutions and Tax Policy in the United States, Sweden, and Britain," *World Politics* 41 (July 1989): 500–535.

68. For a discussion of this process, see Gosta Esping-Andersen, *Politics against Markets* (Princeton, N.J.: Princeton University Press, 1986).

69. This process is similar to the notion of disappointment that Albert Hirschman uses to account for shifts between public and private activity. See his discussion in *Shifting Involvements: Private Interest and Public Action* (Princeton, N.J.: Princeton University Press, 1982).

Chapter Two

1. See the discussion in John A. Garraty, *Unemployment in History: Economic Thought and Public Policy* (New York: Harper and Row, 1978), ch. 7. The notion that unemployment was "a problem of industry" and the phrase itself came from William H. Beveridge, the British social reformer and pioneer in studying unemployment. See William H. Beveridge, *Unemployment: A Problem of Industry* (London, 1930).

2. On Mitchell, see the essays in Arthur F. Burns, ed., *Wesley Clair Mitchell: The Economic Scientist* (New York: National Bureau of Economic Research, 1952). On Commons, see Lafayette G. Harter, Jr., *John R. Commons: His Assault on Laissez-Faire* (Corvallis: Oregon State University Press, 1962).

3. For a discussion of planning ideas in the United States before the National Recovery Administration, see Otis L. Graham, Jr., *Toward a Planned Society* (New York: Oxford University Press, 1976), ch. 1; and Guy Alchon, *The Invisible Hand of Planning: Capitalism, Social Science and the State in the 1920s* (Princeton, N.J.: Princeton University Press, 1985).

4. Ellis Hawley, "Herbert Hoover, the Commerce Secretariat and the Vision of an 'Associative State,' 1921–1928," *Journal of American History* 61 (June 1974): 116–40; Evan B. Metcalf, "Secretary Hoover and the Emergence of Macroeconomic Management," *Business History Review* 49 (Spring 1975): 60–80. For a view of local business opinions on how to alleviate unemployment, see Alexander Keyssar, *Out of Work: The First Century of Unemployment in Massachusetts*, (Cambridge: Cambridge University Press, 1986).

5. Hoover's 1921 Conference on Unemployment advocated this approach. See Carolyn Grin, "The Unemployment Conference of 1921: An Experiment in National Cooperative Planning," *Mid-America* 55 (April 1973): 83–107; and Hawley "Herbert Hoover," 135.

6. Examples of machine politicians creating public work in response to economic downturns appear in numerous accounts of nineteenth-century politics. See, for example, Amy Bridges, *A City in the Republic* (New York: Cambridge University Press, 1984).

7. Grin, "The Unemployment Conference of 1921," 83–107.

8. This "balance wheel" notion is found in the American Association for Labor Legislation program and in the thinking of the leaders of the 1921 conference. See John B. Andrews, "A Practical Program for the Prevention of Unemployment in America," *American Labor Legislation Review* 5 (June 1915): 173–94; Grin, "The Unemployment Conference of 1921," 102.

9. Herbert Stein, *The Fiscal Revolution in America* (Chicago and London: University of Chicago Press, 1969), 10–11, 50–54. See the discussion of the theoretical underpinnings of these early policy recommendations in Donald Patinkin, *Anticipations of the General Theory? and Other Essays on Keynes* (Chicago: University of Chicago Press, 1982).

10. For a survey of the use of public works prior to the 1930s, see Udo Sautter, "Government and Unemployment: The Use of Public Works before the New Deal," *Journal of American History* 73 (June 1986): 59–86.

11. Metcalf, "Secretary Hoover and the Emergence of Macroeconomic Management," 72; Grin, "The Unemployment Conference of 1921," 92–97; Hawley, "Herbert Hoover," 135.

12. Grin, "The Unemployment Conference of 1921," 96–97.

13. Arthur M. Schlesinger, Jr., *The Coming of the New Deal* (Boston: Houghton Mifflin, 1958), 284–87.

14. Quoted ibid., 287.

15. See J. Ronnie Davis, *The New Economics and the Old Economists* (Ames: Iowa State University Press, 1971); and William Barber, *From New Era to New Deal: Herbert Hoover, the Economists and American Economic Policy, 1921–1933* (Cambridge: Cambridge University Press, 1985), for departures from orthodoxy in economic thinking during the 1920s and early 1930s. See also Stein, *The Fiscal Revolution*, chs. 2, 7.

16. For a survey of the evidence, see Bradford Lee, "The Miscarriage of Necessity and Invention: Proto-Keynesianism and Democratic States in the 1930s," *The Political Power of Economic Ideas: Keynesianism Across Nations*, edited by Peter A. Hall (Princeton, N.J.: Princeton University Press, 1989), 129–70. The foremost popularizers of deficit spending were William T. Foster and Waddill Catchings, whose book *The Road to Plenty* (Cambridge, Mass.: Riverside Press, 1928) was widely read as the Depression approached.

17. For a discussion of the diverse views of planning attached to the NIRA, see Ellis Hawley, *The New Deal and the Problem of Monopoly* (Princeton, N.J.: Princeton University Press, 1966), ch. 2.

18. Business interest in planning during the early part of the twentieth century has been well documented, although there are differing interpretations about the depth and character of the business interest in planning. Hawley, *The New Deal and the Problem of Monopoly*, ch. 2, distinguishes between the definitions of planning embraced by government planners and business; Robert M. Collins, *The Business Response to Keynes, 1929–1964* (New York: Columbia University Press, 1981), 27–31, highlights the similarity between the government's approach to planning and that of business; Donald R. Brand, *Corporatism and the Rule of Law: A Study of the National Recovery Administration* (Ithaca and London: Cornell University Press, 1988), 85–86 and ch. 5, takes issue with both interpretations, stressing the

tenuousness of business interest in planning and the differences between business and government.

19. See E. Jay Howenstine, Jr., "Public Works Policy in the Twenties," *Social Research* 13 (December 1946): 486, 495; Stein, *The Fiscal Revolution*, 10.

20. Collins, *The Business Response to Keynes*, 26–27.

21. See Harriman's comments during congressional hearings, in U.S. Congress, House of Representatives, *Hearings on H.R. 5664, National Industrial Recovery Act*, 73d Cong., 1st sess., 1933, 119–44; see also Collins, *The Business Response to Keynes*, 31.

22. See Stein, *The Fiscal Revolution*, 74–81. For other arguments along these lines, see Lee, "The Miscarriage of Necessity and Invention"; see also Michael Bernstein, *The Great Depression: Delayed Recovery and Economic Change in America, 1929–1939* (Cambridge: Cambridge University Press, 1987), especially ch. 7 for an analysis that stresses the importance of divergent sectoral interests among business.

23. Lester V. Chandler, *America's Greatest Depression 1929–1941* (New York: Harper and Row, 1970), 48–51; and James T. Patterson, *Congressional Conservatism and the New Deal* (Lexington: University of Kentucky Press, 1967), 10–11.

24. For an analysis of this process, see Stephen Skowronek, *Building the New American State* (New York: Cambridge University Press, 1982).

25. Patterson, *Congressional Conservatism and the New Deal*, ch. 1.

26. For a discussion of the Progressives and corruption, see James D. Savage, *Balanced Budgets and American Politics* (Ithaca and London: Cornell University Press, 1988), ch. 4; and Dean L. May, *From New Deal to New Economics: The American Liberal Response to the Recession of 1937* (New York and London: Garland Publishing, 1981), ch. 2.

27. See the discussion in Skowronek, *Building the New American State*, ch. 6; and Louis Fisher, *Presidential Spending Power* (Princeton, N.J.: Princeton University Press, 1975), 9–40.

28. May, *From New Deal to New Economics*, 31–36; and Stein, *The Fiscal Revolution*, 44, 64.

29. Stein, *The Fiscal Revolution*, 54.

30. See Hawley, *The New Deal and the Problem of Monopoly*, chs. 3–7; and Donald R. Brand, *Corporatism and the Rule of Law*, especially chs. 5–8.

31. Larry Berman, *The Office of Management and Budget and the Presidency, 1921–1979* (Princeton, N.J.: Princeton University Press, 1979), 3–9; Gerhard Colm, "Fiscal Policy and the Federal Budget," in *Income Stabilization for a Developing Democracy: A Study in the Politics and Economics of High Employment without Inflation*, edited by Max F. Millikan (New Haven: Yale University Press, 1953), 227–32.

32. On Roosevelt's political style in this regard, see Richard Neustadt, *Presidential Power* (New York: Wiley, 1976), ch. 7.

33. Richard Polenberg, *Reorganizing Roosevelt's Government* (Cambridge: Harvard University Press, 1966), 22.

34. May, *From New Deal to New Economics*, ch. 3.

35. Ibid., 45–46.

36. Stein, *The Fiscal Revolution*, 165–67; Alan Sweezy, "The Keynesians and Government Policy, 1933–1939," *American Economic Review* 62 (May 1972): 117–18; and John Kenneth Galbraith, "How Keynes Came to America," in *Economics, Peace and Laughter*, edited by Andrea D. Williams (Boston: Houghton Mifflin, 1971), 47–48.

37. Carol S. Carson, "The History of the United States National Income and Product Accounts: The Development of an Analytic Tool," *Review of Income and Wealth* 21 (June 1975): 165–66. See also Stein, *The Fiscal Revolution*, 165–67; and Sweezy, "The Keynesians and Government Policy," 117–18.

38. Arthur W. MacMahon, John D. Millet, and Gladys Ogden, *The Administration of Federal Work Relief* (Chicago: Public Administration Service, 1941), 200–220.

39. Collins, *The Business Response to Keynes*, ch. 2.

40. Patterson, *Congressional Conservatism and the New Deal*, chs. 4–5. Southern agricultural interests continued to favor spending on established farm programs that benefited large well-to-do farmers; it was new programs that could disrupt the social, political, and economic balance that they feared. See the discussion of the Farm Security Administration in Paul E. Metz, *New Deal Policy and Southern Rural Poverty* (Baton Rouge and London: Louisiana State University Press, 1978), ch. 8.

41. Christina McFayden Campbell, *The Farm Bureau and the New Deal: A Study of National Farm Policy, 1933–40* (Urbana: University of Illinois Press, 1962), 190–91.

42. See Stein, *The Fiscal Revolution*, 109; see also Collins, *The Business Response to Keynes*, 67–71.

43. John Morton Blum, *From the Morgenthau Diaries: Years of Crisis, 1928–1938* (Boston: Houghton Mifflin, 1959), 421.

44. For the details of the 1938 proposal, see Stein, *The Fiscal Revolution*, 109–14; and Collins, *The Business Response to Keynes*, 69–71.

45. See the accounts in Collins, *The Business Response to Keynes*, 69–71; and Stein, *The Fiscal Revolution*, ch. 6. Thus, Ferguson's statement that "Rockefeller advisor Beardsley Ruml proposed a plan for deficit spending, which Roosevelt implemented after versions won approval from [Walter] Teagle [of Standard Oil] and nearly all the important bankers, including Morgan" is a highly misleading account of the 1938 decision favoring spending, particularly as it lacks supporting evidence about how these business interests made their influence felt or why such influence would have been decisive. See Thomas Ferguson, "From Normalcy to New Deal: Industrial Structure, Party Competition, and American Public Policy in the New Deal," *International Organization* 38 (Winter 1984): 92.

46. Henry S. Dennison, Lincoln Filene, Ralph E. Flanders, and Morris E. Leeds, *Toward Full Employment* (New York: Whittlesey House, 1938). For more on the thinking of these business leaders, see Collins, *The Business Response to Keynes*, 63–67. See also the discussion of the BAC in Kim McQuaid, "The Business Advisory Council of the Department of Commerce,

1933–1961: A Study in Corporate/Government Relations," in *Research in Economic History: An Annual Compilation of Research*, edited by Paul Useling (Greenwich, Conn.: JAI Press, 1976), 1:171–93; Kim McQuaid, "The Frustration of Corporate Revival during the Early New Deal," *The Historian* 41 (August 1979): 682–704; Collins, *The Business Response to Keynes*, 59–67.

47. For a description of the stagnationist theory, see Collins, *The Business Response to Keynes*, 10–11, 51. For early expositions of the theory, see Alvin Hansen, *Full Recovery or Stagnation?* (New York: Norton, 1938); and Hansen's 1938 presidential address before the American Economic Association, "Economic Progress and Declining Population Growth," *American Economic Review* 29 (March 1939): 1–15.

48. The early arguments for spending reflected an awareness of the way stagnationist Keynesianism fused social and economic policy objectives. See May, *From New Deal to New Economics*, 142. This fusion became far more pronounced as stagnationist Keynesianism was developed, especially in Alvin Hansen's work. See, for example, Alvin Hansen, "Social Planning for Tomorrow," in *The United States after the War*, edited by Alvin H. Hansen, F. F. Hill, Louis Hollander, Walter D. Fuller, Herbert W. Briggs, and George O. Stoddard (Ithaca, N.Y.: Cornell University Press, 1945); and Alvin H. Hansen, *After the War—Full Employment* (Washington, D.C.: Government Printing Office, 1942).

49. On the recruitment of New Deal lawyers, see Peter Irons, *The New Deal Lawyers* (Princeton, N.J.: Princeton University Press, 1982).

50. On Hansen and the fiscal policy seminar, see the collection of articles in *Quarterly Journal of Economics* 90 (February 1976): 1–37.

51. Byrd L. Jones, "The Role of Keynesians in Wartime Policy and Postwar Planning, 1940–46," *American Economic Review* 62 (May 1972): 125–33; Carson, "The History of the United States National Income and Product Accounts," 173–77.

52. Barry Karl, *Executive Reorganization and Reform in the New Deal* (Cambridge: Harvard University Press, 1963); and Peri Arnold, *Making the Managerial Presidency: Comprehensive Reorganization Planning, 1905–1980* (Princeton, N.J.: Princeton University Press, 1986), ch. 4.

53. For a full account of the recommendations, see President's Committee on Administrative Management, *Report* (Washington, D.C.: Government Printing Office, 1937).

54. In fact, most of the proposals for reorganization that preceded the 1937 plan had economy in government as their goal. See Arnold, *Making the Managerial Presidency*, chs. 1–4.

55. On the opposition, see Polenberg, *Reorganizing Roosevelt's Government*, ch. 8; Patterson, *Congressional Conservatism and the New Deal*, 214–29.

56. Patterson, *Congressional Conservatism and the New Deal*, ch. 7.

57. Ibid., 318–22; Collins, *The Business Response to Keynes*, 46–47.

58. See Hansen, *After the War—Full Employment*; and Alvin Hansen, "Our Coming Prosperity," *Common Sense* 11 (April 1942): 489–500.

59. The most famous of these was written by the NRPB's Committee on

Long-Range Work and Relief Policies, *Security, Work, and Relief Policies* (Washington, D.C.: Government Printing Office, 1942). Congressional opposition to this report sparked the movement to cut off the board's funds.

60. Marion Clawson, *New Deal Planning: The National Resources Planning Board* (Baltimore: Johns Hopkins University Press, 1981), 232.

61. On the bill, see Stephen Kemp Bailey, *Congress Makes a Law* (New York: Vintage Books, 1950), ch. 3; and Collins, *The Business Response to Keynes*, 99–109.

62. The first suggestion for the bill actually came from the National Farmers' Union (NFU), a relatively small organization representing primarily small farmers. Unlike the American Farm Bureau Federation (AFBF), the NFU strongly supported the New Deal's initiatives to deal with rural poverty, and it sought to unite smaller rural interests with urban labor. On the National Farmers' Union and its policies, see Grant McConnell, *The Decline of Agrarian Democracy* (New York: Atheneum, 1969), 37–39, 68–69, 108, 137, 146; and Campbell, *The Farm Bureau and the New Deal*, 169–71.

63. Bailey, *Congress Makes a Law*, 52–53.

64. Both the AFL and the Congress of Industrial Organizations (CIO) continued to have reservations about the bill. According to Bailey, the AFL feared that the CIO was behind the bill and that its passage would be interpreted as a CIO victory. The CIO endorsed the bill with some enthusiasm, but its preferred approach to achieving full employment would have involved a more micro-level approach of adjusting labor supply at the plant level through the use of industry councils. See Bailey, *Congress Makes a Law*, 80, 92–96.

65. The opposition to the bill within the Chamber of Commerce and its local affiliates was very strong, and these groups actively fought against the bill. It is worth noting, however, that Chamber of Commerce President Eric Johnston actually supported the bill, and consequently the Chamber of Commerce did not testify against the bill in committee hearings. Bailey, *Congress Makes a Law*, 140.

66. On the positive-sum nature of Keynesian policies, see Adam Przeworski, "Socialist Democracy as a Historical Phenomenon," *New Left Review*, no. 122 (July–August 1980): 27–58; and Robert Skidelsky, "The Decline of Keynesian Politics," in *State and Economy in Contemporary Capitalism*, edited by Colin Crouch (London: Croom Helm, 1979), 55–87.

67. On the growth of the Farm Bureau during the 1930s and its involvement in congressional politics, see Theodore Saloutos, "The American Farm Bureau Federation and Farm Policy, 1933–1945," *Southwestern Social Science Quarterly* 28 (March 1948): 313–33; and Campbell, *The Farm Bureau and the New Deal*.

68. On the Farm Security Administration, see Sidney Baldwin, *Poverty and Politics: The Rise and Decline of the Farm Security Administration* (Chapel Hill: University of North Carolina Press, 1968), especially ch. 9; on rural complaints about the WPA, see Patterson, *Congressional Conservatism and the New Deal*, 297.

69. Lee J. Alston and Joseph P. Ferrie, "Labor Costs, Paternalism, and Loy-

alty in Southern Agriculture: A Constraint on the Growth of the Welfare State," *Journal of Economic History* 45 (March 1985): 95–117; Jill Quadagno, *The Transformation of Old Age Security: Class Politics in the American Welfare State* (Chicago and London: University of Chicago Press, 1988); for a discussion of the fears of southern agricultural elites about the Full Employment bill, see Bailey, *Congress Makes a Law*, 147–48.

70. On Roosevelt's positions on the issue of race, see Nancy J. Weiss, *Farewell to the Party of Lincoln: Black Politics in the Age of FDR* (Princeton, N.J.: Princeton University Press, 1983).

71. On business's bitterness toward the federal government after the NRA experience, see the discussion in Brand, *Corporatism and the Rule of Law*, chs. 5–8. On business antistatism more generally, see David Vogel, "Why Businessmen Distrust their State: The Political Consciousness of American Corporate Executives," *British Journal of Political Science* 8 (January 1978): 45–78; on business attitudes in the 1920s, see James Prothro, *Dollar Decade: Business Ideas in the 1920s* (Baton Rouge: Louisiana State University Press, 1954).

72. See Collins, *The Business Response to Keynes*, 41, for a discussion of the eclipse of liberal elements within the Chamber of Commerce.

73. Collins, *The Business Response to Keynes*, 36–52; Savage, *Balanced Budgets and American Politics*, 172–75.

74. For a taste of some of the rhetoric, see Bailey, *Congress Makes a Law*, 129–43.

75. Hansen stressed the need for "democratic planning" in postwar America. See Alvin Hansen, "Social Planning for Tomorrow"; id., "The Postwar Economy," in *Postwar Economic Problems*, edited by Seymour Harris (New York: McGraw-Hill, 1943), 12–16; id., "Planning Full Employment," *Nation* 159 (October 21, 1944): 492. Two articles from a special section of *The New Republic* are relevant: "Outline for an American Plan" notes the need for a planning mechanism, and "Shall We Compensate, or Plan Abundance?" argues that the full employment bill could lead either to planning or to a less interventionist economic policy, depending on how it is implemented. See Heinz Eulau, Mordecai Ezekiel, Alvin H. Hansen, James Loeb, Jr., and George Soule, *The Road to Freedom: Full Employment*, special section of *The New Republic*, September 24, 1945, 404–10.

76. For an example of the way concerns about organized labor entered into the hearings on the bill, see Clare Hoffman's (R. Mich.) exchange with Henry Wallace during the House hearings on the bill, quoted in Bailey, *Congress Makes a Law*, 156–57. The wave of strikes at the end of World War II helped to create an employer offensive against labor and provoked strong antilabor sentiment in Congress, which helped defeat a range of legislation that could be construed as prolabor. See the argument in Edwin Amenta and Theda Skocpol, "Redefining the New Deal: World War II and the Development of Social Provision in the United States," in *The Politics of Social Policy in the United States*, edited by Margaret Weir, Ann Shola Orloff, and Theda Skocpol (Princeton, N.J.: Princeton University Press, 1988), 108–19; for a review of postwar labor issues see Arthur F. McClure, *The Truman Admini-*

stration and the Problems of Postwar Labor, 1945–1948 (Cranbury, N.J.: Associated University Presses, 1969).

77. See Collins, *The Business Response to Keynes*, 99–109; and Bailey, *Congress Makes a Law*, 164–71. Key also notes that the New Deal "had stimulated a closer alliance of the black-belt counties with industry." V. O. Key, *Southern Politics in State and Nation* (New York: Knopf, 1949), 329.

78. See Key, *Southern Politics*, especially 302–10 on the political effects of one-party factionalism; Marian Irish, "The Southern One-Party System and National Politics," *Journal of Politics* 4 (February 1942): 80–94.

79. See Patterson, *Congressional Conservatism and the New Deal*, 333.

80. See Amenta and Skocpol, "Redefining the New Deal"; Nelson Lichtenstein, "From Corporatism to Collective Bargaining: Organized Labor and the Eclipse of Social Democracy in the Postwar Era," in *The Rise and Fall of the New Deal Order*, edited by Steve Fraser and Gary Gerstle (Princeton, N.J.: Princeton University Press, 1989), 122–52.

81. Sidney M. Milkis, "FDR and the Transcendence of Partisan Politics," *Political Science Quarterly*, (Fall 1985), 493.

82. See Jerome Bruner, *Mandate from the People* (New York: Duell, Sloan and Pearce, 1944), ch. 9, for surveys showing strong public support for full employment during the war. See Bailey, *Congress Makes a Law*, 179–84, for a discussion of the lack of public attention to the issue of full employment by 1945.

83. On Truman and the Full Employment bill, see Bailey, *Congress Makes a Law*, 161–62.

84. Clawson, *New Deal Planning*, ch. 19, argues that Roosevelt's preoccupation with the war diminished his efforts to save the NRPB. Bailey, *Congress Makes a Law*, 161, maintains that Roosevelt's failure to endorse the full employment legislation presented to him in 1944 was due to his desire to maintain congressional support for the United Nations.

85. Stuart Rice, "Statistical Needs for the Effectuation of Employment Act Objectives," in *The Employment Act Past and Future: A Tenth Anniversary Symposium*, National Planning Association Special Report no. 41, edited by Gerhard Colm (Washington, D.C.: National Planning Association, 1956), 135–41.

86. On intellectual contributions, see Walter Salant, "Some Intellectual Contributions of the Truman Council of Economic Advisers to Policy-Making," *History of Political Economy* 5 (Spring 1973): 36–49. On the Truman Council more generally, see the account by Truman's first CEA chairman in Edwin G. Nourse, *Economics in the Public Service* (New York: Harcourt Brace, 1953); Edward S. Flash, *Economic Advice and Presidential Leadership: The Council of Economic Advisers* (New York: Columbia University Press, 1965), chs. 2–3; see the introductory essay and interview with Leon Keyserling, the second head of the CEA under Truman, in Erwin C. Hargrove and Samuel A. Morley, *The President and the Council of Economic Advisers: Interviews with CEA Chairmen*, (Boulder, Colo.: Westview Press, 1984), ch. 1.

87. Hargrove and Morley, *The President and the Council of Economic Advisers*, 103.

88. In addition to the sources cited in note 79, see William J. Barber, "The United States: Economists in a Pluralistic Polity," *History of Political Economy* 13 (Fall 1981): 513–24.

89. See Charles Maier, "The Politics of Productivity: Foundations of American International Economic Policy after World War II," in *Between Power and Plenty*, edited by Peter J. Katzenstein (Madison: University of Wisconsin Press, 1978), 23–49.

90. Flash, *Economic Advice and Presidential Leadership*, 99–107. Arthur F. Burns, Eisenhower's first CEA chairman, notes that Eisenhower also had serious doubts about whether to continue the CEA. See his remarks in Hargrove and Morley, *The President and the Council of Economic Advisers*, 95–97.

91. See Burns's account of his disputes with Treasury Secretary George Humphrey in Hargrove and Morley, *The President and the Council of Economic Advisers*, 101–8; Stein notes that even Humphrey was not bound by pure orthodoxy and on important occasions pragmatically accepted unbalanced budgets. Stein, *The Fiscal Revolution*, 295–99.

92. On the congressional role in economic decisionmaking, see Victor Jones, "The Political Framework of Stabilization Policy," in Millikan, *Income Stabilization for a Developing Democracy*, 604–10; Alvin Hansen, "The Reports Prepared under the Employment Act," in Colm, *The Employment Act Past and Future*, 92–97; and Edwin Nourse, "Taking Root (First Decade of the Employment Act)," ibid., 62–65.

93. On the Budget Bureau, see Frederick C. Mosher, *A Tale of Two Agencies: A Comparative Analysis of the General Accounting Office and the Office of Management and Budget* (Baton Rouge and London: Louisiana State Press, 1984), 106–7.

94. It was work by the CED's Beardsley Ruml that made possible the tax cut route. In the early 1940s, Ruml devised the withholding plan that became the basis for the American tax system, allowing tax policy to be used for stabilization purposes. On Ruml and the CED's policies, see Stein, *The Fiscal Revolution*, 220–40; Collins, *The Business Response to Keynes*, chs. 5–6.

95. Collins, *The Business Response to Keynes*, ch. 6, presents an excellent account of the CED's extensive campaigns to educate business leaders and government officials about its views on economic policy.

96. On the National Planning Association, see Stein, *The Fiscal Revolution*, 335; Jones, "The Role of Keynesians in Wartime Policy," 131. The Brookings Institution, which was to become the premier liberal think tank in the 1960s, was a stronghold of anti-Keynesians during the 1930s and 1940s. Brookings president Harold Moulton was widely known as a vociferous critic of Hansen and the policies he espoused. By the late 1940s, Brookings was an organization in decline, with little influence on policy. See Donald T. Critchlow, *The Brookings Institution, 1916–1952* (DeKalb: Northern Illinois University Press, 1985), chs. 7–8.

97. William N. Parker, "An Historical Introduction," in *Economic History and the Modern Economist*, edited by William N. Parker (Oxford: Basil Blackwell, 1986), 6–7; on the economics profession in the United States and the

acceptance of Keynesianism, see Marc Trachtenberg, "Keynes Triumphant: A Study in the Social History of Ideas," *Knowledge and Society: Studies in the Sociology of Culture Past and Present* 4 (1983): 17–86.

98. Parker, "An Historical Introduction," 5.

99. On the economists' tendency to favor market mechanisms in policymaking, see Robert H. Nelson, "The Economics Profession and the Making of Public Policy," *Journal of Economic Literature* 25 (March 1987): 49–91.

100. See the discussion in Stein, *The Fiscal Revolution*, 372–84. According to Paul Samuelson, the lawyers in the Kennedy campaign had no clear notion about why they needed economists in the first place, but "wanted to be sure they weren't missing a trick." Oral History Interview with Walter Heller, Kermit Gordon, James Tobin, Gardner Ackley, and Paul Samuelson by Joseph Pechman, August 1, 1964 Fort Ritchie, Maryland, John F. Kennedy Library, 34–35. Oral History Interview quoted with permission.

101. "Ideological heir" is Collins's phrase. *The Business Response to Keynes*, 184. Another strong proponent of spending was Leon Keyserling, former head of Truman's CEA. See the discussion in Oral History Interview with Heller et al., 34.

102. Hargrove and Morley, *The President and the Council of Economic Advisers*, 174, 181–82; Walter Heller, *New Dimensions of Political Economy*, (Cambridge: Harvard University Press, 1966), 26–27.

103. Hargrove and Morley, *The President and the Council of Economic Advisers*, 202.

104. Walter Heller, "Memorandum for the President re: The Economics of the Second Stage Recovery Program," March 17, 1961, President's Office Files, Council of Economic Advisers File 1/61–3/61, John F. Kennedy Library; "Minutes on the President's Request for a Review of the Clark Community Facilities Bill and Allied Projects," June 15, 1961, File 6/1/61–6/15/61, Walter Heller Papers, John F. Kennedy Library.

105. "Recap of Issues on Tax Cuts and the Expenditure Alternative," December 16, 1962, Council of Economic Advisers File, Record Group 174, National Archives, 3; see also Hargrove and Morley, *The President and the Council of Economic Advisers*, 196, 200–1.

106. On Kennedy's relationship with business, see Hobart Rowen, *The Free Enterprisers: Kennedy, Johnson and the Business Establishment* (New York: G.P. Putnam, 1964), ch. 1; and Jim F. Heath *John F. Kennedy and the Business Community* (Chicago: University of Chicago Press, 1969).

107. James Sundquist, *Politics and Policy: The Eisenhower, Kennedy and Johnson Years* (Washington, D.C.: Brookings Institution, 1968), on the role of southern members of Congress in the early Kennedy administration. See also David M. Potter, *The South and the Concurrent Majority* (Baton Rouge: Louisiana State University Press, 1972). For the Kennedy administration's perspective on conservative southern opposition in Congress, see "Memorandum for Lawrence F. O'Brien," July 9, 1962, Congress File, Theodore Sorensen Papers, John F. Kennedy Library.

108. *Congressional Quarterly Almanac, 1961*, 17 (Washington, D.C.: Congressional Quarterly Press, 1961), 642–43.

109. Unemployment was not perceived as one of the top five of the greatest problems the new president would face in a Gallup poll taken in June 1960. The top four problems concerned international security; the fifth was race relations. See George H. Gallup, *The Gallup Poll: Public Opinion 1935–1971* (New York: Random House, 1972), 3:11. According to James Tobin, a member of Kennedy's CEA, Kennedy was at first more concerned about the effect of an unbalanced budget on public opinion than about the effect of unemployment. See Oral History Interview with Heller et al., 292. Oral History Interview paraphrased with permission.

110. These actions accord well with what Stephen Skowronek has called a "regime manager," a president who inherits a set of well-established political relationships and policies, which he or she may seek to extend but not disrupt. See Stephen Skowronek, "Presidential Leadership in Political Time," *The Presidency and the Political System*, edited by Michael Nelson (Washington, D.C.: Congressional Quarterly Press, 1984), 87–132.

111. A 1962 public opinion poll showed that 72 percent of the general public opposed a tax cut if it meant an increase in the national debt. See Heath, *John F. Kennedy and the Business Community*, 115.

112. Hargrove and Morley, *The President and the Council of Economic Advisers*, 205–10.

113. See the discussion in Savage, *Balanced Budgets and American Politics*, 175–79.

114. Andrew Shonfield, *Modern Capitalism: The Changing Balance of Public and Private Power* (London: Oxford University Press, 1965), 333.

Chapter Three

1. See, for example, James Tobin, "The Political Economy of the 1960s," in *Policies for Prosperity: Essays in a Keynesian Mode*, edited by Peter M. Jackson (Cambridge: MIT Press, 1987), 437–38.

2. For this viewpoint, see Charles Murray, *Losing Ground: American Social Policy, 1950–1980* (New York: Basic Books, 1984); and George Gilder, *Wealth and Poverty* (New York: Bantam, 1982).

3. See U.S. Department of Labor, *A Report on Manpower Requirements, Resources, Utilization, and Training* (March 1964), 24–35, for a description of the structure of unemployment in the early 1960s.

4. James L. Sundquist, *Politics and Policy: The Eisenhower, Kennedy and Johnson Years* (Washington, D.C.: Brookings Institution, 1968), 57.

5. See Peter B. Doeringer and Michael J. Piore, *Internal Labor Markets and Manpower Analysis* (Armonk, N.Y.: M. E. Sharpe, 1985); Stephen Amberg, "Revising Regulation for the New Industrial Order: Skills, Sectors, States and Schools" (unpublished mss., June 1990).

6. Henry David, *Manpower Policies for a Democratic Society: The Final Statement of the Council* (New York: Columbia University Press, 1965), viii.

7. Gladys Roth Kremen, "The Origins of the Manpower Development and Training Act of 1962" (unpublished mss., Historical Office, Department of Labor for the Manpower Administration, 1974), 10–13.

8. Ibid., 13.

9. Ibid., 13–14.

10. See Garth Mangum, *MDTA: Foundation of Federal Manpower Policy* (Baltimore: Johns Hopkins University Press, 1968), 11; Kremen, "Origins of the Manpower Development and Training Act," 13–17.

11. Sar A. Levitan, *Federal Aid to Depressed Areas: An Evaluation of the Area Redevelopment Administration* (Baltimore: Johns Hopkins University Press, 1964), 2–3; Roger H. Davidson, *Coalition-Building for Depressed Areas Bills: 1955–1965* (Indianapolis: Bobbs-Merrill, 1966), 4.

12. The hearings produced nine volumes of testimony. See U.S. Congress, Senate, *Unemployment Problems: Hearings before the Senate Special Subcommittee on Unemployment Problems*, 86th Cong., 1st and 2d sess., 1960.

13. See the recommendations in U.S. Congress, Senate, *Report of the Special Committee on Unemployment Problems*, 86th Cong., 2d sess., 1960, Senate Report 1206, 122–26; for a discussion of the committee and its activities, see Sundquist, *Politics and Policy*, 79–83; and Garth Mangum, *The Emergence of Manpower Policy* (New York: Holt, Rinehart, Winston, 1969), 27.

14. Sundquist, *Politics and Policy*, 82–83.

15. Ibid., 83–85.

16. "News from the Ford Foundation," May 13, 1962, File ES-2-1, Administration of State Programs, Record Group 174, National Archives.

17. See E. Wight Bakke, *A Positive Labor Market Policy: Policy Premises for the Development, Operation and Integration of the Employment and Manpower Services* (Columbus, Ohio: Merrill Books, 1963).

18. For evidence along these lines, see "Secretary Wirtz Before the Midwestern Governors Conf.—Chicago, Ill.," December 13, 1962, Speeches File, Record Group 174, National Archives, 5; N. J. Simler, "Memorandum to the Council re: Secretary Wirtz and that Four Percent Figure," November 21, 1962, Council of Economic Advisers File, Record Group 174, National Archives; John F. Henning, "Memorandum to the Secretary re: Suggestions for an Active Manpower Policy," August 8, 1968, IL-Treaties File, Record Group 174, National Archives, 3.

19. Sundquist, *Politics and Policy*, 112.

20. This point has been made by many students of the War on Poverty. See, for example, Allen J. Matusow, *The Unraveling of America: A History of Liberalism in the 1960s* (New York: Harper and Row, 1984), 119–20; Byron Lander, "Group Theory and Individuals: The Origin of Poverty as a Political Issue in 1964," *Western Political Quarterly* 24 (September 1971): 514–26.

21. The argument that the War on Poverty was initiated to help Democrats secure the black vote is made most strongly by Frances Fox Piven and Richard Cloward, *Regulating the Poor: The Functions of Public Welfare* (New York: Vintage Books, 1971), especially ch. 9. For counterarguments, see Carl M. Brauer, "Kennedy, Johnson, and the War on Poverty," *Journal of American History* 69 (June 1982): 111; see also the discussion between Piven and Cloward and some of the people involved in planning the War on Poverty in "Poverty and Urban Policy" (transcript of a conference held in Waltham, Mass., June 16–17, 1973, John F. Kennedy Library), 161–75; 180–215.

22. These political aims do not imply that the president did not also have moral concerns about poverty. See the discussion in Brauer, "Kennedy, Johnson, and the War on Poverty," 103.

23. Sundquist, *Politics and Policy*, 111–12.

24. Adam Yarmolinsky, "The Beginnings of OEO," in *On Fighting Poverty: Perspectives from Experience*, edited by James L. Sundquist (New York: Basic Books, 1969), 37; see also the data presented by Robert Haveman, *Poverty Policy and Poverty Research: The Great Society and the Social Sciences* (Madison: University of Wisconsin Press, 1987), 41–47.

25. Brauer, "Kennedy, Johnson, and the War on Poverty," 107–9.

26. See, for example, *Economic Report of the President* (Washington, D.C.: Government Printing Office, 1964), 178–82.

27. Walter Heller, "Memorandum for the Secretary of Agriculture et al.," November 5, 1963, File LL-2-3, Record Group 174, National Archives.

28. For an excellent discussion of the intellectual foundations of the War on Poverty, see James T. Patterson, *America's Struggle against Poverty, 1900–1980* (Cambridge: Harvard University Press, 1981), ch. 7–8. The emphasis on youth is evident in the initial authorizations for OEO: nearly one-half of the 1965 funds appropriated were specifically for youth programs. See Sar A. Levitan, *The Great Society's Poor Law* (Baltimore: Johns Hopkins University Press, 1969), 46, tabs. 1 and 2. The focus on youth has been much commented upon. See, for example, S. M. Miller and Martin Rein, "The War on Poverty: Perspectives and Prospects," in *Poverty as a Public Issue*, edited by Ben B. Seligman (New York: Free Press, 1965), 288–90; Sundquist, *Politics and Policy*, 141.

29. For the logic of the poverty cycle as the CEA understood it, see the CEA memo quoted in Daniel P. Moynihan, "The Professors and the Poor," in *On Understanding Poverty: Perspectives from the Social Sciences*, edited by Daniel P. Moynihan (New York: Basic Books, 1969), 9; and *Economic Report of the President* (Washington, D.C.: Government Printing Office, 1964), 69–73.

30. On the approach of the economists, see Henry J. Aaron, *Politics and the Professors: The Great Society in Perspective* (Washington, D.C.: Brookings Institution, 1978), 20–23; and Haveman, *Poverty Policy and Poverty Research*, 51. On the culture of poverty, see Patterson, *America's Struggle against Poverty*, ch. 7.

31. Aaron, *Politics and the Professors*, 20.

32. Willard Wirtz, "Memorandum to Theodore Sorensen," January 23, 1964, White House General File, Record Group 174, National Archives, 2.

33. Ibid., 4.

34. *Congressional Record*, 88th Cong., 2d sess., January 27, 1964, 1054–60.

35. Johnson was repeating the CEA argument here. See Gardner Ackley, "Memorandum for the Honorable Sargent Shriver," February 18, 1964, File 2/64, Walter H. Heller Papers, John F. Kennedy Library. For an account of this episode see Daniel P. Moynihan, *Maximum Feasible Misunderstanding: Community Action in the War on Poverty* (New York: Free Press, 1970), 99; see also Sundquist, *Politics and Policy*, 142–45.

36. U.S. Congress, Senate, Subcommittee on Employment and Manpower, *Toward Full Employment: Proposals for a Comprehensive Employment and Manpower Policy in the United States,* 88th Cong., 2d sess., 1964, Committee Print, summarizes the recommendations of the subcommittee. See also the publications of the subcommittee, including the ten volumes of hearings, id., *Nation's Manpower Revolution,* 88th Cong., 1st sess., 1963; and the nine volumes of reading issued by the subcommittee, id., *Selected Readings in Employment and Manpower,* 1964–1966. For a discussion of these publications, see Margaret S. Gordon, "U.S. Manpower and Employment Policy," *Monthly Labor Review* 87 (November 1964): 1314–21.

37. U.S. Congress, *Toward Full Employment,* 47–50.

38. Ibid., 58.

39. Levitan, *The Great Society's Poor Law,* 37–47.

40. See Roger B. Porter, "Economic Advice to the President: From Eisenhower to Reagan," *Political Science Quarterly* 98 (Fall 1983): 403–26; see also Hobart Rowen, *The Free Enterprisers: Kennedy, Johnson, and the Business Establishment* (New York: G. P. Putnam, 1964), 166–67.

41. On Title I of the MDTA, which provided the research money, see Mangum, *MDTA,* 138–45.

42. Ibid., 138–45. Most labor market economists in the 1940s and 1950s had focused their research on trade unionism and collective bargaining. See the essays in Bruce E. Kaufman, ed., *How Labor Markets Work* (Lexington, Mass.: Lexington Books, 1988).

43. See Walter Heller's comments in Erwin C. Hargrove and Samuel A. Morley, *The President and the Council of Economic Advisers: Interviews with CEA Chairmen* (Boulder, Colo.: Westview Press, 1984), 188, 193. For Goldberg's Full Employment bill of 1961, see "Discussion Paper Prepared by the Department of Labor, April 13, 1961: An Act to Implement the Employment Act of 1946," White House Files—President, Department of Labor, Record Group 174, National Archives.

44. U.S. Congress, Senate, *Report of the Special Committee on Unemployment Problems,* 86th Cong., 2d sess., March 30, 1960, Senate Report 1206, 126.

45. *Congressional Record,* 86th Cong., 2d sess., May 16, 1960, 106, pt. 8:10318.

46. After winning office, Kennedy and his advisers rejected the proposal, arguing that they preferred to rely on existing departments and intended to remove many of the committees surrounding the executive office. They also tried to reassure Clark that the presence of at least one economist concerned with employment on the new CEA would obviate the need for a special manpower council. By 1964, Clark had become so dissatisfied with the position of the CEA on manpower issues that he urged President Johnson to appoint an economist more sympathetic to the manpower viewpoint than the council had been for the previous three years. On the administration's position on the manpower council, see Samuel V. Merrick, "Memorandum to the Secretary," February 7, 1963, File MA-1, Record Group 174, National Archives. On the assurance that one member of the CEA would be especially concerned with employment, see Mangum, *MDTA,* 14. On Clark's request to

President Johnson, see "Joseph S. Clark to President," August 13, 1964, File 8/5/64–8/18/64, Walter Heller Papers, John F. Kennedy Library.

47. Hargrove and Morley, *The President and the Council of Economic Advisers*, 210.

48. Sundquist, *Politics and Policy*, 144.

49. William Cannon of the Budget Bureau later noted that the Budget Bureau had tried to dissuade the president from using the "War on Poverty" rhetoric. See his comments in "Poverty and Urban Policy," 301. For an interesting discussion of the president's use of rhetoric in the War on Poverty, see Jeffrey Tulis, *The Rhetorical Presidency* (Princeton, N.J.: Princeton University Press, 1987), 161–72.

50. Richard Blumenthal, "The Bureaucracy: Antipoverty and the Community Action Program," in *American Institutions and Public Policy: Five Contemporary Studies*, edited by Alan Sindler (Boston: Little, Brown, 1969), 149–52.

51. Mangum, *MDTA*, 38–39; Stanley Ruttenberg assisted by Jocelyn Gutchess, *Manpower Challenge of the 1970s* (Baltimore: Johns Hopkins University Press, 1970), 12–17.

52. See Robert M. Solow, "Technology and Unemployment," *Public Interest* 1 (Fall 1965): 17–26.

53. Mangum, *MDTA*, 38–39.

54. Moynihan, *Maximum Feasible Misunderstanding*, 75–82; on the PCJD, see Daniel Knapp and Kenneth Polk, *Scouting the War on Poverty: Social Reform Politics in the Kennedy Administration* (Lexington, Mass.: D. C. Heath, 1971), especially chs. 1, 5, and 7. See the discussion in Matusow, *The Unraveling of America*, 107–26; and Sanford Kravitz, "The Community Action Program—Past, Present, and Its Future," in Sundquist, *On Fighting Poverty*, 52–62.

55. Known as Hackett's guerrillas (after PCJD head David Hackett), PCJD members sought to create ties with other agencies in order to gain access to their resources. See Matusow, *The Unraveling of America*, 107–26.

56. Aaron, *Politics and the Professors*, 29, sums up the various views of the CAPs; see also Sundquist, *Politics and Policy*, 140; on the views of the key Budget Bureau official William Cannon, see Blumenthal, "The Bureaucracy," 146–49. In a memo to Budget Bureau officials, Hackett had stressed that the emphasis on planning ("action-study") would save money by eliminating "overlap, duplication and waste." See David Hackett, "Memorandum to William Capron and Burton Weisbrod," December 5, 1963, Sorensen Papers, Box 37, Poverty (Eastern Kentucky)—Attack on Poverty Program File, John F. Kennedy Library.

57. See the discussion in "Poverty and Urban Policy," 218–19, 261; and the discussion in Piven and Cloward, *Regulating the Poor*, 264–65.

58. Matusow, *The Unraveling of America*, 125–26.

59. Roger Friedland, "Class Power and Social Control: The War on Poverty," *Politics and Society* 6 (1976): 465.

60. Willard Wirtz, "Memorandum for the President," November 3, 1967, Reading File, Record Group 174, National Archives. See also the evaluations of the Concentrated Employment Program in *Manpower Report of the Presi-*

dent (Washington, D.C.: Government Printing Office, 1967), 195–96; and U.S. General Accounting Office, *Review of Economic Opportunity Programs* (Washington, D.C.: Government Printing Office, 1969), 45–50. For a more favorable evaluation of the Concentrated Employment Program, see Sar A. Levitan and Robert Taggart, *The Promise of Greatness* (Cambridge: Harvard University Press, 1976), 183–84.

61. Joseph H. Ball, "The Implementation of Federal Manpower Policy 1961–1971: A Study in Bureaucratic Competition and Intergovernmental Relations," (Ph.D. diss., Columbia University, 1972), 148.

62. See testimony of Frederick Harbison in U.S. Congress, Senate, *Hearings before the Subcommittee on Employment and Manpower of the Committee on Labor and Public Welfare on Manpower Problems of the Sixties*, 86th Cong., 2d sess., June 14, 15, 1960, 39.

63. Sundquist, *Politics and Policy*, 88, reports that the AVA was reputed to have the best lobby on Capitol Hill during the early 1960s.

64. Sundquist, *Politics and Policy*, 87–91; and Mangum, *MDTA*, ch. 2.

65. *Manpower Report of the President* (Washington, D.C.: Government Printing Office, 1969), 238.

66. Ruttenberg and Gutchess, *Manpower Challenge of the 1970s*, 15–23.

67. See, for example, Bakke, *A Positive Labor Market Policy*, 182–87; Eli Ginzberg, "Employment Service—Chosen Instrument of the Manpower Revolution," *Employment Service Review* 4 (March–April 1967): 7–9. A call to turn the Employment Service into a "comprehensive manpower services agency" was issued by the Shultz task force in its 1965 study of the Employment Service. This report is reprinted in *Employment Service Review* 3 (February 1966): 1–29.

68. On the early years of the Employment Service, see Leonard P. Adams, *The Public Employment Service in Transition, 1933–1968: Evolution of a Placement Service into a Manpower Agency* (Ithaca: New York State School of Industrial and Labor Relations, Cornell University, 1969).

69. See Oscar Weigert, "Administrative Problems of Employment Services in Eight States," publication no. 72 (Chicago: Public Administration Service, 1940); William Haber, "Proposals for Reorganization of Unemployment Compensation and the Employment Service," *Social Service Review* 16 (March 1942): 37–56; "A National Employment Service: A Report of the Labor Committee of the National Planning Association" (Washington, D.C.: National Planning Association, 1945).

70. The dispute after the war is discussed in "Control of Employment Services," *Congressional Digest* 25 (April 1946): 97–128. See also William Haber and Daniel Kruger, *The Role of the United States Employment Service in a Changing Economy* (Kalamazoo, Mich.: W. E. Upjohn Institute, 1964), 31–35.

71. Stanley H. Ruttenberg and Jocelyn Gutchess, *The Federal-State Employment Service: A Critique* (Baltimore: Johns Hopkins University Press, 1970), 24–25.

72. The difficulties involved in persuading the Employment Service to serve the disadvantaged are documented in Ruttenberg and Gutchess, *Federal-State Employment Service*, 21–23, 76–78; and Lawyers' Committee for

Civil Rights under Law, *Falling Down on the Job: The United States Employment Service and the Disadvantaged* (Washington, D.C.: National Urban Coalition and Lawyers' Committee for Civil Rights under Law, 1971), especially
ch. 3 and pp. 63–79. See also the case study of San Francisco presented in
Miriam Johnson, *Counterpoint: The Changing Employment Service* (Salt
Lake City: Olympus, 1973), ch. 3; Richard P. Nathan, *Jobs and Civil Rights:
The Role of the Federal Government in Promoting Equal Opportunity in Employment and Training* (Washington, D.C.: Government Printing Office,
1969), 159–62.

73. Ruttenberg and Gutchess, *Federal-State Employment Service*, 52–57;
Arnold Nemore and Garth Mangum, *Reorienting the Federal-State Employment Service*, Policy Papers in Human Resources and Industrial Relations,
no. 8 (Ann Arbor, Mich.: Institute of Labor and Industrial Relations and the
National Manpower Policy Task Force, May 1968), 36–40; "Samuel V. Merrick, Oral History," Lyndon B. Johnson Library, 21.

74. Nemore and Mangum, *Reorienting the Federal-State Employment
Service*, 36–40; Haber and Kruger, *The Role of the United States Employment
Service in a Changing Economy*, 67–70.

75. For the task force recommendations on which the bill was based, see
the Shultz task force report, reprinted in *Employment Service Review* 3 (February 1966): 1–29; for an outline of the Manpower Services Act of 1966 and
the substitute bill proposed by the administration, see U.S. Congress, Senate, *Joint Hearings before the Subcommittee on Employment and Manpower,
Manpower Services Act of 1966 and Employment Service Act of 1966*, 89th
Cong., 2d sess., 1966, 57–60; for the failed effort to reintroduce the bill the
following year and the role of private employment agencies, see Nemore and
Mangum, *Reorienting the Federal-State Employment Service*, 25–26.

76. See Ball, "The Implementation of Federal Manpower Policy 1961–
1971," 154–55; Ruttenberg and Gutchess, *Manpower Challenge of the 1970s*,
76.

77. Ruttenberg and Gutchess, *Manpower Challenge of the 1970s*, 78–81.

78. See the account in Emmette S. Redford and Marlan Blissett, *Organizing the Executive Branch: The Johnson Presidency* (Chicago: University of
Chicago Press, 1981), 180–84; Jonathan Grossman, *The Department of Labor*
(New York: Praeger, 1973), 80–82. One of the central factors behind the opposition of Employment Service administrators to the reform appeared to be
suspicion of the manpower administrator, Stanley Ruttenberg, who had
been director of research for the AFL-CIO and had advocated federalization
of the Employment Service. See "Memo, E. L. Keenan to Governor Price
Daniel," October 23, 1968, Ex FG 160, WHCF, Box 235, Lyndon B. Johnson
Library.

79. The manpower administrator, Stanley Ruttenberg, even maintained
that the governors' protest was engineered by the president to provide him
with an excuse for opposing the reorganization. See Redford and Blissett,
Organizing the Executive Branch, 183; for Ruttenberg's account of this episode, see his oral history interview, "Stanley Ruttenberg, Oral History,"
Lyndon B. Johnson Library, 26–42.

80. Redford and Blissett, *Organizing the Executive Branch*, 142–56; Peri

E. Arnold, *Making the Managerial Presidency: Comprehensive Reorganization Planning, 1905–1980* (Princeton, N.J.: Princeton University Press, 1986), 233–36.

81. E. Wight Bakke, *The Mission of Manpower Policy* (Kalamazoo, Mich.: W. E. Upjohn Institute for Employment Research, 1969), 85.

82. The role of racial issues in the inception of the War on Poverty has been a contentious topic. See the discussion in Michael B. Katz, *The Undeserving Poor: From the War on Poverty to the War on Welfare* (New York: Pantheon Books, 1989), 81–88.

83. Brauer, "Kennedy, Johnson, and the War on Poverty," 110.

84. See Earl Raab, "What War and Which Poverty?" *Public Interest* 3 (Spring 1966): 45–56; Nathan Glazer, "Paradoxes of American Poverty," *Public Interest* 1 (Fall 1965): 77–99; John C. Donovan, *The Politics of Poverty* (New York: Pegasus, 1973), 97–110.

85. Levitan, *The Great Society's Poor Law*, 120–21; Piven and Cloward, *Regulating the Poor*, 258–59; James W. Button, *Black Violence: Political Impact of the 1960s Riots* (Princeton, N.J.: Princeton University Press, 1978), 26.

86. Andrew F. Brimmer, "Economic Developments in the Black Community," *Public Interest* 34 (Winter 1974): 153.

87. Matusow, *The Unraveling of America*, 255–65, details the fate of community action in several cities; see also the case studies presented in J. David Greenstone and Paul E. Peterson, *Race and Authority in Urban Politics: Community Participation and the War on Poverty* (Chicago: University of Chicago Press, 1973), 19–43.

88. On poverty rates, see U.S. Department of Commerce, *Statistical Abstract of the United States, 1967* (Washington, D.C.: Government Printing Office, 1967), 338. On black employment and unemployment, see Ray Marshall, *The Negro Worker* (New York: Random House, 1967), ch. 6.

89. David Zarefsky, *President Johnson's War on Poverty: Rhetoric and History* (University, Ala.: University of Alabama Press, 1986), 102–3.

90. Paul E. Peterson and J. David Greenstone, "Racial Change and Citizen Participation: The Mobilization of Low-Income Communities through Community Action," in *A Decade of Federal Anti-Poverty Programs: Achievements, Failures and Lessons*, edited by Robert H. Haveman (Madison: University of Wisconsin Press, 1977), 248, 251–56.

91. See Button, *Black Violence*, especially chs. 2, 3, 5.

92. Lee Rainwater and William Yancey, *The Moynihan Report and the Politics of Controversy* (Cambridge: MIT Press, 1967), 131. This book provides an excellent account of the politics surrounding the Conference to Fulfill These Rights.

93. Button, *Black Violence*, 160–63.

94. J. Timothy McGinley, "Memorandum to the Secretary of Labor," April 4, 1967, File PE-4-02, McGinley, J. Timothy, Record Group 174, National Archives.

95. See the polls and other public reactions cited in Zarefsky, *President Johnson's War on Poverty*, 104–6.

96. See the House debate on November 8–9, 1967, *Congressional Record,* 90th Cong., 1st sess., 31769–894. These debates are summarized in Donovan, *Politics of Poverty,* 150–51; and William C. Selover, "View from Capitol Hill: Harassment and Survival," in *On Fighting Poverty: Perspectives from Experience,* edited by James Sundquist (New York: Basic Books, 1969), 174–79.

97. Tobin, "The Political Economy of the 1960s," 437.

98. See *Manpower Report of the President* (Washington, D.C.: Government Printing Office, 1967), 73–78; and William J. Spring, "Underemployment: The Measure We Refuse to Take," in *The Political Economy of Public Service Employment,* edited by Harold L. Sheppard, Bennett Harrison, and William

J. Spring (Lexington, Mass.: D.C. Health and Co., 1972), 187–94.

99. James R. Wetzel and Susan S. Holland, "Poverty Areas of Our Major Cities," *Monthly Labor Review* 89 (October 1966): 1106.

100. See the discussion in *Manpower Report of the President* (Washington, D.C.: Government Printing Office, 1967), 73–78; and *Manpower Report of the President* (1968), 34–36.

101. U.S. Congress, Senate, Subcommittee on Employment, Manpower, and Poverty, *Comprehensive Manpower Reform,* app. 1, " 'A Report on Employment and Unemployment in Urban Slums and Ghettos,' Memo for the President, December 23, 1966," 92d Cong., 2d sess. (Washington, D.C.: Government Printing Office, 1972), 2301.

102. Ibid., 2287–2312.

103. The report is reprinted in Rainwater and Yancey, *The Moynihan Report and the Politics of Controversy,* 41–124.

104. Cited in *Congressional Quarterly Almanac, 1966* (Washington, D.C.: Congressional Quarterly Press, 1967), 257.

105. See the Kerner Commission report, U.S. National Advisory Commission on Civil Disorders, *Report of the National Advisory Commission on Civil Disorders* (New York: Bantam Books, 1968), 413–24; on the Poor People's Campaign, see Charles Fager, *Uncertain Resurrection: Poor People's Washington Campaign* (Grand Rapids, Mich.: Eerdmans, 1969).

106. On the 1967 effort to enact the tax surcharge, see the interview with CEA heads Gardner Ackley and Arthur Okun in Hargrove and Morley, *The President and the Council of Economic Advisers,* 247–60, 302–6; Lawrence C. Pierce, *The Politics of Fiscal Policy Formation* (Pacific Palisades, Calif.: Goodyear Publishing Co., 1971), 146–59; *Congressional Quarterly Almanac, 1967,* 643–53.

107. Memorandum for the President, July 28, 1967, Reading File, Record Group 174, National Archives.

108. After its first six months of operation, the Department of Labor's experimental job development program claimed to have developed 62,213 jobs in service occupations. See "Memorandum to the President from Secretary of Labor Willard Wirtz," November 13, 1965, White House—President File, Record Group 174, National Archives. For descriptions of some of these early experiments in job development, see "The President's Job Development Program," *Employment Service Review* 2 (December 1965): 3, 35; Law-

rence A. Still, "Chicago's JOBS-NOW: An Answer for Ghetto Youth," *Employ-ment Service Review* 14 (August–September 1967): 36–41; and *Manpower Re-port of the President* (Washington, D.C.: Government Printing Office, 1967), 54–55.

109. *Public Papers of the Presidents of the United States, Lyndon B. John-son, 1968–69,* book 1 (Washington, D.C.: Government Printing Office, 1970), 46–53.

110. Sar A. Levitan, Garth L. Mangum, and Robert Taggart, *Economic Op-portunity in the Ghetto: The Partnership of Government and Business* (Balti-more: Johns Hopkins University Press, 1970), 20–21.

111. On the problems in the JOBS program by 1970, see *Manpower Report of the President* (Washington D.C.: Government Printing Office, 1971), 44.

112. Jack Barbash, "Union Interests in Apprenticeship and Other Train-ing Forms," *The Journal of Human Resources* 3 (Winter 1968): 84.

113. See Gary Burtless, "Are Targeted Wage Subsidies Harmless? Evi-dence from a Wage Voucher Experiment," *Industrial and Labor Relations Review* 39 (October 1985): 105–14.

114. See Doeringer and Piore, *Internal Labor Markets and Manpower Analysis.*

115. Michael K. Brown and Steven P. Erie, "Blacks and the Legacy of the Great Society: The Economic and Political Impact of Federal Social Policy," *Public Policy* 29 (Summer 1981): 315.

116. On the rise in welfare expenditures during the 1960s, see Piven and Cloward, *Regulating the Poor,* ch. 10. For the argument about public sector employment, see Brown and Erie, "Blacks and the Legacy of the Great Soci-ety," 299–330.

117. On the positions that black organizations took on social and eco-nomic policy during the Great Society period, see Charles V. Hamilton and Dona C. Hamilton, "Social Policies, Civil Rights and Poverty," in *Fighting Poverty: What Works and What Doesn't,* edited by Sheldon H. Danziger and Daniel H. Weinberg (Cambridge: Harvard University Press, 1986), 298–303.

118. For the mobilization against the Moynihan report see Rainwater and Yancey, *The Moynihan Report and the Politics of Controversy.*

119. The WIN program is discussed in Levitan and Taggart, *The Promise of Greatness,* 54–57; on the imposition of work requirements more generally, see Lawrence Mead, *Beyond Entitlement: The Social Obligations of Citizen-ship* (New York: Free Press, 1985).

120. Martin Luther King, Jr., *Where Do We Go from Here? Chaos or Com-munity* (Boston: Beacon Press, 1967), especially ch. 2.

121. The Freedom Budget is printed in U.S. Congress, Senate, Subcom-mittee on Employment, Manpower, and Poverty, *Examination of the War on Poverty,* part 1, 90th Cong., 1st sess., 1967, 407–504; see also the report of the conference, *The Report of the White House Conference to Fulfill These Rights* (Washington, D.C.: Government Printing Office, 1966), especially 44–55.

122. See the exchange between Senator Joseph Clark and Bayard Rustin during the 1967 hearings on the War on Poverty in U.S. Congress, Senate,

Subcommittee on Employment, Manpower, and Poverty, *Examination of the War on Poverty*, part 1, 90th Cong., 1st sess., 1967, 242–43.

123. Bayard Rustin to Mrs. Lenore Marshall, November 22, 1966, Bayard Rustin Papers (Frederick, Md.: University Publications of America, 1988), Reel 13, 00257.

124. See Peterson and Greenstone, "Racial Change and Citizen Participation"; and Peter K. Eisinger, "The CAP and the Development of Black Political Leadership," in *Urban Policy Making*, edited by Dale Rogers Marshall (Beverly Hills and London: Sage Publications, 1979), 127–44.

125. Edward G. Carmines and James A. Stimson, *Issue Evolution: Race and the Transformation of American Politics* (Princeton, N.J.: Princeton University Press, 1989), 116–19, 134–37.

126. On the increasing racial conservatism of the Republican party, see ibid., 52–55.

127. On the 1968 election, see Matusow, *The Unraveling of America*, ch. 14; see also Philip E. Converse, Warren E. Miller, Jerrold G. Rusk, and Arthur C. Wolfe, "Continuity and Change in American Politics: Parties and Issues in the 1968 Election," *American Political Science Review* 63 (December 1969): 1083–1105.

128. Everett Carll Ladd, Jr., with Charles D. Hadley, *Transformations of the American Party System: Political Coalitions from the New Deal to the 1970s* (New York: W. W. Norton, 1978), 240–41. This pattern and the possibilities of building a new political coalition based upon it are discussed by Walter Dean Burnham, *Critical Elections and the Mainsprings of American Politics* (New York: W. W. Norton, 1970), 169–74.

129. Ladd and Hadley, *Transformations of the American Party System*, 233–35; on organized labor see Matusow, *The Unraveling of America*, 432–33.

130. For a discussion of the "selectivist" strategy that characterized American social policy in the 1960s, see Walter Korpi, "Approaches to the Study of Poverty in the United States: Critical Notes from a European Perspective," in *Poverty and Public Policy: An Evaluation of Social Science Research*, edited by Vincent T. Covello (Cambridge, Mass.: Schenkman, 1980), 301–5.

Chapter Four

1. For a survey of developments in postwar macroeconomic thought, see Robert J. Gordon, "Postwar Macroeconomics: The Evolution of Events and Ideas," in *The American Economy in Transition*, edited by Martin Feldstein (Chicago: University of Chicago Press, 1980), 101–58. On the activist strategy, see Arthur M. Okun, *The Political Economy of Prosperity* (Washington, D.C.: Brookings Institution, 1970). For a summary of the Phillips curve approach, see Helmut Frisch, "Inflation Theory 1963–1975: A 'Second Generation' Survey," *Journal of Economic Literature* 15 (December 1977): 1289–1317.

2. On the early economic policies of the Nixon administration, see Herbert Stein, *Presidential Economics: The Making of Economic Policy from*

Roosevelt to Reagan and Beyond (New York: Simon and Schuster, 1984), ch. 5; Erwin Hargrove and Samuel A. Morley, eds., *The President and the Council of Economic Advisers* (Boulder, Colo.: Westview Press, 1984), 319–57; George P. Shultz and Kenneth W. Dam, *Economic Policy beyond the Headlines* (New York: W. W. Norton, 1977); Leonard Silk, *Nixonomics: How the Dismal Science of Free Enterprise Became the Black Art of Controls* (New York: Praeger, 1972); *Economic Report of the President* (Washington, D.C.: Government Printing Office, 1970), 31–32.

3. See Henry J. Aaron, *Politics and the Professors: The Great Society in Perspective* (Washington, D.C.: Brookings Institution, 1978), ch. 4, for a summary of these new issues in understanding unemployment. See also George L. Perry, "Changing Labor Markets and Inflation," *Brookings Papers on Economic Activity*, no. 3 (1970): 411–39.

4. Aaron, *Politics and the Professors*, ch. 4, and Lester Thurow, *Dangerous Currents: The State of Economics* (New York: Vintage Books, 1983), ch. 7, have general surveys of the breakdown in the theoretical consensus about the operations of labor markets. See also Ray Marshall, "Implications of Labor Market Theory for Employment Policy," in *Manpower Research and Labor Economics*, edited by Gordon I. Swanson and Jon Michaelson (Beverly Hills, Calif.: Sage, 1979), 17–59.

5. Charles C. Holt, C. Duncan MacRae, Stuart O. Schweitzer, and Ralph E. Smith, *The Unemployment Dilemma: A Manpower Solution* (Washington, D.C.: Urban Institute, 1971); id., *Manpower Programs to Reduce Inflation and Unemployment: Micro Lyrics for Macro Music* (Washington, D.C.: Urban Institute, 1971); id., "Manpower Policies to Reduce Inflation and Unemployment," in *Manpower Programs in the Policy Mix*, edited by Lloyd Ulman (Baltimore: Johns Hopkins University Press, 1973), 51–82.

6. On the changing composition of the labor force, see Robert E. Hall, "Why Is the Unemployment Rate So High at Full Employment?" *Brookings Papers on Economic Activity*, no. 3 (1970): 369–410; on the emergence of the search-turnover theory of unemployment, see Clair Brown, "Unemployment Theory and Policy, 1946–1980," *Industrial Relations* 22 (Spring 1983): 168–69.

7. Holt et al., *Manpower Programs to Reduce Inflation and Unemployment*, p. II-3.

8. Holt et al., "Manpower Policies to Reduce Inflation and Unemployment," 82. NMAC director Eli Ginzberg makes a similar argument in "Manpower Training: Boon, Not Boondoggle," *Challenge* 16 (September–October 1973): 52–56.

9. See, for example, the publications of a project on "Unemployment and the American Economy," funded by the Ford Foundation in the 1960s, including Arthur M. Ross, ed., *Unemployment and the American Economy* (New York: John Wiley, 1964); Arthur M. Ross, ed., *Employment Policy and the Labor Market* (Berkeley: University of California Press, 1967); and Robert Aaron Gordon, *Toward a Manpower Policy* (New York: Wiley, 1967). For elaborations of these viewpoints in the 1970s, see Robert Aaron Gordon, "Some Macroeconomic Aspects of Manpower Policy," in Ulman, *Manpower*

Programs in the Policy Mix, 10, 49; U.S. Congress, Joint Economic Committee, *The 1972 Economic Report of the President*, 92d Cong., 2d sess., 1972, 710, 723–24; Lloyd Ulman, "The Uses and Limits of Manpower Policy," *Public Interest* 34 (Winter 1974): 83–105.

10. For an overview of the NMAC policy positions, see the collected letters of the group to government officials in *Manpower Advice for Government: National Manpower Advisory Committee Letters to the Secretaries of Labor and of Health, Education, and Welfare, 1962–1971* (Washington, D.C.: U.S. Department of Labor, 1972).

11. Support for public service employment was also increasingly voiced by some of the macroeconomists who had served in the Kennedy and Johnson administrations. See James Tobin, *The New Economics One Decade Older* (Princeton, N.J.: Princeton University Press, 1974), 95–96.

12. Peter B. Doeringer and Michael J. Piore, *Internal Labor Markets and Manpower Analysis* (Armonk, N.Y.: M. E. Sharpe, 1985); Peter B. Doeringer, *Low-Income Labor Markets and Urban Manpower Programs: A Critical Assessment* (Washington, D.C.: U.S. Department of Labor, 1972); Michael J. Piore, "On-the-Job Training in the Dual Labor Market: Public and Private Responsibilities in On-the-Job Training of Disadvantaged Workers," in *Public-Private Manpower Policies*, edited by Arnold R. Weber, Frank Cassell, and Woodrow L. Ginsburg (Madison, Wisc.: Industrial Relations Research Association, 1969), 101–32; Michael J. Piore, "The Importance of Human Capital Theory to Labor Economics—A Dissenting View," in *Proceedings of the 26th Annual Winter Meeting of the Industrial Relations Research Association, 1973* (Madison, Wisc.: IRRA, 1974), 251–58. For a critical discussion of dual labor market theories, see Glen G. Cain, "The Challenge of Segmented Labor Market Theories to Orthodox Theory: A Survey," *Journal of Economic Literature* 14 (December 1976): 215–57.

13. Doeringer, *Low-Income Labor Markets and Urban Manpower Programs*, 38–39; Peter B. Doeringer and Michael J. Piore, "Unemployment and the Dual Labor Market," *Public Interest* 38 (Winter 1975): 76–77. Doeringer and Piore believed that the supply of primary sector employment should be increased. Although the complexity of this task put it beyond the reach of policymakers, they argued that a strong commitment to achieve full employment by means of aggregate stimulation was the best route to encourage structural transformations that would reduce labor market inequalities. See "Unemployment and the Dual Labor Market," 78–79.

14. Bennett Harrison, "Public Service Jobs for Urban Ghetto Residents," in *Political Economy of Public Service Employment*, edited by Harold L. Sheppard, Bennett Harrison, and William J. Spring (Lexington, Mass.: D. C. Heath, 1972), 231–68; Barry Bluestone, "Economic Theory, Economic Reality and the Fate of the Poor," ibid., 117–28.

15. Milton Friedman, "The Role of Monetary Policy," *American Economic Review* 58 (March 1968): 1–17.

16. Friedman, "The Role of Monetary Policy," 9.

17. U.S. Congress, Joint Economic Committee, *Lowering the Permanent Rate of Unemployment*, 93d Cong., 1st sess., 1973, Committee Print; a ver-

sion of this report was published by its author, see Martin Feldstein, "The Economics of the New Unemployment," *Public Interest* 33 (Fall 1973): 3–42.

18. Feldstein, "Economics of the New Unemployment," 10.

19. Shultz and Dam, *Economic Policy beyond the Headlines*, 23–24; Joseph H. Ball, "The Implementation of Federal Manpower Policy, 1961–1971: A Study in Bureaucratic Competition and Intergovernmental Relations" (Ph.D. diss., Columbia University, 1972), 181.

20. *Manpower Report of the President* (Washington, D.C.: Government Printing Office, 1970), 10.

21. Ibid., 83–85.

22. For a description of the administration's proposed act, see ibid.

23. Harry Frumerman, *Job Vacancy Statistics in the United States* (Washington, D.C.: National Commission on Employment and Unemployment Statistics, 1978).

24. On the Philadelphia Plan, see Hugh Davis Graham, *The Civil Rights Era: Origins and Development of National Policy* (New York: Oxford University Press, 1990), chs. 11, 13; *Manpower Report of the President* (Washington, D.C.: Government Printing Office, 1970), 97–98.

25. Ball, "The Implementation of Federal Manpower Policy, 1961–1971," 181–85; *Manpower Report of the President* (Washington, D.C.: Government Printing Office, 1970), 79.

26. *Manpower Report of the President* (Washington, D.C.: Government Printing Office, 1970), 79.

27. See Ball's discussion in "The Implementation of Federal Manpower Policy, 1961–1971," 182–85. See also the memo from Manpower Administrator Arnold Weber to the secretary of labor outlining the strategy for reorganization in which he states: "The previous reorganization aborted because of the failure to obtain adequate support from the Executive Branch and the sharp resistance of some of the State Employment Security administrators and governors. However, it should be noted that most of the states, especially the larger industrial states with the greater proportion of the labor force, did not react negatively to the plan. Nonetheless, we hope to engage in a wide process of consultation to build understanding and support of what we are trying to do." Arnold Weber, "Memorandum to the Secretary of Labor," February 7, 1969, 1969 White House Urban Affairs Council (January–March) File, Record Group 174, National Archives.

28. For a description of the predecessors of ASPER, see "History of the Department of Labor under Nixon and Ford: Section on the Assistant Secretary for Policy Evaluation and Research," Historical Office, Department of Labor, 1977, 1–3. The material on ASPER that follows is from Erwin C. Hargrove, "Knowledge and Organization: The Bureaucratic Politics of Analysis, Evaluation, and Research in the Department of Labor" (unpublished mss., Historical Office, Department of Labor, 1976).

29. Hargrove, "Knowledge and Organization," pp. II-2–3.

30. Ibid., pp. II-1–2.

31. Roger Davidson, *The Politics of Comprehensive Manpower Legislation* (Baltimore: Johns Hopkins University Press, 1972), 17–19.

32. *Congressional Quarterly Weekly Report* 28 (December 18, 1970): 2992.

33. See the president's veto message ibid., 2993.

34. Stein, *Presidential Economics,* 135.

35. On Nixon's New Federalism, see Richard P. Nathan, *The Administrative Presidency* (New York: John Wiley, 1983), 17–22; Paul R. Dommel, *The Politics of Revenue Sharing* (Bloomington: Indiana University Press, 1974).

36. On the Nixon administration's hopes of securing blue-collar support, see *New York Times,* June 30, 1970, 1; and Silk, *Nixonomics,* 28–35. On the strategic political position of blue-collar workers in the late 1960s, see Howard L. Reiter, "Blue Collar Workers and the Future of American Politics," in *Blue Collar Workers: A Symposium on Middle America,* edited by Sar A. Levitan (New York: McGraw-Hill, 1971), 101–29; Everett Carll Ladd, Jr., with Charles D. Hadley, *Transformations of the American Party System: Party Coalitions from the New Deal to the 1970s* (New York: W. W. Norton, 1978), 232–34.

37. George Shultz, "Memo for John Ehrlichman," June 20, 1970, 1970 White House Committee on the Blue Collar Workers File, Record Group 174, National Archives.

38. On programs supporting "black capitalism," see Graham, *The Civil Rights Era,* 313–16.

39. Nathan, *The Administrative Presidency,* especially ch. 3.

40. See Nathan, *The Administrative Presidency,* 28–33; for evidence that the staff in the new programs created under Johnson had beliefs that differed from those of the Nixon administration, see Joel D. Aberbach and Bert A. Rockman, "Clashing Beliefs within the Executive Bureaucracy: The Nixon Administration Bureaucracy," *American Political Science Review* 70 (June 1976): 456–68.

41. On the administration's strategy of dividing civil rights leaders and organized labor through the Philadelphia Plan, see Graham, *The Civil Rights Era,* 325. Clarence Mitchell, director of the NAACP, charged that the administration's handling of the plan revealed "a calculated attempt coming right from the President's desk to break up the coalition between Negroes and labor unions." See *Congressional Quarterly Weekly Report* 28 (November 27, 1970): 2859–61.

42. Nathan, *The Administrative Presidency,* 34–38.

43. Daniel J. Baltz, "Economic Report/Civil Servant, Statistician Named Chief of Troubled Bureau of Labor Statistics," *National Journal* 5 (July 7, 1973): 995. The Joint Economic Committee sought to keep up the tradition of BLS interpretation of the statistics by scheduling monthly hearings to discuss newly released labor statistics. See U.S. Congress, Joint Economic Committee, *Current Labor Market Developments,* 92d Cong., 2d sess., 1972.

44. Hargrove, "Knowledge and Organization," pp. II-2–3.

45. Ibid., p. IV-3.

46. On the administration's proposal for manpower revenue sharing, see *Congressional Quarterly Almanac, 1971* (Washington, D.C.: Congressional Quarterly Press, 1972), 698–709.

47. For the text of Nixon's manpower message, see *Congressional Quar-*

terly Weekly Report 28 (December 18, 1970): 57-A–59-A; William H. Kolberg, *Developing Manpower Legislation: A Personal Chronicle* (Washington, D.C.: National Academy of the Sciences, 1978), 13.

48. Howard Hallman, *Emergency Employment: A Study in Federalism* (University, Ala.: University of Alabama Press, 1977), 28.

49. Kolberg, *Developing Manpower Legislation,* 6–29; "New Federalism III/Manpower," *National Journal* 5 (March 3, 1973): 299–300; *Congressional Quarterly Almanac, 1971,* 698–709, 57-A.

50. Among the many accounts of the New Economic Policy, see Stein, *Presidential Economics,* 176–82; A. James Reichley, *Conservatives in an Age of Change: The Nixon and Ford Administrations* (Washington, D.C.: Brookings Institution, 1981), 221–25; see McCracken's perspective in Hargrove and Morley, *The President and the Council of Economic Advisers,* 244–57.

51. Reichley, *Conservatives in an Age of Change,* 213–14.

52. See, for example, the testimony of United Auto Workers president Leonard Woodcock and Senator Philip Hart (D. Mich.) in the Joint Economic Committee's hearings on the New Economic Policy, U.S. Congress, Joint Economic Committee, *The President's New Economic Program,* pt. 4, 92d Cong., 1st sess., 510–73, 592–607; *Congressional Quarterly Weekly Report* 29 (August 12, 1971): 1759; John F. Burby, "Economic Report/No Letup for President's Economic Advisers Despite Good Second Quarter," *National Journal* 4 (August 12, 1972): 1282.

53. "The U.S. Economy: Nixon's Failure," *American Federationist* 79 (March 1972): 9–11.

54. On the reforms in the Democratic party, see Nelson Polsby, *The Consequences of Party Reform* (New York: Oxford University Press, 1983).

55. John F. Burby, "Campaign '72 Report/Complex McGovern Economics Plan Dissolves in Campaign Heat," *National Journal* 4 (September 16, 1972): 1449–58.

56. Ladd, *Transformations of the American Party System,* 235.

57. Hargrove, "Knowledge and Organization," p. II-6.

58. Charles Culhane, "Labor Report/Mayors, Labor Leaders Add Political Muscle to Hill Challenge of Manpower-Training Cuts," *National Journal* 5 (April 7, 1973): 489, 496; Kolberg, *Developing Manpower Legislation,* 7.

59. On the increasingly powerful and political role of the OMB in this era, see Joel Havemann, "White House Report/OMB's Legislative Role Is Growing More Powerful and More Political," *National Journal* 5 (November 27, 1973): 1589–98; see also Hugh Heclo, "OMB and the Presidency—The Problem of Neutral Competence," *Public Interest* 38 (Winter 1975): 80–98.

60. Hargrove, "Knowledge and Organization," II-65.

61. Reichley, *Conservatives in an Age of Change,* 228; John F. Burby, "$268.7 Billion Blueprint/President's Budget Requests Seek to Reshape Domestic Government," *National Journal* 5 (February 3, 1973): 142.

62. Stein, *Presidential Economics,* 287–90, characterizes Nixon's entire postelection economic policy as a return to the old-time religion.

63. Richard B. DuBoff, "Full Employment: History of a Receding Target," *Politics and Society* 7 (1977): 1–25.

64. Daniel J. Baltz, "Economic Report/JEC Recommendations Refuel Debate over Appropriate Full-Employment Target," *National Journal* 5 (March 31, 1973): 443–49.

65. Quoted in Helen Ginsburg, *Full Employment and Public Policy: The United States and Sweden* (Lexington, Mass.: Lexington Books, 1983), 33.

66. *Congressional Quarterly Weekly Report* 28 (May 1, 1970): 1182.

67. See the testimony in U.S. Congress, Joint Economic Committee, *The 1970 Midyear Review of the State of the Economy*, 91st Cong., 2d. sess., 1970, 321, 520–23, 528–32.

68. Baltz, "Economic Report/JEC Recommendations," 443–49.

69. Gary Orfield, *Congressional Power: Congress and Social Change* (New York: Harcourt Brace Jovanovich, 1975), 220; see Hallman, *Emergency Employment*, chs. 3–4, for an account of the passage of the legislation.

70. Orfield, *Congressional Power*, 236–39; see a summary of the testimony during congressional hearings on public jobs in 1972 in *Congressional Quarterly Almanac, 1972*, 572–77.

71. On the termination of the EEA, see Culhane, "Labor Report/Mayors, Labor Leaders Add Political Muscle to Hill Challenge of Manpower-Training Cuts," 491–92; on the popularity of EEA, see, for example, the comment that the EEA was "the most popular federal manpower program ever run in North Carolina," cited in Sar Levitan and Robert Taggart, eds., *Emergency Employment Act: The PEP Generation* (Salt Lake City: Olympus Publishing Co., 1974), 6. The 1975 *Manpower Report of the President*, 49, also mentioned the popularity of the program, noting that PEP had helped to counterbalance the negative assessment of public employment that had been left over from the New Deal.

72. On the passage and early provisions of CETA, see Donald C. Baumer and Carl E. Van Horn, *The Politics of Unemployment* (Washington, D.C.: Congressional Quarterly Press, 1985), 59–65; Grace A. Franklin and Randall B. Ripley, *CETA: Politics and Policy, 1973–1982* (Knoxville: University of Tennessee Press, 1984), 12–18; Kolberg, *Developing Manpower Legislation*, 30–44; Charles Culhane, "Manpower Report/Revenue Sharing Shift Set for Worker Training Programs," *National Journal* 6 (January 12, 1974): 51–58.

73. Baumer and Van Horn, *The Politics of Unemployment*, 59, 66–67.

74. Cited in ibid., 75.

75. For a survey of changes in congressional policymaking during the 1970s, see Samuel C. Patterson, "The Semi-Sovereign Congress," chapter 4 in *The New American Political System*, edited by Anthony King (Washington, D.C.: American Enterprise Institute, 1978). On Congress and the politics of grant programs, see R. Douglas Arnold, "The Local Roots of Domestic Policy," chapter 8 in *The New Congress*, edited by Thomas E. Mann and Norman Ornstein (Washington, D.C., and London: American Enterprise Institute, 1981).

76. Secretary Wirtz had a difficult time getting the kind of indicators he wanted. The BLS was resistant to new social indicators that did not conform to traditional definitions of unemployment. See Hargrove, "Knowledge and Organization," p. IV-4.

77. See the correspondence between Senator Gaylord Nelson and Secretary of Labor J. D. Hodgson, March 2, 1972, May 26, 1972, File LL-2-2, Labor and Public Welfare, 1972, Record Group 174, National Archives. The Urban League sought to raise concern on this issue by publishing its own report on unemployment in ghetto areas, using the Joint Economic Committee's definition of unemployment. See the editorial in the *Washington Post*, August 10, 1972, and the reply by Geoffrey H. Moore, commissioner of the Bureau of Labor Statistics, defending the conventional definitions, in the *Washington Post*, September 11, 1972.

78. Hargrove, "Knowledge and Organization," p. II-65.

79. On Nixon's urban strategy, see John Mollenkopf, *The Contested City* (Princeton, N.J.: Princeton University Press, 1983), 122-35.

80. On mayors' initial enthusiasm for revenue sharing, see Dommel, *The Politics of Revenue Sharing*, ch. 4; see also William Lilley, III, "Campaign '72 Report/Nixon Inroads among Democratic Mayors Weaken Party's Old Coalition," *National Journal* 4 (July 15, 1972): 1143-50.

81. Orfield, *Congressional Power*, 242-43. A congressional report echoed these charges, see Levitan and Taggart, *Emergency Employment Act*, ch. 1. The Department of Labor found the Urban Coalition's report to be a "serious misunderstanding of the Emergency Employment Act...." Secretary Hodgson called it "outrageous . . . [a] politically inspired drive and nothing else." See William Mirengoff, "Memorandum to Malcolm Lovell," August 29, 1972, and Carl Uehlein to Malcolm Lovell, December 6, 1971, Malcolm Lovell Papers, Historical Office, Department of Labor.

82. On the early hopes of the Department of Labor for WIN, see *Manpower Report of the President* (Washington, D.C.: Government Printing Office, 1971), 52-54. On WIN's performance see Mildred Rein, "Work in Welfare: Failures and Future Strategies," *Social Service Review* (June 1982): 211-27.

83. For a review of WIN's performance, see Demetra Smith Nightingale and Lynn C. Burbridge, *The Status of State Work-Welfare Programs in 1986: Implications for Welfare Reform*, (Washington, D.C.: Urban Institute, July 1987), 14-20; Lawrence Mead, *Beyond Entitlement: The Social Obligations of Citizenship* (New York: Free Press, 1985).

84. Department of Labor officials were puzzled by this change in the ratio. See Bradley C. Reardon, "Memorandum to King Carr," December 9, 1971, Malcolm Lovell Papers, Historical Office, Department of Labor.

85. Hargrove, "Knowledge and Organization," pp. II-91-96, IV-60-67.

86. Baumer and Van Horn, *The Politics of Unemployment*, 66-68, 84-85.

87. See the polls collected in Robert Y. Shapiro, Kelly D. Patterson, Judith Russell, and John T. Young, "Report: Employment and Social Welfare," *Public Opinion Quarterly* 51 (Summer 1987): 274-77.

88. For a survey of the publications of the commission, see National Commission on Employment Policy, *The First Five Years, 1974-1979* (Washington, D.C.: U.S. Department of Labor, 1979).

89. Ray Marshall, "Selective Employment Policies to Achieve Full Em-

ployment," *Industrial Relations Research Association, Proceedings of the 30th Annual Meeting, 1977* (Madison, Wisc.: IRRA, 1978), 1–9.

90. Ray Marshall, "Full Employment: The Inflation Myth," *American Federationist* 83 (August 1976): 7; James W. Singer, "Administration Adjusts Its Aim at Job Training Targets," *National Journal* 19 (April 30, 1977): 680–83. At a presentation before the National Association of Manufacturers, Marshall argued that general macroeconomic measures that put people back to work only indirectly were much more expensive than public service employment, estimating that general measures cost $20,000 per job, in contrast to $5,000 per job for public service employment. See "Presentation by the Honorable Ray Marshall before the National Association of Manufacturers," March 24, 1977, Speech Files, Historical Office, Department of Labor.

91. Hargrove and Morley, *The President and the Council of Economic Advisers*, 476–77.

92. *Congressional Quarterly Almanac, 1977,* 397–98.

93. Ibid., 100.

94. See Robert J. Samuelson, "Don't Knock Experience," *National Journal* 9 (January 1, 1977): 30.

95. For a sense of the views of the Brookings Institution economists on economic policy during the 1970s, see the annual policy volumes *Setting National Priorities* (Washington, D.C.: Brookings Institution), beginning in 1970.

96. Hargrove and Morley, *The President and the Council of Economic Advisers*, 476–78.

97. See the comments of the chief academic proponent of the structural thesis during the 1960s, Michigan State University economist Charles Killingsworth, "The Fall and Rise of the Idea of Structural Employment, *"Industrial Relations Research Association, Proceedings of the 31st Annual Meeting, 1978* (Madison, Wisc.: IRRA, 1979), 13.

98. Baumer and Van Horn, *The Politics of Unemployment,* 91, 96.

99. Ibid., 130–32; on the incentives of local officials to use CETA funds for political purposes, see Erwin C. Hargrove and Gillian Dean, "Federal Authority and Grassroots Accountability: The Case of CETA," *Policy Analysis* 6 (Spring 1980): 127–49.

100. Baumer and Van Horn, *The Politics of Unemployment,* 95–104.

101. See the examples cited in Baumer and Van Horn, *The Politics of Unemployment,* 104–9, 130–32.

102. Ibid., 106–13.

103. See the correspondence between Marshall and White House public relations expert Gerald Rafshoon, Ray Marshall, "Memorandum for Gerald Rafshoon Re: Proposed One-Year Public Strategy for Highlighting Employment Issues," October 11, 1978, White House (General) File, Ray Marshall Papers, Department of Labor; Jerry Rafshoon, Memorandum for Secretary Ray Marshall Re: Employment Credit-Taking Strategy, November 7, 1978, White House (General) File, Ray Marshall Papers, Department of Labor; Ray Marshall, "Memorandum for Gerald Rafshoon Re: Public Strategy on the

Employment Issue," November 17, 1978, White House (General) File, Ray Marshall Papers, Department of Labor.

104. James Singer and Robert J. Samuelson, "Labor's Marshall—A Believer in the Workability of Government Programs," *National Journal* 9 (September 10, 1977): 1406.

105. *Congressional Quarterly Almanac, 1978,* 272–79.

106. Baumer and Van Horn, *The Politics of Unemployment,* ch. 5.

107. Ibid., 127–28; *Congressional Quarterly Almanac, 1978,* 287–300.

108. Roger Davidson, *The Politics of Comprehensive Manpower Legislation* (Baltimore: Johns Hopkins University Press, 1972), 17–19.

109. On abuse and fraud, see Baumer and Van Horn, *The Politics of Unemployment,* 133; on fiscal substitution, see Richard P. Nathan, Robert F. Cook, V. Lane Rawlins, and Associates, *Public Service Employment: A Field Evaluation* (Washington, D.C.: Brookings Institution, 1981), ch. 2.

110. On corruption as a political issue in the United States, see Ann Shola Orloff and Theda Skocpol, "Why Not Equal Protection? Explaining the Politics of Public Social Spending in Britain, 1900–1911 and the United States, 1880–1920," *American Sociological Review* 49 (December 1984): 741–43.

111. On the CWA, see Bonnie Fox Schwartz, *The Civil Works Administration, 1933–34: The Business of Emergency Employment in the New Deal* (Princeton, N.J.: Princeton University Press, 1984), 95–101; on the WPA, see Searle F. Charles, *Minister of Relief: Harry Hopkins and the Depression* (Westport, Conn.: Greenwood Press, 1963), ch. 9.

Chapter Five

1. The most thoroughgoing of these arguments is presented in Thomas Ferguson and Joel Rogers, *Right Turn: The Decline of the Democrats and the Future of American Politics* (New York: Hill and Wang, 1986).

2. For a sophisticated analysis of unemployment and inflation that points in this direction, see Douglas Hibbs, Jr., "The Mass Public and Macroeconomic Performance: The Dynamics of Public Opinion toward Unemployment and Inflation," *American Journal of Political Science* 23 (November 1979): 705–31. Both public opinion and business mobilization are considered as determinants of economic policy in Thomas Byrne Edsall, *The New Politics of Inequality* (New York: W. W. Norton, 1984).

3. *New York Times,* March 14, 1974, 37.

4. See the interview with Leontief in "What an Economic Planning Board Should Do," *Challenge* 17 (July–August 1974): 36.

5. Ibid., 35.

6. Ibid., 37.

7. *New York Times,* February 28, 1975, 43, 48; "A New Push behind Economic Planning," *Business Week,* March 10, 1975, 21. Among the economists supporting the plan were John Dunlop, who was secretary of labor designate at the time. Business supporters included Robert V. Roosa, former undersecretary of the treasury during the Kennedy administration, at the time, a senior vice president of the investment house Brown Brothers Harriman & Co.,

as well as Irwin Miller, president of Cummins Engine Company, Stanley Marcus, of Neiman-Marcus, and John R. Bunting, Jr., chairman of First Pennsylvania Corporation. See David Vogel, *Fluctuating Fortunes: The Political Power of Business in America* (New York: Basic Books, 1989), 143–44.

8. Wassily Leontief and Herbert Stein, *The Economic System in an Age of Discontinuity: Long-Range Planning or Market Reliance?* (New York: New York University Press, 1976), 8.

9. The Initiative Committee for National Economic Planning, "For a National Economic Planning System," *Challenge* 18 (March–April 1975): 52; "A New Push behind Economic Planning," 21.

10. *New York Times*, February 28, 1975.

11. See Humphrey's comments in "Planning Economic Policy," *Challenge* 18 (March–April 1975): 21–25; see also Clarence J. Brown et al., *National Economic Planning: Right or Wrong for the U.S.?* (Washington, D.C.: American Enterprise Institute, 1976), 32.

12. See Helen Ginsburg, *Full Employment and Public Policy: The United States and Sweden* (Lexington, Mass.: Lexington Books, 1983), 64–73. For a summary of the bill and an explanation of its provisions by Hawkins, see *Congressional Record*, 93d Cong., 2d sess., June 26, 1974, H5803–8.

13. "The New Humphrey-Hawkins Bill," *Challenge* 19 (May–June, 1976): 22.

14. See the description in James W. Singer, "The Humphrey-Hawkins Bill–Boondoggle or Economic Blessing?" *National Journal* 8 (June 12, 1976): 814.

15. On the political chances of the Humphrey-Hawkins bill during the spring of 1976, see James W. Singer, "Humphrey-Hawkins Hangs On," *National Journal* 9 (May 7, 1977): 724.

16. See Ginsburg, *Full Employment and Public Policy*, 67–68.

17. Singer, "The Humphrey-Hawkins Bill," 813; on the Business Roundtable, see Kim McQuaid, "The Roundtable: Getting Results in Washington," *Harvard Business Review* 59 (May–June 1981): 114–23.

18. See Kim McQuaid, *Big Business and Presidential Power: From FDR to Reagan* (New York: William Morrow and Co., 1982), 158–75.

19. Most prominent among them were maverick representatives of Wall Street investment houses, such as Felix Rohatyn of Lazard Freres. See Gar Alperovitz and Jeff Faux, "What Kind of Planning?" *Working Papers* 3 (Fall 1975): 68.

20. See Keyserling's critique of "the new economics" in Leon Keyserling, "What's Wrong with American Economics?" *Challenge* 16 (May–June 1973): 18–25.

21. On the move from institutionalist to neoclassical analyses of unemployment, see Clair Brown, "Unemployment Theory and Policy, 1946–1980," *Industrial Relations* 22 (Spring 1983): 164–85.

22. On the problems that congressional representatives interested in alternatives to macroeconomic measures encountered in finding expert direction for their concerns, see Jerrold E. Schneider, *Ideological Coalitions in Congress* (Westport, Conn.: Greenwood Press, 1979), ch. 6.

23. For a sympathetic critique of the bill, see James K. Galbraith, "Why We Have No Full Employment Policy," *Working Papers* 6 (March–April 1978): 27–33.

24. U.S. Congress, Senate, Committee on Labor and Public Welfare, *Full Employment and Balanced Growth Act, 1976: Hearings on S. 50 and S. 472,* 94th Cong., 2d sess., May 1976, 141–65.

25. Singer, "Humphrey-Hawkins Hangs On," 724.

26. Galbraith, "Why We Have No Full Employment Policy," 29; see the critique of the anti-inflation measures in this version of the bill in Michael C. Barth, "The Full Employment and Balanced Growth Act of 1976: An Analysis and Evaluation," Institute for Research on Poverty Discussion Papers (University of Wisconsin–Madison, June 1976), 13–14.

27. Legislative authority for the controls was passed on August 15, 1970, and controls were applied in the construction industry in March of the following year. Not until the New Economic Policy were broad controls in the form of a freeze on wages and prices applied. See John T. Dunlop, "Inflation and Incomes Policies: The Political Economy of Recent U.S. Experience," *Public Policy* 23 (Spring 1975): 135–66.

28. Moreover, the power of these junior members of Congress had been enhanced by changes in the organization of the House of Representatives. See Edsall, *The New Politics of Inequality,* 39–49; James Sundquist, *The Decline and Resurgence of Congress* (Washington, D.C.: Brookings Institution, 1981), 373–90; see also *Congressional Quarterly Weekly Report* 33 (June 28, 1975): 1333–35; Daniel Rapoport, "A New Old Guard Has Come Forward in the House," *National Journal* 9 (August 13, 1977): 1264–67.

29. Singer, "The Humphrey-Hawkins Bill," 815.

30. On the "ethnic purity" incident, see Singer, "The Humphrey-Hawkins Bill," 815; on Carter's view of the Humphrey-Hawkins bill after his election, see id., "Humphrey-Hawkins Hangs On," 724.

31. The move to the bill occurred after the failure of Carter's welfare reform plan, which would have provided jobs to welfare recipients. On welfare reform, see Laurence E. Lynn and David deF. Whitman, *The President as Policymaker: Jimmy Carter and Welfare Reform* (Philadelphia: Temple University Press, 1981); on the administration's identification of Humphrey-Hawkins as a black measure, see Arnold Packer, "Memorandum for the Secretary Re: Humphrey-Hawkins Bill," April 20, 1977, File LL-2, National Legislation (April–May), Ray Marshall Papers, Department of Labor.

32. "Supporters See Passage of Humphrey-Hawkins Bill Next Year," *National Journal* 9 (November 19, 1977): 1824.

33. *Congressional Quarterly Almanac, 1978* (Washington, D.C.: Congressional Quarterly Press, 1979), 272–79.

34. On the expansion of unemployment insurance during the 1970s, see James M. Rosbrow, *Fifty Years of Unemployment Insurance—A Legislative History: 1935–85,* Unemployment Insurance Service Occasional Paper no. 86–5 (Washington, D.C.: U.S. Department of Labor, 1986), 16–18.

35. Edward J. Harpham, "Federalism, Keynesianism, and the Transformation of the Unemployment Insurance System in the United States," in

Nationalizing Social Security in Europe and the United States, edited by Douglas E. Ashford and E. W. Kelley (Greenwich, Conn.: JAI Press, 1986), 155–79. Although President Nixon also supported such changes, unlike Kennedy and Johnson, he sought to effect them within the existing federal-state framework. See Sar A. Levitan and Martha R. Cooper, *Business Lobbies: The Public Good and the Bottom Line* (Baltimore and London: Johns Hopkins University Press, 1984), 106–7.

36. The comment about piecemeal remedies was made by Senator Jacob Javits, (R. N.Y.). See James W. Singer, "Labor Report/ Unemployment Pay Reform Unlikely to Occur in Near Future," *National Journal* 7 (January 25, 1975): 135.

37. On the development of TAA, see Daniel J. B. Mitchell, "Trade-Related Injuries and Adjustment Assistance," in *Proceedings of the 28th Annual Winter Meeting of the Industrial Relations Research Association, 1975* (Madison, Wisc.: IRRA, 1975), 205–11; and Steve Charnovitz, "Worker Adjustment: The Missing Ingredient in Trade Policy," *California Management Review* 28 (Winter 1986): 156–73.

38. Michael R. Gordon, "Trade Adjustment Assistance Program May Be Too Big for Its Own Good," *National Journal* 12 (May 10, 1980): 766.

39. For the views of organized labor, see Elizabeth R. Jager, "Adjustment Assistance for Import-Impacted Workers," in *Proceedings of the 28th Annual Winter Meeting of the Industrial Relations Research Association, 1975*, 217–23.

40. On TAA's failure to act as an adjustment tool, see Charnovitz, "Worker Adjustment," 156–73.

41. See Stephen E. Baldwin, *Trade Adjustment Assistance: Part of the Solution or Part of the Problem* (Washington, D.C.: National Commission for Employment Policy, 1987), iii.

42. Daniel S. Hamermesh, "Prospects for Integrating Unemployment Insurance and Employment Policy," *Labor Law Journal* 28 (August 1977): 466–72, showed that nonwhites provided a much larger percentage of those enrolled in remedial job training programs than of those receiving unemployment insurance in 1974 and 1975.

43. Levitan and Cooper, *Business Lobbies*, 107–10.

44. John T. Dunlop, "Industrial Relations, Labor Economics, and Policy Decisions," *Challenge* 20 (May–June 1977): 7. Dunlop laid out the theory of wage contours in "The Task of Contemporary Wage Theory," in *The Theory of Wage Determination*, edited by John T. Dunlop (London: Macmillan, 1957), 3–27.

45. For the differences between Dunlop and Nixon's Council of Economic Advisors during 1974, see Daniel J. Baltz, "Economic Report/Policy Makers Disagree on How to Solve the Problem," *National Journal* 6 (March 30, 1974):472–74. For a brief summary of Dunlop's career, see John T. Dunlop, "Labor Markets and Wage Determination: Then and Now," in *How Labor Markets Work*, edited by Bruce E. Kaufman (Lexington, Mass.: Lexington Books, 1988), 77–80.

46. James W. Singer, "Dunlop: The Professor with a Flair for the Practical," *National Journal* 7 (November 22, 1975): 1595–96.

47. See Singer, "Dunlop," 1597, for a list of the members of the committee and some of the issues it considered.

48. See Herbert Stein, *Presidential Economics: The Making of Economic Policy from Roosevelt to Reagan and Beyond*, 2d rev. ed. (Washington, D.C.: American Enterprise Institute, 1988), 159–61; A. James Reichley, *Conservatives in an Age of Change: The Nixon and Ford Administrations* (Washington, D.C.: Brookings Institution, 1981), 220.

49. See "History of the Department of Labor under Nixon and Ford: Secretary Dunlop Section," February 14, 1977, Historical Office, Department of Labor, 26–29.

50. Dunlop was considering the possibilities of building similar committees in the retail food, health care, and maritime industries. See ibid., 38.

51. For a description of the mobilization, see ibid., 35–36.

52. See the account in Reichley, *Conservatives in an Age of Change*, 395–96.

53. See Secretary of Labor, "Memorandum for W. Michael Blumenthal et al. Re: Implementing the President's Anti-Inflation Program," March 8, 1978; Arnold Packer, "Memorandum for EPG Deputies Re: Sanctions or Reducing Anti-Inflationary Pressures?" August 8, 1978; Arnold Packer, "Memorandum to the Secretary Re: Your Meeting," March 15, 1978; Secretary of Labor, "Memorandum for Stu Eizenstadt Re: Administrative Structure of the Anti-Inflationary Program," September 18, 1978; and Arnie Packer, "Memorandum to Ray Marshall Re: Comments on the Draft EPG Anti-Inflation Paper," November 9, 1978, all in White House—President's Anti-Inflation Program File, Ray Marshall Papers, Department of Labor.

54. See William J. Barber, "The Kennedy Years: Purposeful Pedagogy," in *Exhortation and Controls: The Search for a Wage Price Policy, 1945–1971*, edited by Craufurd D. Goodwin (Washington D.C.: Brookings Institution, 1975), 135–91; and James L. Cochrane, "The Johnson Administration: Moral Suasion Goes to War," ibid., 193–293.

55. See the account in Stein, *Presidential Economics*, 176–82; Reichley, *Conservatives in an Age of Change*, 221–25.

56. *Congressional Quarterly Weekly Report* 29 (July 30, 1971), 1591; Stein, *Presidential Economics*, 167–68; Reichley, *Conservatives in an Age of Change*, 216–17; Neil De Marchi, "The First Nixon Administration: Preludes to Controls," in *Exhortation and Controls*, edited by Craufurd D. Goodwin, 338–43.

57. For an evaluation of the experience of controls under Nixon, see Marvin H. Kosters, in association with J. Dawson Ahalt, *Controls and Inflation: The Economic Stabilization Program in Retrospect* (Washington, D.C.: American Enterprise Institute, 1975).

58. See Meany's testimony before the Joint Economic Committee in *Meany on Controls* (Washington, D.C.: AFL-CIO, 1972); for a summary of labor reaction to the announcement of the New Economic Policy, see *Congressional Quarterly Weekly Report* 29 (August 21, 1971), 1760–61.

59. See Stein, *Presidential Economics*, 186–87; for an examination of monetarist and Keynesian views of controls, see Lloyd Ulman, "Unions, Economists, Politicians, and Incomes Policies," in *Economics in the Public Sector*,

edited by Joseph Pechman and N. J. Simler (New York: W. W. Norton, 1982); Kosters, *Controls and Inflation.*

60. Jack Meyer, *Wage-Price Standards and Economic Policy* (Washington, D.C.: American Enterprise Institute, 1982), 3–5.

61. Erwin C. Hargrove and Samuel A. Morley, *The President and the Council of Economic Advisers: Interviews with CEA Chairmen* (Boulder, Colo.: Westview Press, 1984), 488.

62. On various forms of tax-based incomes policies, see Arthur Okun, "An Efficient Strategy to Combat Inflation," in *The Battle against Unemployment and Inflation,* edited by Martin N. Baily and Arthur M. Okun (New York: W. W. Norton, 1982), 179–83; and Henry Wallich, "The Tax-Based Incomes Policies," ibid., 84–88.

63. *Congressional Quarterly Almanac, 1978,* 218.

64. See W. Kip Viscusi, "The Political Economy of Wage and Price Regulation: The Case of the Carter Pay-Price Standards," in *What Role for Government: Lessons from Policy Research,* edited by Richard J. Zeckhauser and Derek Leebaert (Durham, N.C.: Duke Press Policy Studies, 1983), 159.

65. For a sense of the broad discontent with the administration's policies, see the testimony at the hearings held on a bill to increase the authorization and extend the duration of the Council on Wage and Price Stability in 1980, U.S. Congress, House, Committee on Banking, Finance, and Urban Affairs, Subcommittee on Economic Stabilization, *To Authorize the Extension of the Council on Wage and Price Stability: Hearings on H.R. 6777,* 96th Cong., 2d sess., March 19, 26 and May 6, 1980.

66. Viscusi, "The Political Economy of Wage and Price Regulation, 174.

67. Erwin C. Hargrove, *Jimmy Carter as President: Leadership and the Politics of the Public Good* (Baton Rouge and London: Louisiana State University Press, 1988), 85–87. For Dunlop's views of what the Pay Advisory Committee sought to do, see his testimony at the hearings *To Authorize the Extension of the Council on Wage and Price Stability,* 293–306.

68. Viscusi, "The Political Economy of Wage and Price Regulation," 159.

69. On the congressional reaction to these proposals, see *Congressional Quarterly Weekly Report* 37 (January 20, 1979): 82–84.

70. See John T. Dunlop, "Inflation and Incomes Policies: The Political Economy of Recent U.S. Experience," *Public Policy* 23 (Spring 1975): 135–66.

71. Herbert Stein, "Memorandum to Secretary Kennedy et al.," June 5, 1970, Councils, Economic Advisers File, Record Group 174, National Archives, 3.

72. Vogel, *Fluctuating Fortunes,* chs. 3–4.

73. See Levitan and Cooper, *Business Lobbies,* chs. 2–3.

74. Vogel, *Fluctuating Fortunes,* 203–13.

75. Ibid., 200.

76. Ibid., 153–57; Andrew Levison, *The Full Employment Alternative* (New York: Coward, McCann, and Geoghegan, 1980), 186–88.

77. Hargrove, *Jimmy Carter as President,* 28.

78. Hargrove and Morley, *The President and the Council of Economic Advisers,* 478; Hargrove, *Jimmy Carter as President,* 87–99.

79. See Joel Havemann, "Reorganization—How Clean Can Carter's Broom Sweep?" *National Journal* 9 (January 1, 1977): 4–8.

80. Hargrove, *Jimmy Carter as President*, 30, 47–60; on the effort to reform welfare policy, see also Lynn and Whitman, *The President as Policymaker*.

81. On Carter's campaign themes, see Charles O. Jones, *The Trusteeship Presidency: Jimmy Carter and the United States Congress* (Baton Rouge and London: Louisiana State University Press, 1988), ch. 2.

82. See Samuel Kernell, *Going Public: New Strategies of Presidential Leadership* (Washington, D.C: Congressional Quarterly Press, 1986), 226.

83. James W. Ceaser, "The Theory of Governance of the Reagan Administration," in *The Reagan Presidency and the Governing of America*, edited by Lester M. Salamon and Michael S. Lund (Washington, D.C.: Urban Institute Press, 1984), 77.

84. A study by the Congressional Budget Office in 1980 reported that a balanced budget would reduce inflation by less than 1 percent. See James Savage, *Balanced Budgets and American Politics* (Ithaca, N.Y.: Cornell University Press, 1988), 201.

85. Ray Marshall, "Memorandum for the EPA Re: Anti-Inflation Program," White House—President's Anti-Inflation Program File, Ray Marshall Papers, Department of Labor, 3.

86. The business economist Alan Greenspan, who served as President Ford's chairman of the CEA, based his economic policy recommendations on this argument. See Reichley, *Conservatives in an Age of Change*, 387–90.

87. Edsall, *The New Politics of Inequality*, 215–19; see also Joseph Peschek, *Policy-Planning Organizations: Elite Agendas and America's Rightward Turn* (Philadelphia: Temple University Press, 1987).

88. See James A. Smith, "Think Tanks and the Politics of Ideas," in *The Spread of Economic Ideas*, edited by David C. Colander and A .W. Coats (New York: Cambridge University Press, 1989), 188.

89. Vogel, *Fluctuating Fortunes* 220–27.

90. Savage, *Balanced Budgets and American Politics*, 200.

91. On the antitax crusade and public opinion about taxes during the late 1970s, see Edsall, *The New Politics of Inequality*, 211–13.

92. See Edward G. Carmines and James A. Stimson, *Issue Evolution: Race and the Transformation of American Politics* (Princeton, N.J.: Princeton University Press, 1989), ch. 5.

93. On this general problem, see Robert M. Solow, "How Economic Ideas Turn to Mush," in Colander and Coats, *The Spread of Economic Ideas*, 75–83.

94. See the polls reported in Robert Y. Shapiro, Kelly D. Patterson, Judith Russell, and John T. Young, "The Polls—A Report, Employment and Social Welfare," *Public Opinion Quarterly* 51 (Summer 1987): 273–74. In polls conducted from 1972 to 1982, a majority of those favoring more government action also generally voiced approval for increased taxes to support that activity if necessary. The exception was an April 1979 poll, in which 48 percent of the respondents who favored government action disapproved of taxes and 43 percent approved.

95. See Timothy B. Clark and Robert J. Samuelson, "Now That Carter's 1980 Budget Is Out, Let the Battle Begin," *National Journal* 11 (January 27, 1979): 124–39.

96. On Volker's appointment, see William Greider, *Secrets of the Temple: How the Federal Reserve Runs the Country* (New York: Simon and Schuster, 1987), 32–47.

97. John T. Wooley, *Monetary Politics: The Federal Reserve and the Politics of Monetary Policy* (New York: Cambridge University Press, 1984), 103–5.

98. On the political appeal of supply-side economics, see Stein, *Presidential Economics*, ch. 7.

99. See Donald C. Baumer and Carl E. Van Horn, *The Politics of Unemployment* (Washington, D.C.: Congressional Quarterly Press, 1985), ch. 6.

100. For a discussion of the changed logic expressed in hearings on the extension of unemployment insurance in the 1980s, see Alan Weil, "The Triumph of Economics: The Debate over Unemployment Insurance in the 1980s" (unpublished mss., Harvard University, 1986).

101. These declines reflected state-level action to increase the solvency of state unemployment insurance programs as well as the actions of the Reagan administration. See the discussion in Wayne Vroman, "The Aggregate Performance of Unemployment Insurance, 1980–85," in *Unemployment Insurance: The Second Half Century*, edited by W. Lee Hansen and James F. Byers (Madison: University of Wisconsin Press, 1990), 27–37.

Chapter Six

1. See Ira Katznelson, "Rethinking the Silences of Social and Economic Policy," *Political Science Quarterly* 101 no. 2 (1986): 307–25.

2. Paul E. Peterson and J. David Greenstone, "Racial Change and Citizen Participation: The Mobilization of Low-Income Communities through Community Action," in *A Decade of Federal Anti-Poverty Programs: Achievements, Failures and Lessons*, edited by Robert H. Haveman (Madison: University of Wisconsin Press, 1977), 248, 251–56.

3. On the resurgence of interest in institutions, see James G. March and Johan P. Olsen, *Rediscovering Institutions: The Organizational Basis of Politics* (New York: Free Press, 1989); for a perceptive analysis of economic policy that highlights the importance of institutional factors, see Peter A. Hall, *Governing the Economy: The Politics of State Intervention in Britain and France* (New York: Oxford University Press, 1986).

4. On public education and employment concerns early in the century, see Ira Katznelson and Margaret Weir, *Schooling for All: Class, Race, and the Decline of the Democratic Ideal* (New York: Basic Books, 1985), ch. 6.

5. For the importance of connecting ideas with politics and administration, see Peter A. Hall, "Conclusion: The Politics of Keynesian Ideas," in *The Political Power of Economic Ideas: Keynesianism Across Nations*, edited by Peter A. Hall (Princeton, N.J.: Princeton University Press, 1989), 361–91.

6. See the discussion of public philosophy in Samuel H. Beer, "In Search of a New Public Philosophy," in *The New American Political System*, edited

by Anthony King (Washington, D.C.: American Enterprise Institute, 1978), 5–44.

7. Ideas of this sort are often the product of social research. See Carol H. Weiss, "Improving the Linkage between Social Research and Public Policy," in *Knowledge and Policy: The Uncertain Connection*, edited by Lawrence E. Lynn, Jr. (Washington, D.C.: National Academy of Sciences, 1978), 23–81.

8. See the strongly worded critique of John T. Dunlop, "Policy Decisions and Research in Economics and Industrial Relations," *Industrial and Labor Relations Review* 30 (April 1977): 275–82. The call for more attention to institutions has been central to critiques of Keynesianism and neoclassical economics. See Leon Lindberg, "The Problems of Economic Theory in Explaining Economic Performance," *Annals* 459 (January 1982): 14–27; and Lester C. Thurow, *Dangerous Currents: The State of Economics* (New York: Vintage Books, 1983), especially 230–35.

9. Henry J. Aaron, *Politics and the Professors: The Great Society in Perspective* (Washington, D.C.: Brookings Institution, 1978), 31–33.

10. Ibid., 156–57.

11. Harold Wilensky, "Nothing Fails Like Success: The Evaluation-Research Industry and Labor Market Policy," *Industrial Relations* 24 (Winter 1985): 8–10.

12. Jeffrey K. Tulis, *The Rhetorical Presidency* (Princeton, N.J.: Princeton University Press, 1987), 165.

13. See Beer, "In Search of a New Public Philosophy."

14. See Emma Rothschild, "The Real Reagan Economy," *New York Review of Books* 35 (June 30, 1988): 46-53; see also Benjamin M. Friedman, *Day of Reckoning: The Consequences of American Economic Policy under Reagan and After* (New York: Random House, 1988). For a discussion of policymaking under conditions of economic and political uncertainty, see Richard Rose, "The Political Appraisal of Employment Policies," *Journal of Public Policy* 7 (July–September 1987): 285–305.

15. E. E. Schattschneider, "Party Government and Employment Policy," *American Political Science Review* 39 (December 1945): 1154.

16. On social security, see Martha Derthick, *Policymaking For Social Security* (Washington, D.C.: Brookings Institution, 1979); on the development of health policy, see Theodore Marmor, *The Politics of Medicare* (New York: Aldine, 1970).

17. On tax policy, see David R. Beam, Timothy J. Conlan, and Margaret T. Wrightson, "Solving the Riddle of Tax Reform: Party Competition and the Politics of Ideas," *Political Science Quarterly* 105 (Summer 1990): 193–217; on deregulation, see Martha Derthick and Paul J. Quirk, *The Politics of Deregulation* (Washington, D.C.: Brookings Institution, 1985).

18. See, for example, Michael J. Piore and Charles F. Sabel, *The Second Industrial Divide: Possibilities for Prosperity* (New York: Basic Books, 1984); and Peter Gourevitch, *Politics in Hard Times: Comparative Responses to International Economic Crises* (Ithaca and London: Cornell University Press, 1986). See also Thomas Byrne Edsall, "The Changing Shape of Power: A Re-

alignment in Public Policy," in *The Rise and the Fall of the New Deal Era, 1930–1980*, edited by Steve Fraser and Gary Gerstle (Princeton, N.J.: Princeton University Press, 1989), 269–93.

19. For a strong argument in favor of enforcing an obligation to work, see Lawrence Mead, *Beyond Entitlement: The Social Obligations of Citizenship* (New York: Free Press, 1985).

20. These views are presented in Martin Feldstein, "The Economics of the New Unemployment," *Public Interest* 33 (Fall 1973): 3–42; Robert Lucas, "Unemployment Policy," *American Economic Review* 68 (May 1978): 353–57. For a summary description, see Clair Brown, "Unemployment Theory and Policy," *Industrial Relations* 22 (Spring 1983): 164–85. For a broad critique of "the new orthodoxy," see Michael Piore, "Historical Perspectives and the Interpretation of Unemployment," *Journal of Economic Literature* 25 (December 1987): 1834–50.

21. The 1980s saw an outpouring of writing on the underclass. The best structural perspective is presented by William Julius Wilson, *The Truly Disadvantaged: The Inner City, The Underclass and Public Policy* (Chicago: The University of Chicago Press, 1987); for an analysis that emphasizes behavioral problems, see Isabel Sawhill, "The Underclass: An Overview," *Public Interest* 96 (Summer 1989): 3–15; see the discussion of the way "underclass" has been used in political discussion in Herbert J. Gans, "Deconstructing the Underclass: The Term's Dangers as a Planning Concept," *Journal of the American Planning Association* 56 (Summer 1990): 271–77.

22. On these programs, see Demetra Smith Nightingale and Lynn C. Burbridge, *The Status of State Work-Welfare Programs in 1986: Implications for Welfare Reform* (Washington, D.C.: Urban Institute, July 1987).

23. The debate over welfare reform that led to the Family Support Act of 1988 was heavily influenced by the debate about the underclass. See Andrew Hacker, "Getting Rough on the Poor," *New York Review of Books* 35 (October 13, 1988): 12–17.

24. William Julius Wilson stresses this point. See Wilson, *The Truly Disadvantaged*, 150.

25. On the decline of wages for men without college educations, see McKinley L. Blackburn, David E. Bloom, and Richard B. Freeman, "The Declining Economic Position of Less Skilled American Men," in *A Future of Lousy Jobs? The Changing Structure of U.S. Wages*, edited by Gary Burtless (Washington, D.C.: Brookings Institution, 1990), 31–67. Broader claims about the increase in low-wage jobs are made by Bennett Harrison and Barry Bluestone, *The Great U-Turn: Corporate Restructuring and the Polarizing of America* (New York: Basic Books, 1988), ch. 5. For a fascinating discussion of different "postindustrial employment trajectories," see Gosta Esping-Andersen, *The Three Worlds of Welfare Capitalism* (Princeton, N.J.: Princeton University Press, 1990).

26. On the way employers and government policies have and have not responded to women in the labor force, see the essays in Sharon L. Harlan and Ronnie J. Steinberg, eds., *Job Training for Women: The Promise and*

Limits of Public Policies (Philadelphia: Temple University Press, 1989); for an emphasis on employer responses, see Sheila B. Kamerman and Alfred J. Kahn, *The Responsive Workplace: Employers and a Changing Labor Force* (New York: Columbia University Press, 1987).

27. See the description of Milwaukee in Isabel Wilkerson, "How Milwaukee Has Thrived While Leaving Blacks Behind," *New York Times*, March 19, 1991, 1.

28. See Wilson, *The Truly Disadvantaged*. These conditions have been extensively described by journalists. See, for example, Nicholas Lemann, "The Origins of the Urban Underclass," *The Atlantic*, June 1986, 31–61. For a discussion of the corrosive effects of crime on poor neighborhoods, see John J. DiIulio, Jr., "The Impact of Inner-City Crime," *Public Interest*, no. 96 (Summer 1989); 28–46.

29. See the argument of Albert O. Hirschman that "neglected" policy problems can be more easily addressed if they are attached to "privileged" policy problems that are the focus of broad public concern, Albert O. Hirschman, "Policymaking and Policy Analysis in Latin America—A Return Journey," in id., *Essays in Trespassing: Economics to Politics and Beyond* (Cambridge: Cambridge University Press, 1981), 150–52.

30. Concern about the preparation of the American labor force became a common theme in the 1980s. See, for example, Edward B. Fiske, "Impending U.S. Jobs 'Disaster': Workforce Unqualified to Work," *New York Times*, September 25, 1989, 1. The newsletter *Challenges*, published monthly by the Council on Competitiveness, has made problems with American workforce preparation a central theme. See also Paul Osterman, *Employment Futures: Reorganization, Dislocation, and Public Policy* (New York: Oxford University Press, 1988), especially ch. 7; Ray Marshall, *Unheard Voices: Labor and Economic Policy in a Competitive World* (New York: Basic Books, 1987).

31. Among the many discussions about the links between public education and work, see *Non-College Youth in America* (Washington, D.C.: William T. Grant Commission on Work, Family, and Citizenship, 1988).

32. For an argument in favor of creating a broad apprenticeship program in the United States, see Robert I. Lerman and Hillard Pouncy, "The Compelling Case for Youth Apprenticeships," *Public Interest* 101 (Fall 1990): 62–77.

33. See Wilson, *The Truly Disadvantaged*.

34. On the growth of state-level capacities during the 1980s, see David Osborne, *Laboratories of Democracy* (Boston: Harvard Business School Press, 1988); and R. Scott Fosler, *The New Economic Role of American States: Strategies in a Competitive World Economy* (New York: Oxford University Press, 1988).

35. For an argument in favor of an employment policy organized along these lines, see Osterman, *Employment Futures*, ch. 7; another argument for a broader approach to employment policy is made by Isabel Sawhill, "Rethinking Employment Policy," in *Rethinking Employment Policy*, edited by D. Lee Bawden and Felicity Skidmore (Washington, D.C.: Urban Institute Press, 1989), 9–36.

36. This formulation is John. T. Dunlop's. See his essay "Involving Gov-

36. This formulation is John. T. Dunlop's. See his essay "Involving Government as a Catalyst, Not as Regulator," *The Dislocated Worker, Preparing America's Workforce*, edited by William Kilberg (Washington, D.C.: Seven Locks Press, 1983), 14–17.

Index